THE PICKERING MASTERS

THE ECONOMIC WRITINGS OF WILLIAM THORNTON

Volume 1

THE ECONOMIC WRITINGS OF WILLIAM THORNTON

Edited by
Philip Mirowski and
Steven Tradewell

Volume 1
Introduction
Miscellaneous Works

Routledge
Taylor & Francis Group
LONDON AND NEW YORK

First published 1999 by Pickering & Chatto (Publishers) Limited

Published 2016 by Routledge
2 Park Square, Milton Park, Abingdon, Oxon OX14 4RN
605 Third Avenue, New York, NY 10017

Routledge is an imprint of the Taylor & Francis Group, an informa business

BRITISH LIBRARY CATALOGUING IN PUBLICATION DATA

Thornton, William
The economic writings of William Thornton
1.Economics
I.Title II. Mirowski, Philip, 1951– III. Tradewell, Steven
330.1

ISBN 13: 978-1-13875-947-3 (hbk) (Vol-1)

LIBRARY OF CONGRESS CATALOGING-IN-PUBLICATION DATA

Thornton, William Thomas, 1813–1880.
The economic writings of William Thornton / [introduction and edited by Philip Mirowski and Steven Tradewell].
v. cm.
Includes bibliographical references and indexes.
Contents: v. 1 Letters to the economist concerning Thornton – v. 2 – Over-population and its remedy (1846) – v. 3. A plea for peasant proprietors (1848) – v. 4 – On labour (1869) – v. 5 Old fashioned ethics and common sense metaphysics (1873).
ISBN 1-85196-388-X
Thornton, William Thomas, 1813–1880. 2. Economics—Great Britain—History—19th century Sources. 3. Great Britain—Economic conditions—19th century Sources. 4. Supply and demand. 5. Population—Economic aspects. 6. Land tenure–Economic Aspects. I. Mirowski, Philip, 1951– . II. Tradewell, Steven. III. Economist (London, England : 1843) IV. Title.
HB103.T514A25 1999
330.1—dc21 99-28820
CIP

Typeset by Antony Gray, London

CONTENTS OF THE EDITION

CONTENTS

Volume 1

* Contributions are Thornton's unless otherwise stated

COPY TEXTS

Some of the material included in this edition is reproduced in facsimile.

In order to fit texts comfortably to the pages of the edition, certain liberties have been taken with the format of the original: occasionally right-hand pages have become left-hand pages (and vice versa) and text from consecutive pages has been fitted onto a single page.

Texts are reproduced by kind permission of the British Library Board and the British Library of Political and Economic Science.

INTRODUCTION

Why Put Together a Collected Economic Works for William Thomas Thornton?

WHEN mentioning this project to a number of our friends and acquaintances, the most frequent reaction we encountered was: William *Who?* This may hardly be the most propitious start to our aim of fostering a greater level of historical sophistication in the appreciation of the traditions which led to modern economics. Other scholars have given us wonderful editions of the works of Adam Smith, David Ricardo, Karl Marx and John Maynard Keynes, which have immeasurably enhanced our appreciation of their endeavours and contexts. Many economists might never have considered the works of William Thomas Thornton (1813–80) as a candidate for similar treatment. Neither of the present authors is much of an antiquarian for its own sake, nor do we nurture an especially fond fixation upon the more obscure corners of Victorian British history, nor do we especially admire the Quixote in tilting at windmills. So why have we taken this opportunity to make a wider audience acquainted with Thornton's ideas?

Amongst specialists in the history of Victorian social and economic thought, Thornton is widely regarded as little more than a bit player: perhaps someone bearing resemblance to Rosencrantz and Guildenstern in Shakespeare's *Hamlet*. The comparison is more apt than it might at first appear. In the play, Rosencrantz and Guildenstern are reputed to be close friends of Hamlet, but they are summoned by Hamlet's nemesis in order to try and penetrate his rather odd behaviour and cryptic utterances. They are subsequently treated rather rudely by both sides in the larger dramatic conflict and to such an extent that they are often confused and conflated with one another.[1] Hamlet then stage manages a play within the play, which Rosencrantz and Guildenstern protest is not a credible performance. Hamlet treats them with stiff cordiality when he is in their presence, but conspires to send them to their deaths at the hands of the English, unwittingly bearing their own death sentence as a message from the Prince, a demise which (in the opinion of many critics) is even more senseless and tragic than the trademark Shakespearian bloodbath at the conclusion of the play. In the end, the huge chess game of duplicity and feints is all for naught, since the surfeit of jockeying for political advantage in Denmark merely clears the way for the ruthless invader Fortinbras to assume the throne and bring down the curtain on a century or more of royal rule. It is only in the twentieth century that we have realised that interpretation of the play need not dwell so insistently upon the vicissitudes of Hamlet himself, and that some more subtle bathos inheres in the experience of Rosencrantz and Guildenstern as pawns in a larger game for which they never enlisted and could never adequately comprehend (Stoppard, 1967).

Lest we ourselves be accused of speaking in riddles after the manner of Hamlet, let us proceed to describe Thornton's fate in more prosaic terms. William Thornton is treated in the orthodox history of economic thought literature, if at all, as the person who created the occasion for John Stuart Mill's celebrated "recantation of the wages fund doctrine", a doctrinal revision of near-eschatological significance for his contemporaries, which we shall treat in some detail below. This crisis in English classical political economy, it is often said, was putatively triggered by the publication of the first edition of Thornton's book *On Labour* (1869). What is notable about modern accounts of this incident is the cavalier disdain assumed by all and sundry towards Thornton and his role. It has been our experience that almost no modern commentator (with one or two honourable exceptions to be noted below) has deemed that Thornton's ideas merited serious scrutiny, then or now. No effort is therefore expended by these authors to explicate his writings in any sympathetic detail, instead they concentrate all their hermeneutic powers upon such revered figures as John Stuart Mill or Alfred Marshall. To offset the impression that we generalise about this contempt in a hasty and unwarranted manner, let us just sample some of the calumny which has been heaped upon Thornton's head.

George Stigler sniffed that Thornton's *On Labour* was "absurd" (1965, p. 9). Krishna Bharadwaj opined that his arguments "were rather confusing and weak" (1978a, p. 260). William Breit accused Thornton of "fatuous" examples and "flimsy criticism" (1967, pp. 519, 521). Lujo Brentano once wrote, "Mr. Thornton's chapter 'On the Origins of Trades Unions' bears the same relation to the real origin of Trades-Unions as Rousseau's *Contrat Sociale* to the historical origins of States" (1870, p. clxv). The economist Robert Ekelund finds himself unable to repress his roiling scorn, launching into a barrage of *ad hominem* accusations, such as: "Thornton's purpose appears not to be a scientific search for truth, but rather to find an argument that will support his preconceived political conclusions"; that he "was inappropriately applying the method of the natural sciences to the social sciences"; that "there is no textual evidence that Thornton ever understood Mill's simple but servicable theory"; and that his book could not be considered "anything more than an unsophisticated stab in the dark" (Ekelund and Thommesen, 1989). Evelyn Forget, in a somewhat more cautious mood, asserts with confidence that Thornton's "contribution does not reach the same level of analytical sophistication as does Mill's or Longe's" and his "economic analysis did not transcend the level of popular debate of the era" (1991, pp. 207, 215). From this litany of disdain – and we have by no means exhausted its breadth or extent – one would seemingly be driven to infer that Thornton would not deserve even the attention it would take to do a serious job of refutation.

Yet here we confront one of the first of a sequence of paradoxes which seem to hover about the historical personage of William Thomas Thornton. If he really was such an intellectual lightweight, a literary leper, a sad specimen of someone who couldn't think his way out of his own inkwell, then why was it that so many of the acknowledged giants of nineteenth-century political economy took him so very seriously? It is indeed wondrous to see how the modern paragons of scientific logic and sober orthodoxy squirm around the abundance of contemporaneous testimonials to his intellectual acuity and conceptual consequence – that is, if they even deign to acknowledge their existence. For instance, John Stuart Mill, in promoting the intellectual merits of *On Labour*, wrote, "The present work, though popular and attractive in style, is strictly scientific in its principles and reasonings" (1967, p. 633). J. E. Cairnes, in acknowledging the impetus to his own work, praised "the one living writer whose abilities and acquirements I feel high respect, and whose practical aims I not unfrequently sympathise . . . I trust I have profited by the example he has set me of courtesy towards opponents" (1874, pp. 1–2). The *Economist* opined, "This is a book all true economists should welcome." An anonymous reviewer in the *Examiner* of 4 November 1871 wrote that Thornton's book was so "revolutionary in its effects that it rendered obsolete all existing economical works." The *Westminster Review* essayist of July 1869 wrote, "Admirable as the work is in itself, embodying the results of a lifetime of disinterested study, and full of new lights on obscure questions of economical science, it has done the most service perhaps by calling imperatively upon every man of note to revise and test his opinions upon this momentous subject . . . . for though there is a good deal in his scientific reasoning to which exception may be taken . . . we cannot fail to recognise in his work the result of independent thought, high moral aim, and a generous intrepidity in a noble cause" (p. 37). The *British Quarterly* reviewer enthused, "His style is at once popular and precise; so perfectly clear and sparkling that his readers can follow him with ease through subtle and complicated discussions . . . Mr. Thornton makes us realize that the conclusions of the economist both need the perpetual verification of experience, and, in fact, receive it; while he questions anew those formulas which, by reason of their very excellence as abbreviations of an enormous multitude of particular facts, are liable to lose their meaning when, like algebraic symbols, they are applied to long and complicated problems" (Anon., 1869c, p. 448). A less starry-eyed reviewer in the *Athenaeum* was still prompted to admit, "He is given to digression, and uses everywhere from twice to ten times as many words as are needed to set forth his meaning; nevertheless, it may, on the whole, be doubted whether any considerable economic work of equal merit has appeared since the first publication of Mr. Mill's Political Economy" (Anon., 1869a, p. 275). There were other Victorian contemporaries who attained much more exulted academic position than Thornton – one thinks of Henry Fawcett at Cambridge, the aforementioned John Elliott Cairnes at University College, or Bonamy Price at Oxford – who, in their cautious orthodoxy and placid commonplaces never achieved a vanishing fraction of the attention and (more importantly) scrutiny which was lavished upon Thornton. Of course, not all commentators would equally attest to his analytical perspicuity or resort to unchecked praise; but the enervated levels of rhetoric, pro and con, did suggest something rather more significant had occurred than the inept frothings of an inadequate intellect.

But that is only the most obvious paradox. To repress or disparage the judgment of those long dead is one thing; but to condemn the living is quite another. If Thornton really was the minor character that so many make him out to be, then he must be the single most-discussed minor character in the modern history of economics. A survey of just the primary English-language journals dealing in history reveals more than ten articles concerned with Thornton over the last decade (see the appended bibliography). The incongruous spectacle of repeated seriatim attempts by different scholars either to explain away his writings or simply thrust him unceremoniously back into his grave, reprises of an uneasy variant *Economists of the Living Dead*, has begun to itself call into question blithe assertions of his indubitable irrelevance. Recently, this phenomenon of a growing secondary literature on Thornton has provoked the redoubtable Robert Ekelund to an academic frenzy, redoubling his efforts to smear Thornton – calling him an "idiot", saying "Thornton should receive a grade of 'F' (with strongly worded advice to return to the pursuit of poetry and sociology)", proleptically insisting his "(in)famous arguments were worse than nonsense" – and to extend his assessments to modern writers who study Thornton (1997, p. 21). Lecturing skulls in graveyards, especially those belonging to persons supposedly deemed Fools when alive, is not calculated to foster confidence in the Royal House of economic orthodoxy. Perhaps something really is rotten in the state of Denmark.

This brings us back full circle to the need for a readily accessible *Collected Works* of William Thomas Thornton. It seems that his writings, but especially his book *On Labour*, touched a pervasive chord for many writers in that crucial period of the 1860s and 1870s in Britain: that is, right when British classical political economy began to be superseded by what has become known in retrospect as "neoclassical" economic theory. Indeed, we shall argue that Thornton's book played a major role in the actual configuration of events which led up to the initial statements of the fledgling doctrine by such figures as Fleeming Jenkin, William Stanley Jevons, Francis Ysidro Edgeworth, and Alfred Marshall. The importance of the controversy swirling about Thornton in the 1860s and 1870s has not been adequately appreciated by historians, at least in part, because of the inaccessibility of his works and a convenient summary of the reactions. Thornton the gadfly was in a large measure responsible for the condensation out of the specifically British form of microeconomics prevalent around the turn of the last century. This remains the format of "introductory economics" in countless university courses down to the present.

Secondly, Thornton was also relevant in the influence he had upon the rise of political trade unionism in Britain and its changing relationship to academic political economy, something which has gone relatively unnoticed in the literature of the social history of labour. Again, we attribute much of this neglect to the lack of a convenient compendium of his writings, accompanied by pointers to the relevant contemporary discussions. There was a period in which much of social history was concerned with searching for the influence (or more pertinently, explaining the absence thereof) of Marxist doctrines upon working-class politics in Britain. A newer generation of scholars has initiated an inquiry into the relevance of middle-class reformist movements in the normalisation of union activity (Finn, 1993); and it is our opinion that Thornton should be considered as one of the major intellectual resources for those movements in Britain in the critical period of the legal legitimation of union activity.

Third, there is the question of Thornton's relevance to modern understandings of economic theory. It is our view that recent controversies over his significance are symptomatic of larger-scale transformations happening within our *fin de siècle* theoretical orthodoxy of neoclassical economics. In effect, new questions opened up by the modern projects of game theory, experimental economics, and the fascination with the phenomenon of evolutionary processes fosters a situation in which Thornton can be read in a new, perhaps more user-friendly light. An earlier generation of historians of economics were generally partisans of a Marshallian mode of price theory. One of the most important events of the last forty years has been a progressive repudiation and sloughing off of the Marshallian approach by the neoclassical high theory, especially consequent upon the demonstrations that market supply and demand functions *cannot* generally be derived from more rigorous specifications of neoclassical general equilibrium models.[2] Dramatic transformations in modern understanding of the so-called "law of supply and demand" within the orthodoxy of economics cannot but prompt re-evaluations of the nineteenth-century traditions which attempted to wed such laws to the neoclassical organon of the optimisation of utility subject to constraints (Mirowski, 1990). Furthermore, the blossoming of the literature of experimental economics in the last two decades, particularly with regard to the exploration of the nature of differential market outcomes conditional upon alternative institutional formats – double auction, posted price, Dutch auction, and so forth – has proven a tonic against the earlier neoclassical attitude that "all markets are alike" (Davis & Holt, 1993). Here is where a reconsideration of Thornton's significance for modern economics becomes relevant. Thornton famously insisted that there were no "laws of supply and demand", even though invocation of such laws had become conventional wisdom in the British classical tradition; yet far from preaching paralysis, he insisted that one could still make fruitful theoretical statements about the operation of the economy in their absence. In this opinion, he was rebutted most vigorously by various economic theorists, but most effectively by Alfred Marshall, who forged an alliance between utilitarianism and a revised conception of such laws. Now that Marshall's hundred years of solicitude has been torn asunder (however much some Marshallian holdouts may persist in denying it), it now becomes interesting to trace the filiation back to the fork in the path where the fateful choice was made, and explore the first few steps on the road not taken. Hence, Thornton assumes a new relevance for a generation searching for precursors who could be read as sharing its own concerns.

Fourth, we offer these texts and our interpretation of them as a small contribution to a larger dispute over the future of the history of economic thought. Since the end of World War II, the economics profession has precipitously withdrawn its support for scholarship in the history of economics. The motivations here have been many and complex, but one reaction of those remaining scholars engaged in the enterprise has to become more narrowly focused themselves, specialising in perhaps one or two "great men" and subjecting the same canonical texts to repeated microscopic close readings, as though that extra modicum of blinkered attention might finally arrive at the "correct" interpretation, the one which vindicates the prejudices of the modern profession, to stand unchallenged for all time. We think there has been no more sure prescription for utter irrelevance and total oblivion than this. Trying to phrase this in a language we hope they can understand, we believe this sort of history has entered a region of sharply diminishing returns. One possible antidote would come in widening the context, expanding the roster of players, augmenting the body of archival evidence, and appealing to traditions of scholarship which have been ostracized by the anti-historical biases of the economics profession. One particularly apposite example of these alternatives applies to an incident central to the career of William Thomas Thornton, namely, John Stuart Mill's so-called "recantation of the wages fund doctrine". This incident has been a favourite of the "close reading" camp of historians for years, since it constitutes a major challenge to their project of presenting the last two centuries of economics as a single homogeneous continuous progress narrative. Perhaps the most extreme exponent of this practice, Samuel Hollander, is therefore forced to admit that Mill's "retraction of support from the wages fund doctrine constitutes one of the most difficult problems in the history of economics" (1985, p. 409). Yet no amount of compilation of quotes from Mill's published texts on the part of Hollander nor anyone else has served to illuminate this incident in a satisfactory manner. We shall instead assert that it is only when we shift our perspective to adopt Thornton's point of view, and then entertain the notion that much of our own heritage of understanding is a function of what the immediate contemporaries made of Thornton, can much of the intractable and problematic character of this incident be dissolved.

For all these reasons, we have undertaken to present in a convenient format the *Collected Works* of William Thomas Thornton.

A Brief History of the "Law" of Supply and Demand to Cournot

There is a surfeit of writing in the history of economics which seeks to discover the Marshallian laws of demand and supply in numerous texts all the way back to Aristotle, if not before. While the topic of what happens to price and quantity in various market situations was a subject of interested commentary as far back as the beginnings of recorded history, it makes a mockery of the history to simultaneously assert that there is some Platonic economic essence of "supply and demand" which remained intact through the millennia;[3] and worse, that Alfred Marshall did little more than provide a textbook codification of what everyone already implicitly knew. This genre of writing, which Richard Rorty has dubbed "doxography", exists primarily to smother curiosity and stifle any sophisticated appreciation of how we arrived at our present predicaments; it certainly makes it all but impossible to understand the role of William Thornton in the history of British classical political economy.

The indispensable prerequisite for comprehension of the very idea that there could exist such a thing as a "law" or "laws" of supply and demand is to acknowledge that the phrase did not refer to any single concept or phenomenon over time: rather, it was repeatedly recast in conjunction with some rather critical variables over the course of the history of economic thought. The conditioning variables to which we shall make passing reference are: transformations in the economic history of diverse market structures; relationships to notions of "science" and scientific explanation; the strength of conviction in the unity of human social experience and the fundamental identity of human cognitive structures; the role of geometry and mathematics in British science and in economic expression; and the pivotal importance of theories of value, and especially the critical difference between "classical" or substance theories of value (Mirowski, 1989) and neoclassical or "field" theories of value. In brief, notions of supply and demand were continuously adjusted to conform to some matrix of these variables, and this process continues down to the present day. One simply cannot comprehend Adam Smith, Antoine Cournot, William Thornton, Alfred Marshall, Henry Schultz or Werner Hildenbrand without taking each and every one of these factors into account; this has been one of the glaring weaknesses of previous historical narratives from Joseph Schumpeter to Mark Blaug to John Creedy.

Joseph Schumpeter once asserted that the laws of supply and demand "proved unbelievably hard to discover" (1954, p. 602). Perhaps the reason this seemed so interminably protracted a quest was not any failing on the part of the protagonists in our drama; rather, it was a necessary consequence of Schumpeter's project to squeeze something so promiscuous and profoundly variable onto the Procrustean Bed of a single brace of "laws" uniformly applicable to all market phenomena, grounding the totality of economic analysis. Because the famous Marshallian scissors still serve as the arch over the entranceway into the discipline of orthodox economics, the geometrical Checkpoint Charlie of Economics 101, it may seem almost perverse to insist that these ideas are neither obvious nor well-defined in such a way that they could extend back to the very dawn of economic analysis. Perverse or not, it remains the truth, a truth intimately related to William Thornton's role in the history of economics.

The Constitution of Subsistence Markets

We shall embark upon our narrative in the late seventeenth century, since this is the context most relevant to the history of British conceptions of supply and demand, and latterly, to the writings of Thornton. The single most significant fact to notice about economic writers in this era is that they did not uniformly presume that all markets were fundamentally alike; certain markets identified by the specific commodity and geographic provenance were felt to obey alternative principles of legitimate operation, and thus require alternative formats of explanation. Land markets were heavily informed by kinship procedures and distinctions, which in practice could lend appreciable flexibility to land measurement (Kula, 1986); household items would be negotiated on a personal basis with itinerant peddlars; in some instances, labour obligations partook of a customary character. The market for bread in urban centres was always acknowledged as operating according to distinct sets of principles. The very notion of an impersonal and standardised market was a relatively circumscribed phenomenon, and for good reasons: apart from a few metropolises, units of measurement and legal relations were anthropomorphic and narrowly local, most people had great difficulty with even simple forms of calculation, and consequently, sellers were just as likely to alter the character or physical constitution of the commodity offered as adjust the money price in the face of altered circumstances of what we would now call scarcity. Standardisation, monetary and metrological, was plainly a function of the spread of political hegemony; few contemporaries would have associated it with the spread of a generic "market" or disembodied "division of labour". Because most trade was ineluctably local and personalised, the most common mental model of exchange was one of "fair trade", which is why the earliest attempts to portray a generic market function are derived from moral and political philosophy. The European fascination with the "just price" had appreciable justification in the actual configuration of lived economic experience.

Indulging briefly in bald generalisation, the dynamism of the Western polities in the seventeenth century had profound consequences for these patchy, disconnected and fundamentally heterogeneous markets, and for the patterns of thought which underwrote their operations. Without getting into the controversy over whether notions of natural science induced ambitions of market standardization or vice versa (Hadden, 1994), clearly models of fair trading were giving way to something altogether more general and mechanistic at the end of the century. Fairs and itinerant peddlers went into decline, and were being replaced by all manner of other forms of structured retail activities, especially in large and burgeoning cities. Standardisation of weights and measures became a rallying cry for reformers, who used the state to impose it from above; merchants increased their reliance on the judiciary to settle disputes about the terms of trade and discharge of obligations; the maintenance of double-entry accounts became the *sine qua non* of the prosperous merchant, and even the proto-industrialist. The model of idiosyncratic personalised fair trade was being displaced by another model, one with higher turnover, greater interaction with strangers, layered abstractions for the gauging of success, and limited manipulation of the constitution of the goods sold. The spread of standardisation and price-regulated markets proceeded hand in glove, although this did not resemble the "spontaneous order" so beloved of those who would rather recount fairy tales about virtual origins than study actual history. In order to render the market more impersonal and mechanical, it was thought necessary to relegate it to a limned and well-policed space, so that supervision and surveillance could insure that increased dependence upon price-regulated adjustment did not backfire and undermine the state which had set it in motion.

The shift from "fair" to "price-regulated" trade did not proceed along a uniform front, either geographically or across commodities. Neither was the substitution without friction: much of the literature of the "moral economy" of spontaneous revolts documents the clash of the former with the latter (Thompson, 1993, pp. 200–7). Although a synoptic history of this "great transformation" is still notable primarily by its absence, one cannot read the contemporary literature discussing markets without noting that a fair proportion of writers felt that the market for bread warranted special care and attention due to its distinctive features, and that British attitudes and analysis diverged sharply from those prevalent across the Channel in France. Initially, both England and France engaged in elaborate intervention and regulation of the production and sale of bread, regarded as "subsistence", particularly in urban settings; the fear was that intermittent crises of subsistence could not be adequately contained by a price-regulating market structure, and therefore required vigilance and overt control. However, by the eighteenth century, England and France had diverged in their approach to the problem of bread markets. In England, the Assize of Bread was allowed to lapse; forestalling, regrating and engrossing were essentially decriminalised (Webb, 1904; Barnes, 1930). In 1795, England suffered the worst grain shortage of the entire century, and yet there was no renewal of targeted market controls. If there was any attempt to offset crises of subsistence, it took the form of policies like Speenhamland: rather than stipulate the correct operation of the market, relief was scaled to the local price of bread. In effect, the British did not subject the operation of the bread market to close scrutiny, trusting Nature and their conveniently appointed island situation to effect most of the required alterations in the channels of trade. This would have subtle consequences for their subsequent conceptual picture of commerce.

The situation in France was altogether different. Grain police and micro-management of grain market operations were a hallowed tradition, only to be redoubled in the eighteenth century (Kaplan, 1976, 1984). The French also had their champions of trust in Nature: the Physiocrats made it one of their crusades to revoke this doctrine of supervision of grain sales. In 1763 their followers managed to lift most market controls, but this resulted in political and economic disaster, and the system of close market scrutiny was reimposed in 1770. Upon the accession of Louis XVI, A. R. J. Turgot was appointed Controller-General of Finances, and immediately ordered the abolition of the grain police once again. Serious dearth beset France in 1775, and yet in the teeth of hunger Turgot tried to force through further market liberalisations, and was sacked for his efforts in 1776. The plague of the sequence of dearths of subsistence is still widely credited as one of the triggers of the French Revolution. Beyond the political consequences, this litany of woe was also the defining moment in the development of French political economy. Every attempt to come to grips with price theory in France, from Turgot to Galiani to Lavoisier to Canard to Say, was in one way or another a struggle to come to terms with this distressing sequence of failures to understand how the bread market worked. Every evocation of the "naturalness" of the commerce found itself compelled to confront this particular market, and to explain the utter disarray of the grain police in their efforts to render markets fair and transparent.

Modern commentators often attribute the failure of the grain police to the hubris of the Enlightenment project of rational planning – they pass over the failures of the attendant market liberalisations in silence. These superficial reactions ignore one of the more important common denominators of the Physiocrats and the grain police: both more or less shared a common understanding of how grain markets worked. Both would cite an array of forces under the dual rubrics of demand and supply to organise their causal accounts of price movements; the difference was that the grain police believed they were not countermanding or suppressing these forces, but instead rendering them more transparent and above board, so that justice and equity would be better served. This was the motivation behind such strictures as restricting all commerce to a public marketplace, prohibitions on resale, forced offer of inventory within three market days at the risk of seizure and sale by grain police, and explicit public encouragement of higgling and bargaining activity. In practice, the grain police were seeking to render demand and supply visible and palpable and accessible to all, so that there would be no hint of corruption or exploitation in its justice and operation. By *imposing* a specific format of the clearing of the market and *defining* demand and supply in terms of palpable quantities and clearly posted prices, it was the French regulatory tradition which first made it possible to even conceive of a market as a Natural configuration which equilibrated a relatively decontextualised set of price-quantity relationships focusing upon the activities of buying and selling. It is due to this development that the tradition of treating demand and supply as *functions* was first nurtured in France, and found its initial expression in French political economy.

The Impact of Enlightenment Natural Philosophy

Since most histories of the sciences tend to restrict themselves to a single line of inquiry or subject matter, it has been difficult in the past to recognise the essential commonalities across disciplines of the movement of ideas and technologies in specific historical eras and geographic contexts. Of late, this situation has been remedied to some extent, with historians of the natural sciences paying more attention to the social sciences, and some historians of the social sciences achieving greater acquaintance with the literatures of the natural sciences. There are two signal themes from this interdisciplinary endeavour which bear direct relevance for the history of price theory. The first, which we cannot adequately summarise here, identifies the seventeenth and eighteenth century predilection for the explanation of trade as motion, and the explanation of motion in turn as the transmission and exchange of a unified "substance" which inheres in all massy bodies (Mirowski, 1989, ch. 2). The upshot of this structure of explanation is that it was "second nature" to depict market trade as being controlled by some embodied substance inherent in all commodities, be it *blé* for the Physiocrats, or embodied labour in the British context.

The second theme has recently been adumbrated by Norton Wise (1993). He argues that much of enlightenment thought was unified by the idea and the technology of the "balance", ranging from the calorimeter to the treatment of *vis viva*, from the products of fermentation to the manipulation of probabilities, and from animal health to the balance sheet. Although the centrality of the icon of balance was pervasive in European thought, the French were the acknowledged virtuosi of the balancing act. *Vis viva* was balanced in mechanics; caloric was balanced in the calorimeter; debit and credit were counterbalanced in the balance sheet. Nevertheless, there existed a noticeable equivocation on the correct application of the balance in various scientific contexts. On the one hand, "balance" might denote deterministic harmonic fluctuations about a predefined equilibrium position, themselves attributed to external perturbations of a second order of significance; here, classical mechanics provided the exemplar. In this case the laws governing the equilibrium and the perturbations were essentially identical. On the other hand, "balance" might connote a cancelling out of numerous accidental disturbances to a system, where the aggregate of disturbances would be presumed to have no special bias in any particular direction; the exemplar here was testimony in legal settings. In this version, the disturbances might originate from causes having nothing to do with the laws governing the central tendency. This ability to shift back and forth in explanatory resources when explicating balance would have direct implications in the elaboration of the concepts of supply and demand.

There is a collateral theme which also deserves a passing glance. It is a commonplace in the history of mathematics that by the eighteenth century, styles of mathematical expression had diverged in pronounced ways as between England and France. The British tended to hew to their Newtonian heritage, preferring geometric arguments and the rather awkward notation of fluxions, whereas the French tended to favour algebra and the Leibniz notation. Of course one could be translated into the other, but persistent biases in matters of perceived rigour and elegance of expression tended to have real consequences in terms of the areas of mathematics which exemplified these standards and thus were deemed to warrant concerted attention. British pedagogy would stress the timeless quality of Euclid's *Elements*, whereas the French would find their ideal in Descartes's analytical geometry and Lagrange's celestial mechanics. The British fondness for geometric curves over the French penchant for functions would extend even to the presentation of data in scientific reports, although few outside the history of science have come to appreciate just how rare it actually was until well into the nineteenth century to present observations as points plotted on graphs or freehand curves (Tiling, 1975).

The Debut of the Discourse of Supply and Demand

William Thweatt (1983) has performed the invaluable service of compiling an inventory of the uses in English of terminology of supply and demand in early classical political economy, and has come up with a number of unexpected findings. It seems that in the seventeenth century "supply" was rarely used as a noun, and never in conjunction with "demand". Prices were instead situated in a context of scarcity and plenty, or "quantity in proportion to vent". It was only in the early eighteenth century that one finds prices being related to "quantity in proportion to Demand", and that notably in an author steeped in French discourse, namely, John Law. This language of proportionality echoes early discussions of rational mechanics in English, and points towards incipient metaphors of balance. The political economist who deserves the laurels for the introduction of the terminology of "supply and demand" is the under-appreciated Sir James Steuart in 1767; however, the personage who most often garners the credit for promulgation of the discourse of demand and supply is Adam Smith in his *Wealth of Nations.* Since it is Smith rather than Steuart who serves as a touchstone for much which follows, we will briefly examine his usage of the terms.

Whatever else Smith may have intended, he was by no stretch of the imagination an advocate of the later Marshallian organon of supply and demand. Smith discusses his theory of price in Book 1 Chapter 7 of the *Wealth of Nations.* There, price was divided up into the two phenomena of "natural price" and "market price". The former was of course the primary analytical concept, and was determined by a set of natural cost considerations, often called his "adding-up" theory in the literature of the history of economic thought. The latter was intended to denote the observable day-to-day price quotations, which were said to be determined by "supply and demand". There is no question that Smith believed that market price was superimposed upon yet subordinate to natural price, although his discussion of both their determinants and interactions left much to be desired. Market price was said to be propelled by the *ratio* of supply to demand: a common enough locution before Smith, but also one which would readily conjure Newtonian affiliations for his audience. The quarantine of market from natural determinants was achieved through the use of the natural science metaphor of "gravitation": market price would "gravitate" towards natural price over time. However, this recourse embroiled Smith in the trademark enlightenment equivocation over whether market price was the playing out of law-governed harmonic motions, or instead the cancelling-out of externally acausal accidents. This equivocation itself is responsible for a fair number of the non-Marshallian features of Smith's discussion: no notion of price-quantity schedules, no law of one price outside of natural price, no dictum that the market must be cleared. A major consideration is the ability to reserve participation in the market, a theme which will assume ever greater significance in our narrative: "The market price will sink more or less below the natural price . . . according as it happens to them to be more or less important to them to get immediately rid of the commodity" (1976, p. 65).

The French predicament is also a significant subtext of Smith's discussion of price. He praises the Physiocrats in Book 4 Chapter 9, thanks to whom "the agriculture of France has been delivered of several of the oppressions which it before laboured under" (p. 199). At the very least, this was premature when it was written, given the history recounted above. Book 4 Chapter 5 is scathingly dismissive of those who believe the bread market requires state intervention: "famine has never arisen from any other cause but the violence of government attempting, by improper means, to remedy the inconveniences of a dearth" (p. 33); "popular fear of engrossing and forestalling may be compared to the popular terrors and suspicions of witchcraft" (p. 41). It was far and away easier to compose such statements in the 1770s comfortably ensconced in Edinburgh than to be precariously perched in Paris, but there was also the differential willingness to ignore all the various details of the specific market operation, since they were all deemed the outcome of an inexorable Natural process.

Most aspects of Smith's brief foray into demand and supply would have been recognised as standard operating procedure in Enlightenment discourse. Natural price was proposed to be regarded as an expression of enduring substance – and many pounced upon Smith's brief comments on the labour content of commodities – whereas market price (and therefore supply and demand) could be relegated to the realm of the temporary balance. For instance, Lavoisier could write in 1786: "One may compare the increase in price that accompanies the [grain] shortage to the fevers of illness; the fevers are nothing other than the effort that nature makes to re-establish in the animal oeconomy the order that has been troubled" (in Wise, 1993, p. 220). Yet, there remained differences of emphasis and concern, and when the French read Smith, they were not entirely convinced. Perhaps he was thought a little too cavalier about the operation of supply and demand; perhaps he did not quite grasp what the French meant by balance; perhaps the section on labour costs was unseemly; perhaps he displayed a tin ear when it came to an understanding of (early) modern science. At minimum, the French would feel the deficit of system in his presentation with acute displeasure. This would be a complaint of even his major French supporters, Germain Garnier and Jean-Baptiste Say. The differences started small, but gained force and gravitas over time. These differences matter, because supply and demand was more the province of the French economic community than the British, at least until the advent of late British classical political economy.

France at the turn of the century was replete with Enlightenment balancing acts. Nicholas-François Canard's 1801 prize essay marked the birth of mathematical political economy in France, and stood as the only work of political economy that Cournot read before setting out to compose his own *Recherches*. Canard, an engineer, initiated the French practice of fully and unapologetically disengaging market price from natural price, and in explicit analogy with the balance beam, wrote down an equation of forces which determined price under nonspecific circumstances. Here the sellers and buyers were accorded a single function each, with price as the shared variable; psychological need is identified as the ultimate source of each function; equilibrium is equated with the balance of those forces. Unfortunately, all specification of the sequence of actions by which equilibrium is brought about is absent, in a clear analogy with d'Alembert's principle in mechanics.

Jean-Baptiste Say attracted much more attention and commentary than Canard, and although he was opposed to mathematical expression of political economy, he resembles Canard more than he diverges from him. Say objects to the idea of natural price in Smith, collapsing all lawlike regularities to market price determined solely by supply and demand. "Demand and supply are opposite extremes of the beam, whence depend the scales of dearness and cheapness; the price is the point of equilibrium, where the momentum of one ceases, and that of the other begins . . . the rise of price is in direct ratio of the demand, and inverse ratio to the supply" (1830, p. 232). Say's lack of facility with mathematics did not prevent him from attempting to mould his doctrine into a geometrical format in his *Cours complet d'économie politique practique*. The only diagram in the entire work is a triangle, which was intended to represent the number of "fortunes" which (who?) were able to purchase the given commodity at a price represented on the vertical axis (1852, p. 358, Forget, 1994). The relationship to "balance" was more visual than analytical – the figure resembled nothing so much as a fulcrum – and although it made little sense, even with the help of Say's commentary, it did capture the French ambition to develop a theory of supply and demand in critical dialogue with Smith's text which would unify all of political economy and help it to ascend to scientific status through explication of the natural operation of market pricing. Government intervention is denounced in no uncertain terms, and the bread market was cited as one of the relevant examples (p. 362).

Antoine-Augustin Cournot is a landmark figure in our narrative, and not just because he was the one author identified by Marshall as the source of his own inspiration in price theory. Since a geometric portrayal of supply and demand curves can be found in Cournot's 1838 *Recherches*, his work is often used to suggest a long and continuous history for the theory of demand and supply, but such inferences are premature and critically flawed. There exist two very perceptive studies of Cournot's *oeuvre* in French (Menard, 1978; Vatin, 1998), but because they languish untranslated into English, appreciation of Cournot's career has been stunted in the Anglophone world. While Cournot is a recognisable member of the sequence of authors in the French engineering tradition (Etner, 1987), it is necessary to understand why he was largely ignored in his own country, and why it was that his stock began to rise only at the end of the century in Britain, long after his demise.

Cournot, unlike Canard and Say, had a very strong background in mathematics and physics by the standards of his contemporaries; he also demonstrated a deep concern for the pedagogical relationship of geometry to algebra, something which paved the way for later appreciation in the British context. However, he was largely innocent of any previous literature of political economy, which permitted him to venture some rather unorthodox opinions once he came to write his *Recherches*; it was these opinions which rendered him virtually invisible to his economist contemporaries. The paramount fact of his career, and the source of embarrassment to all who wish to elevate him to precursor status, is that this text met with such resounding failure that Cournot himself repudiated his earlier doctrines later in his life (de Ville & Menard, 1989). They had failed by the very criteria for which he had hoped to proselytise: it was deemed poor applied mathematics, and an inadequate codification of Reason.

Cournot began his text by considering how exchange could and could not be considered as amenable to mathematical treatment; it is significant that he explicitly identified that favoured concept of Francophone political economy, *utilité*, as falling into the unsuitable category. After a passing glance at the problem of money, Cournot then confronted the trademark distinction between natural and market prices: "Here, as in astronomy, it is necessary to recognize *secular* variations, which are independent of *periodic* variations" (1971, p. 28). As with his predecessors, Cournot opted to restrict the analysis entirely to short-run or "periodic" phenomena, without any further justification. But that should not be confused with observable prices, as we learn in his Chapter 4, "De la loi de debit".[4] Cournot tells us that he intends his curve to correspond to realized sales – and not, we must insist, virtual unfulfilled desires. He then invokes "the single axiom . . . that each one seeks to derive the greatest possible value from his goods or his labour" (p. 44). This axiom is pivotal, since it justifies recourse to the calculus for Cournot.

At this point we are introduced to the central analytical device of the book: "Let us admit therefore that the sales or annual demand D is, for each article, a particular function F(p) of the price p of such article. To know the form of this function would be to know what we call the *loi de débit*" (p. 47). It will now be necessary to quote *in extenso*:

> Since so many moral causes capable neither of enumeration nor measurement affect the law of sales, it is plain we should no more expect this law to be expressible by an algebraic formula than the law of mortality . . . Observation must therefore be depended on for furnishing the means for drawing up, between proper limits, a table of the corresponding values of D and p; after which, by familiar interpolation of graphical techniques, an empirical formula or curve can be given to represent the function; and solutions can be extended into numerical applications. But even if this objective were unattainable (on account of the difficulty of obtaining observations of sufficient number and accuracy, and also because of progressive variations which the law must undergo in a country not yet at the stationary state), it would nevertheless not be improper to introduce the unknown law of demand into analytical schemes, by means of an undetermined symbol . . . Thus without knowing the law of the decrease of capillary forces, and starting from the principle that these forces are insensible at sensible distances, mathematicians have demonstrated the general laws of the phenomenon of capillarity, and these laws have been confirmed by observation" (pp. 47–8).

The nonspecific reference is to Laplace's work of 1805–7 on capillary action (Grattan-Guinness, 1990, pp. 442–9); Cournot's mentor Poisson had also been involved in elaborations of the theory. Thus, it was all the more damning that Cournot suppressed the comparison after raising it, since Laplace had physical (and not just mathematical) reasons for positing the undetermined capillary function in his theory, and these underwrote the application of various integrals and other mathematical devices in his theory. Further, when subjected to experiment, the results were mixed, and this caused Laplace himself to doubt the legitimacy of his analysis. Those cognoscenti familiar with the case would doubt its relevance; and everyone else would simply be passively dazzled by the references to the physical sciences.

It is very difficult to imagine that Cournot himself was unaware of the disanalogies with his economic model. Hard upon the above quote, Cournot posited that his F(p) function was continuous; this was justified by the assumption of a thick market and a large number of consumers (p. 50). Since continuity was a requirement for every mathematical manipulation that followed, Cournot uncharacteristically devoted it much consideration, acknowledging that there might be "exceptions", but conjuring them away with the comment that, "just as friction wears down roughnesses and softens outlines, so the wear of commerce tends to suppress these exceptional cases" (p. 51). To pile ignominy on top of unreliability, he then posits that "the price of an article may vary notably in the course of a year, and strictly speaking, the law of sales may also vary in the same interval, if the country experiences a movement of progress or decadence", and therefore "the curve which represents the function F must itself be an average of all the curves which would represent this function" (p. 52). In the midst of this litany of pleading, the all-important negative slope of the function F is inserted as an unmotivated assumption. Time frames, assertions of continuity and regularity, statistical means and individual instances, realisations versus virtual realities, renunciations of mental causes with appeals to human nature – all become hopelessly jumbled in the headlong rush to concoct a function, *any function*, which might be manipulated in the manner of physics: that is, subjected to an optimisation procedure. Is it any wonder that Cournot ends this section with the disturbing concession? – "We may admit that it is impossible to determine the function F(p) for each article" (p. 53), all the while proposing that economic agents are going to use this function in order to inform their own behaviour.

In their unseemly rush to award laurels, modern economists overlook that this was deemed a sorry performance, a sad sequence of *non sequiturs* understandably shunned by Cournot's contemporaries. The idea that anything other than the rhetorical power of physical analogy, much less the "law of demand", was "discovered" by Cournot is a travesty of the actual historical events. The incongruous imposition of "already completed" price arbitrage with a putative variable state of the thickness of the market and strength of competition was difficult to swallow. Since the law of one price was only plausible in the case of monopoly, that accounts for the fact Cournot's next chapter begins there; and the analysis works solely in terms of the single curve. Since the curve purportedly depended upon "the kind of utility of the article, on the nature of services it can render or the enjoyments it can procure, on the habits and customs of the people, on the average wealth, and on the scale which wealth is distributed" (p. 47), and none of these held out the promise of any stability or invariance, it would have been wishful thinking to regard the function F(p) as anything other than a will-o'-the-wisp, much less continuous with first and second derivatives.

We do not mean to suggest the majority of Cournot's peers thrust the volume away in disgust over the dubious character of its formal arguments (although Bertrand's 1883 review could be cited as one instance). Indeed, it is more likely that they were put off by the text's politics, that is, if they managed to reach the last chapter. There Cournot explicitly set his work in opposition to "the school of Adam Smith, with a view to removing the barriers between nation and nation, has always argued from the uncontestable increase in wealth, which has been the invariable result of the removal of barriers" to international trade (p. 160). Cournot's argument was that the extension of markets could either raise or lower incomes relative to the pre-trade *status quo*. This alone would have been sufficient to alienate the author from the orthodoxy of French political economy.

No historian other than Menard has paid any attention to Cournot's career after the *Recherches,* which extended for another four decades and numerous books, including two more on political economy. Somehow it is deemed legitimate to ignore the later books because they had no impact on contemporaries; but by those standards, neither should we take a second look at the *Recherches.* The young Cournot relied heavily upon a belief in the inexorable spread of the market and of rationality (with the metric system as exemplar) to rationalise his own project of a mathematical political economy. He thought that as markets became more thick and competitive, and people became increasingly rational, it would become legitimate to rely upon the law of large numbers to treat participants as homogeneous, markets as frictionless, and hence F(p) as continuous and well-behaved. Menard explicitly links this to a common engineering mentality. However, later in life Cournot grew disenchanted with trends he thought he had observed – the relative failure of metricisation, lack of progress towards greater competition, and less evidence of rationality amongst the masses. This provoked a growing philosophical conviction that economics should look more like biology than rational mechanics. For just these reasons, his later works on political economy contain no mathematical content, and thus, no law of sales. It was on just these grounds that Cournot rejected Walras's *Élements* (Walras, 1965, letter 294).

British Treatments of Supply and Demand in the Nineteenth Century prior to Thornton

The discourse of laws of supply and demand was noticeably slower to catch on in Britain than in France. Indeed, as Thweatt (1983, p. 289) demonstrates, after Steuart and Smith there were no substantial discussions for a quarter-century. The silence was broken by Thomas Malthus's pamphlet *The High Price of Provisions* in 1800 and Henry Thornton – no relation to William Thomas – and James Mill in 1802. But soon thereafter, the number of texts escalates rapidly, with numerous mentions of "supply and demand" in Parliamentary debates by 1810. The primary camp which appears to have adopted the terminology as their own were the "Philosophical Radicals" such as Francis Horner, Henry Brougham and Richard Torrens (Halévy, 1972). It is safe to say that by the end of the Napoleonic Wars the laws of supply and demand were common currency in the British context; but there are many curious and counterintuitive aspects of this sea change which have yet to attract major scrutiny.

The first incongruous aspect of the rise of supply and demand theory in Britain is that this discourse gains purchase right in the period of the genesis and development of the Ricardian orthodoxy in British classical political economy. David Ricardo's hostility to supply and demand as generic explanations of price and quantity in his *Principles* of 1817 and elsewhere are well known, and need not be reiterated here. Thus it is all the more noteworthy that many of the proponents of supply and demand theories were engaged in close contact with Ricardo and his notions of a scientific political economy during their genesis – all the more reason why classical political economy should never be treated as a monolithic doctrine. Secondly, it is also well known that the primary context for these debates were disputes over the corn laws and the "high price of provisions". Hence, just as in the French case, it was the vexed issue of the question of special treatment accorded to the bread or grain markets which called forth the conceptual clarification of notions of supply and demand. Third, this similarity in the conditions of genesis is no mere coincidence, since it was precisely those figures most heavily influenced by French writers and French ideas, especially Malthus, Horner and Mill Sr. (Halévy, 1972, p. 270) who became proponents of the doctrine of the primacy of supply and demand as scientific political economy. Nevertheless, once the doctrine recrossed the Channel, it tended to assume a different tenor and tone; and this specific historical manifestation requires description in depth in order to begin to grasp the impact of Thornton's work in the later 1860s. We shall sketch the outlines of such a description by briefly relating the conceptions of supply and demand proposed by a number of key texts in the period from Thomas Robert Malthus to John Stuart Mill.

From a historiographic distance, Thomas Malthus's *High Price of Provisions* would resemble a rather standard broadside against those who would seek to regulate bread markets, such as one would find in that era in France. Britain had just suffered a terrible dearth of grain in 1795, and even though harvests had subsequently recovered, prices were still high by historical standards. Malthus's pen was mobilized by the fact that, "Many men of sense have joined in the universal cry of the common people, that there must be roguery somewhere; and the general indignation has fallen upon the monopolizers, forestallers and regraters" (1986, p. 6). The problem was that a sophisticated understanding of the laws of political economy was absent: "When any commodity is scarce, its natural price is necessarily forgotten, and its actual price is regulated by the excess of demand over supply." In times of crisis people needed an understanding of the short-term workings of markets; appeals to long-run natural determinants were essentially unavailing. Parson Malthus could not restrain himself from also blaming the Poor Laws and Speenhamland; but the paramount message was that the operation of the market, here explicitly equated with the balance of demand and supply, was not at fault. One observes that even in the British context, the advantages of downgrading the theory of "natural" price relative to some lawlike supply and demand doctrines were becoming apparent to a few key figures.

It is now frequently forgotten that Jeremy Bentham entered this fray on the opposing side in his *Defence of* a *Maximum* (1801), supporting temporary price controls on corn. Such heresy, especially among the clique of Radicals, cried out for a response; and James Mill responded to the call in his 1804 essay on the trade in corn. His major weapon against market intervention was the assertion that "the demand will always be proportioned to the supply, however great that supply may be" (1966, p. 56). In 1805, Mill was the first to acknowledge Say and his "loi de débouchés" as a theoretical and political ally. In 1806, Mill wrote an elaborate review of Sir James Steuart's *Principles* – the first systematic treatise to extensively use the language of supply and demand – as a pretext to discuss the corn trade. Mill subsequently developed a close personal relationship with Say, serving as his intermediary with the British luminaries of political economy and facilitating correspondence with Bentham, Malthus and Ricardo, among others. By 1820, their personal and intellectual careers were so intertwined that Mill Sr. arranged for his adolescent son John Stuart Mill to reside with Say during his first visit to Paris (Bain, 1882, p. 190; Mill, 1960). Thus it was not unexpected that when Mill Sr. produced his own *Elements of Political Economy* in 1821, asking in Chapter 3 "What Determines the Quantity in Which Commodities Exchange for One Another?" the answer should be, "the principle of supply and demand, in the first instance" (1966, p. 255). With Mill, the doctrine of the determination of price by supply and demand and the doctrine of the impossibility of a general glut became inextricably yoked together, so that mere assertion of "laws" of demand and supply were taken as shorthand for a belief that markets always operated for the benefit of the common weal in a problem-free fashion.

Hence, by the 1820s, at least in the hands of the "Millians" (as they were then called), the mantra of "supply and demand" became a sort of litmus test to divine the soundness of someone's position on political economy. The assertion that grain markets always correctly represented the state of scarcity reigning in any given situation shaded over into a dogma that markets would never allow the existence of overproduction in general (although disproportionalities between industries might make for temporary disruption), and therefore all unemployment was merely a matter of frictions, temporary imbalances or external interference with the wage mechanism. This was a defining moment in British classical political economy: French concern over the specific problems of a grain market with its own characteristic rules and practices, provoking a French liberal backlash hostile to attempts to regulate and regularise subsistence markets, slowly transmuted into a British belief that all markets exhibited the same generic mechanisms described by "laws" of supply and demand, and therefore constituted the primary explanation why free markets for labour could not result in pervasive unemployment or impoverishment of the workforce.

Consequently, by the 1820s, the language of supply and demand was coming to be deployed as a shorthand in England for a very specific political position (Groenewegen, 1973, p. 509): for instance, in Parliamentary debates, to signal adherence to a position which denounced subsistence aid to the poor or any organised interference in the wage labour nexus. Its transformation was so swift that it went from a tentative hypothesis to a proposition so well-established that one violated it only under the most dire of circumstances, all in little more than two decades. One observes it used unselfconsciously in speeches from the floor, like that of the Marquis of Lansdowne in 1822: "That it is mischievous to interfere with the regular course of supply and demand in the market was a principle no less generally recognized; but, so singular was the situation of Ireland, that this great principle of political economy must be violated" (in Fetter, 1980, p. 59). This was the orthodox use of supply and demand which Charles Dickens savaged in his 1854 novel *Hard Times*:

> For the first time in her life Louisa had come into one of the dwellings of the Coketown hands . . . She knew them in crowds passing to and from their nests, like ants or beetles. But she knew from her reading infinitely more of the ways of the toiling insects than of these toiling men and women. Something to be worked so much and paid so much, and there ended; something to be infallibly settled by the laws of supply and demand; something that blundered into those laws and floundered into difficulty; something that was a little pinched when wheat was dear and overrate themselves when wheat was cheap; . . . something that occasionally rose like the sea, and did some harm and waste (chiefly to itself), and fell again; this she knew the Coketown hands to be. (1961, p. 160)

However, the stronger were the links forged between the British discourse of demand and supply and this construction of the political lessons of political economy, the less precise were the specifications of what the imperious "laws" actually implied or ruled out. "Laws" they might very well be, but it was noticeable that British political economists expended appreciably less effort than their contemporary French counterparts in shoring up their expression with mathematics or empirical data. Perhaps this might be attributed to the uneasy coexistence of the discourse of demand and supply with the stated tenets of the Ricardian school, perhaps the relative quarantine of British political economists from trained engineers and natural sciences (in contrast to the situation of the French) could also have played a role. In any event, the configuration of forces did have the result of producing a much less coherent and sustained discussion of demand and supply in Britain from roughly 1820 to 1870, a period punctuated by intermittent unresolved controversies over the meaning and significance of demand and supply.

Especially in the 1820s and 1830s, one cannot help but notice a proliferation of positions vis-a-vis the theory of supply and demand. As De Quincey once noted, "that one desperate enormity of vicious logic which takes place in the ordinary application to price of the relation between supply and demand has secured more arguments dispersed through speeches, books, journals than a long life could fully expose" (1897, p. 118). In the interests of brevity, we shall identify three major categories.[5] First, there were the hardcore Ricardians who sought to defend the central doctrinal primacy of the labour theory of value; this would include McCulloch, popularisers such as Jane Marcet, Ricardo himself, and later Thomas De Quincey. Natural price as cost of production was deemed the pre-eminent theoretical device; the accidental and imponderable aspects of the day-to-day operation of markets were to be disposed of under the portmanteau rubric of supply and demand. This group, understandably, bore the least stake, and thus exerted the least effort, in trying to stabilise the precise theoretical referent of supply and demand. "You must, however, recollect that it is the cost of production of a commodity which constitutes its exchangeable value; the proportion of supply and demand should be considered as only accidentally affecting it" (Marcet, 1827, p. 317). "Variations of demand and supply occasion corresponding variations of price; but it is essential to remark that these valuations are temporary only. The cost of production is the grand regulator of price – the centre of all those transitory and evanescent oscillations on the one side and the other . . . wherever industry is unrestricted and competition allowed to operate, the average price of the various products of art and industry coincides with the cost of production" (McCulloch, 1864, pp. 252, 257). "It is a metaphysical impossibility that Supply and Demand, the relation of which is briefly expressed by the term 'market value,' could ever affect price except by a *secondary* force" (De Quincey, 1897, p. 121).

Then there was a second camp seeking to occupy something like a middle ground: unwilling to wholly repudiate the labour theory in its guise as a "cost of production" approach, but seeking to downgrade it to something resembling a special case of the more general laws of supply and demand. The best representatives of this group were Malthus and his sympathisers such as Longfield and Scrope; but the tent was sufficiently large to encompass the rather more venturesome Mills, the antipodean William Hearn and Ricardian sometimes-fellow-travellers like Torrens. This was the group who frequently sought to engage with Say on his own ground, often flirting to a greater or lesser extent with "utility" as an ur-principle of value, and less frequently looking to French liberals for a modicum of their own political inspiration. As Mill Jr. wrote, "The principle, that value is proportional to cost of production, being consequently inapplicable, we must revert to a principle anterior to that of cost of production, and from which this last flows as a consequence, – namely, the principle of demand and supply" (1897, p. 13). One implication of the inversion of importance was that the theory of supply and demand should, in principle, enjoy explication of the conditions under which it would operate freely and the environments in which it would dominate cost of production; yet precious few of the authors in this second group ultimately devoted much effort to that task. Nevertheless, their rallying cry, this figure/ground reversal as regards the labour theory of "natural price" and the supply/demand locution would soon prove their downfall, since the need to expand supply/demand to broaden the tent, all the while doggedly maintaining agnosticism on what was "natural" about natural price, tended to rob this crew of all conceptual precision or political efficacy. It is no surprise that this bloated and disorganised middle ground would be where William Thornton would choose to mount his attack in the 1860s upon political economy, its confusions on price and its strictures on wages.

Finally, there did exist a third group of writers rooted primarily in the natural sciences – outsiders to the Ricardian orthodoxy – who had no interest in defending past verities or recent French fashions. They, too, sought "laws" of the economy; in their no-nonsense instrumental world, the language of "supply and demand" would serve as well as any other to demarcate their quest. However, all notions of reconciliation with the classical labour doctrine were dismissed as futile. They are sometimes identified in the modern literature as the "Whewell group" of political economists (Henderson, 1996) – Edward Rogers, William Whewell, Dionysius Lardner – although by all rights, Fleeming Jenkin would fit very neatly into this category as well. Although they may look very modern in retrospect, they had almost no lasting impact upon their contemporaries in Britain. Partly, this was due to the fact that the demand/supply organon was deployed in their writings more as a tool of critique than as engine of analysis, at least prior to the 1870s; and in part, it was confounded by the hostility to algebraic models in the British context.

Because it was the second, largest group that provided the millieu and target for Thornton's later work, it may prove worthwhile to take a somewhat closer look at a few of the key texts which constituted the mid-nineteenth century orthodoxy concerning the theory of supply and demand. The leitmotiv of this literature is repeated accusations launched at others of dire confusions over the deployment of the laws of supply and demand, and endless reiteration of the desperate need for sound definitions, although each subsequent proposal never seemed to satisfy much of anyone. Malthus, for one, could never make others understand just what it was he meant by the laws of demand and supply. In his 1820 *Principles* he appeals to Turgot and Say, but still feels he must enter a note of caution: "The terms Demand and Supply are so familiar to the ear of every reader . . . [yet] are by no means applied with precision" (1966, p. 36). Paradoxically, everyday usage is held as arbiter: "[When] society has been divided, in common language, into buyers and sellers, demand may be defined to be the will combined with the power to purchase, and supply, the production of commodities with intention to sell them" (p. 37). What one blade giveth, the other immediately taketh away: "existing market prices are, at the moment they are fixed, determined upon a principle quite distinct from cost of production, and that these prices are in reality almost always different from what they would have been if this cost had regulated them . . . the great principle of Demand and Supply is called into action to determine what Adam Smith calls natural as well as market prices" (pp. 45–6). Perhaps one can sympathise with Ricardo's vexation with this passage, reproduced in his notes on Malthus: "The author forgets Adam Smith's definition of natural price, or else he would not say that Demand and Supply could determine natural price."

Malthus cluttered up the end of his career with screeds chiding all and sundry concerning the inadequacies of their definitions, surely the very last refuge of the pedant. As frequently is the case, the guns were turned on those closest to his own position: "the most culpable confusion of terms which Mr. Mill has fallen into, is in relation to demand and supply; and as he has a more original and appropriate claim to this error than any other English writer . . . the notice of it is particularly called for" (1827, p. 44). This prefaced a rambling critique of the surfeit of meanings of demand then prevalent in political economy, only to end up with his preferred specification(s) – "two distinct meanings: one, in regard to the extent, or the quantity of commodities purchased; and the other, in regard to the intensity, or sacrifice which the demanders are willing and able to make in order to satisfy their wants" (p. 244). To preserve a semblance of continuity, this "intensity" was further equated with the labour commanded by the commodity.

No one could rest content with this; everyone felt impelled to propose some variation upon it. Poulett Scrope wrote: "the value (or selling price) of an article at any time and place is determined by the proportion of the demand to the supply at that time and place . . . The extent of the Demand for a thing depends upon the intensity of desire for its possession among a larger or smaller group of persons, and likewise upon the means of purchasing it . . . The supply of goods is determined by the circumstances that affect their production, and is subject to greater variations than the demand" (1969, pp. 185–7). Mountifort Longfield took the dramatic step of attempting to restrict its meaning in the interest of rendering the definition more general: "that portion of any commodity which any one possesses and does not intend to consume is supply; the disposition to give something in exchange for it is demand . . . . if the quantity of the article to be sold is more than sufficient to supply all those who are willing to pay the natural price for it, the competition among the sellers . . . will sink the price until the supply comes equal to the effective demand . . . In this case the equality between the Demand and the Supply is produced not by diminishing the supply, but by the increased demand consequent upon a diminution of price" (1834, pp. 45, 49). Perhaps one can conjure some empathy with the frustration of the author of *Observations on Certain Verbal Disputes* . . . who complained: "If the degree of demand can itself be altered by the degree of supply, what information is given us by saying, that something depends upon the balance of forces (as it were) between the two?" (in Smith, 1951, p. 253).

Stranded in this morass, the writings of John Stuart Mill must have appeared as welcome *terra firma* amidst an endless Sargasso Sea of shifting definitions. In his youthful work *Some Unsettled Questions in Political Economy* (written 1829/30), he already set about the task of judiciously distancing himself from the hardcore Ricardian position, but equally so from his father's advocacy of Say. It is noteworthy that this takes place within the context of one of the first extended commentaries on supply and demand in English not explicitly devoted to either the corn trade or the wages question. The first essay is concerned rather with the theory of international trade – not insignificantly one of the exceptions to the primacy of natural price in Ricardo's system – whereas the second essay tends to mitigate the insistence made by Say upon the ironclad impossibility of a general glut. Mill here insists upon a construction of his version of supply and demand as predicated upon market clearing: "Whatever be the commodity – the supply in any market being given, there is some price at which the whole of the supply will find purchasers, and no more. That, whatever it be, is the price at which, by the effect of competition the commodity will be sold" (1897, p. 13). Nevertheless, the precision promised by this point of satiation was still treated as eluding the effective grasp of the science of political economy: "The result of our most fortunate inquiries will seldom assume a very definite form: it will be more frequently a genus than an individual: we shall seldom be able to accurately measure its dimensions, or to express it precisely in numbers. It is not unlikely, however, that an artificial science might be formed, which should promote the practical discovery of political truth" (p. 70).

Such circumspection, while laudable in an essay format, has no place in a textbook; and thus Mill's *Principles of Political Economy* approached the problem of price in an aggressively confident manner. This change in tone had something to do with Mill's rather dramatic hardening of his view of the central place of natural science-style laws and their relationship to the role of the expert in social theory:

> I already regarded the methods of the physical sciences as the proper models for the political; but one important point in the parallelism much insisted on by M. Comte, had not before occurred to me, in mathematics and physics what is called the liberty of conscience . . . is merely nominal: though in no way restrained by law, liberty is not exercised . . . [I]f any one rejected what has been proved by demonstration or experiment, he would be thought to be asserting no right but the right of being a fool: those who have not studied the sciences take their conclusions on trust from those who have . . . Hitherto, it had not occurred to me that the case would be the same in the moral, social and political branches of speculation if they were equally advanced with the physical . . . From this time by hopes of [mankind's] improvement rested less on the reason of the multitude, than on the possibility of effecting such an improvement in the methods of political and social philosophy, as should enable all thinking and instructed persons who have no sinister interest to be so nearly of one mind on these subjects, as to carry the multitude with them by their writed authority. (Mill, *Collected Works*, 1967, vol. 1, pp. 615–16)

This rather paternalistic naturalism pervades Mill's discussion of the theory of price in the *Principles*. His unfortunate assertion there that "there is nothing in the laws of Value which remains for the present or any future writer to clear up" (1965, p. 456) has oft been quoted as a masterpiece of imprescience; but few seem to have realised the extent to which he so qualified Ricardo's cost of production strictures that the "theory" of supply and demand became the *de facto* doctrinal core of his political economy, or as he put it in an important emendation of the phrase from his earlier Essay, "we must revert to a law of value anterior to cost of production and more fundamental, the law of demand and supply" (1965, p. 583). Much of this doctrinal hubris, this drastic innovation retailed as doctrinal faithfulness to Ricardo plus some unalloyed common sense, has been praised in retrospect[6] as an anticipation of the Marshallian orthodoxy of a half-century later:

> Thus we see that the idea of a *ratio*, as between demand and supply, is out of place . . . the proper mathematical analogy is that of an *equation*. Demand and supply, the quantity demanded and the quantity supplied, will be made equal. If unequal at any moment, competition equalizes them, and the manner in which this is done is by adjustment of the value" (1965, p. 467).

Yet it is important to take note of the ways in which Mill's doctrine was less forward-looking than profoundly conservative (Packe, 1954, p. 312). This is best signalled by the fact that Mill only cited two authors in his discussion of the theory of supply and demand: De Quincey and Say. Say is credited with a "clear exposition" (p. 466) of the theory, whereas De Quincey is upbraided for not realising the extent to which the doctrine remains fully supportive of the Ricardian tradition. For those familiar with the latter two authors, these two statements would in essence imply a contradiction, something often encountered in Mill's *ex cathedra* mode. The sense of misplaced concreteness undoubtedly derived from Mill's desire to uphold the Ricardian catechism that "production" [read:substance] was the root determinant of value, with exchange operations treated as secondary perturbations superimposed upon the fundamental relationships, to such an extent that they could be dealt with as analytically separable. Thus Mill could still insist that supply and demand constituted "the Law of Value, with respect to commodities not susceptible of being multiplied at pleasure" (p. 468); but then genuflect towards Ricardo by adding, "the value of things which can be increased in quantity at pleasure, does not depend (except accidentally, and during the time necessary for production to adjust itself) upon demand and supply; on the contrary, demand and supply depend upon it" (p. 475). Here, as in many other instances, Mill was simultaneously retailing the two alternative Enlightenment conceptions of balance, with no attempt to distinguish or differentiate them. Were divergences from the theoretically correct price due to accidents not covered in the theory but averaged out in large numbers, or a set of determinants fundamentally separate from the law of normal price, or the same lawlike determinants as account for the normal price, just operating on a meta-level, such as perturbations around equilibrium?

In Mill's *Principles*, the theory of supply and demand was both delimited and confirmed in its previous doctrinal associations. In their prior incarnations, the "laws" of demand and supply were never intended to encompass every possible market phenomenon under every conceivable circumstance; and here Mill's version was no different. He notoriously exempted supply and demand from what would become the paradigm case of catallactics in the neoclassical era, namely, the case of the isolated individual purchasing goods for private use. Said Mill, "Purchases for private use, even by people in business, are not always made on business principles" (p. 460). Since psychological motives were not deemed sufficiently regular to underpin economic laws, Mill proposed that the laws of supply and demand might not capture pricing behaviour in retail markets, but would be best exemplified in wholesale markets, where "values and prices are determined by competition alone". Thus the notion was promulgated that it was men of business who were most capable and trustworthy representatives serving as conduits and mouthpieces for the inanimate forces of production; only they were driven by impersonal dictates of competition, which overrode all specifics of the actual organization and structure of the marketplace. Rather than a description of a process, competition tended to be conflated with the "axiom", viz, "that there cannot be for the same article, of the same quality, two prices in the same market". For Cournot, the *loi de débit* would be most transparently expressed in the case of monopoly, since it was only there that one would expect the one-price rule to hold; whereas for Mill, the fullness of competition in the guise of the one-price rule was the only regime under which there might obtain a "law" of demand at all. Not only was this an inversion of the usual understanding of the significance of price dispersion in a market: this was equally the ushering in of a long tradition of the repression of distinctive market processes under various rubrics of degrees of "competition" (Dennis, 1977).

There was another way in which real existing markets were acknowledged as diverse: foreigners might be exempt from the idealisation of "economic man" and full competition to a greater or lesser degree.

> In political economy . . . empirical laws of human nature are tacitly assumed by English thinkers, which are calculated only for Great Britain and the United States. Among other things, an intensity of competition is constantly supposed, which, as a general mercantile fact, exists in no country in the world except in those two . . . . Yet those who know the habits of the Continent of Europe are aware how apparently small a motive often outweighs the desire of money-getting, even in the operations which have money-getting as their direct object. (Mill, *Collected Works*, 1967, vol. 8, p. 906)

We can thus observe that the boundaries of the set of markets to which the "laws" of supply and demand would pertain was conveniently imprecise and highly variable: a fact that will shortly prove relevant to Mill's own attempts to defend these laws against critics, as well as in understanding the ways in which he diverged from the subsequent neoclassical doctrine.

Mill's textbook bears responsibility for another, rather dismal doctrine in the history of Anglophone economics. Mill took the prior political valence of popular appeals to supply and demand and hardened it into a rigid dictum about the impotence of workers to do anything about the level of their own wages, which he himself popularised under the label of the "wages-fund". In Books I and II of the *Principles*, the wages fund is described in the context of a stationary economy: wages "depend mainly on the demand and supply of labour; or as is often expressed, on the proportion between population and capital . . . nothing can permanently alter general wages, except an increase or diminution of capital itself (always meaning by the term the funds of all sorts devoted to the payment of labour) compared with the quantity of labour offering itself to be hired" (Mill, *Collected Works*, 1967, vol. 2, pp. 337–9). In Book III this became indissolubly linked to the primacy of supply and demand as a causal explanation of price: "there are commodities of which, though capable of being increased to a great, or even an unlimited extent, the value never depends upon anything but demand and supply. This is the case, in particular, with the commodity Labour" (1965, p. 469). In Books IV and V, a more fluid and dynamic perspective was taken, whereby the working class as a whole might eventually improve its lot through population control, education, and Mill's favourite Golden Mean of "Co-operation" between Labour and Capital; but after all was said and done, in editions of the *Principles* prior to the late 1860s there was very little hope held out for the working man in his or her own lifetime.

It is a topic of extended commentary the extent to which Mill tended to change his mind about political economy under the influence of Harriet Taylor after 1848 (Packe, 1954, p. 313; Hayek, 1951). Nevertheless, it does appear that Mill suffered reservations about how the doctrine of the wages-fund was being used, especially after Henry Fawcett's 1860 *Westminister Review* article on strikes. These reservations, in conjunction with the links forged between the wages-fund, the condemnation of the economic impact of trades unions, and the burgeoning significance of the demand/supply doctrine as an explanation of price, set the stage for the momentous intervention of William Thomas Thornton in the 1860s.

The Life of William Thomas Thornton

Part of the explanation for the neglect of Thornton in the historical literature is the palpable fact that someone of his particular station in life, not to mention his publications prior to *On Labour*, would present a most unlikely candidate for having a lasting impact upon the evolution of British political economy. To a certain extent, his obscurity has masked his role behind the scenes in the 1860s and 1870s, over and above his publications.

According to the *Dictionary of National Biography*, William Thomas Thornton was born in the British town of Burnham, Buckinghamshire, on 14 February 1813. William was the youngest son of Sophie Zohrab, the daughter of a Greek merchant, and Thomas Thornton, a man involved with international commerce from an early age. Thomas Thornton is best known for his 1807 book *The Present State of Turkey*. This tract was a detailed description of the social, political and military institutions of the Ottoman Empire. Most of Thomas Thornton's familiarity with the Levant derived from his many years of residence in Constantinople and the surrounding region, pursuing British mercantile interests.

Unfortunately for the young William, his father died on 28 March 1814, on the eve of his voyage to Alexandria to assume the position of counsel to the Levant Company. While this left William bereft of a father at a young and tender age, subsequent to an initial residence in the Moravian settlement at Ockbrook, he was nonetheless able to experience a wide variety of educational experiences abroad upon reaching his majority. Most notable are his three years' residence with the auditor-general of Malta, William Thomas's cousin W. H. Thornton, and five years in Constantinople from 1830–35 with the consul-general Cartwright. In August 1836 William Thornton obtained a position with the India House at the very height of its power and prestige. His preferment was due to the intervention of Sir James Carnac, then chairman of the East India Company. This clerkship was not only the beginning of a long and successful career in the colonial bureaucracy, but also served to bring William into contact with many of the leading businessmen, politicians and intellectuals of the time. One notable example was the Prime Minister of Britain (1788–1850) Sir Robert Peel; another was the Duke of Argyll. Previously unpublished letters in the British Library archives addressed to Peel suggest that Peel was partially instrumental in William Thomas's early advancement within India House. We reproduce these letters below.[7]

58 Upper Berkeley Street
Portman Square
February 4, 1845

Sir,
I trust that I shall be excused for laying before you the following statement and that the peculiar circumstances of my case may be considered a sufficient apology for the intrusion.
Above twenty one years age I was appointed at the instance of the late Mr. Canning to the situation I now hold, that of Clerk of Securities in the Excise at a salary of £600 per annum, the office having just been vacated by Mr. Henry Canning on his receiving a Consulship.

I also received from Mr. Canning the distinct promise of a higher office which induced me to relinquish all ideas of following any other profession. Mr. Canning's friends indeed were so well aware of the flattering interest which he took in my advancement, that after that Premier's death the late Mr. Haskiper(?) assured me that if it should ever be in his power to further my career, he should consider it his duty to fulfill the promise made to me by Mr. Canning.

I venture therefore from my long services, and on the strength of the promises I have received to address this statement to you, and feeling confident that the Board of Excise will bear testimony to the manner in which I have for so many years discharged the duties of my present office, I am induced to hope that you may be inclined to take my case into your consideration, and to confer upon me a Commissionership(?) at one of the Public Boards (the appointment which I have reason to believe was designed for me by Mr. Canning) or any other office of superior station to that which I now hold, and for which you may consider me eligible.

The changes of Administration, and an unwillingness to prefer an application of this kind at an unseasonable moment have hitherto precluded me from mentioning these circumstances; at the present time however I am more particularly desirous of stating them, as owing to the developed state of the West Indies (where my property is situated) my income flow thence has entirely ceased. This I am aware is a matter completely of a private nature, but I still venture to think that it may be regarded by you as an aggravation of the disappointment of those prospects of investment which were apparently so well guarded.

I am fully sensible of the liberty I have taken in thus addressing you, whilst at the same time I cannot forget the sense which is universally entertained of the kindness and justice which have ever distinguished your decisions, and which encourages me to hope that you may look favourably upon the statement I have now ventured to lay before you.

I have the honour to be
Sir
Your most obedient Servant,
W. T. Thornton

Excise
October 3, 1845

Sir,
Having just learnt from the Chairman of this board that the arrangements for the abolition of the Office which I now hold in this department have been submitted to you, and have been pleased to entertain the proposition for appointing me to the situation of Receiver General of Excise. I beg to offer you my most sincere acknowledgments, and to assure you that I shall always entertain a grateful recollection of your kindness.

I have the honor to be
Sir
Your most obedient Servant,
W. T. Thornton

Thornton's elevation to Receiver General of Excise coincided with his debut as an author. *Overpopulation and Its Remedy* (1846) was an anti-Malthusian tract, which inverted the conventional wisdom in maintaining that "the original cause of over-population is almost invariably misery", rather than vice versa. At this early stage one can observe Thornton's nascent fascination with the wages fund doctrine, accepting at that stage that wages were determined by the ratio between the "fund" and the population of labourers, but questioning the extent to which the denominator conformed to simple stories of immiseration. Thornton there first stated his life-long theme that the cultural experience of being lifted out of poverty would not render the subject feckless and lazy and profligate, but rather was the most generally assured method of fostering a set of behaviours which would maintain prosperity. His indictment of Malthus was that he "overlooked or undervalued the tendency which the possession of property has to engender prudence, and seems, indeed, to have thought that the quality is rarely to be found among members of the labouring class, except under the pressure of misery" (p. 270). Thornton instead believed that there existed the possibility of a low-level trap in economic development, wherein the hardscrabble struggle for existence would actually serve to lower living standards. He revealed a nascent scepticism in the benevolent progress of natural forces, one which would subsequently loom increasingly larger in importance, pointing to situations where workers "are too numerous to earn a competent subsistence for themselves and their families, competition takes place amongst them: each, in his anxiety to obtain employment, offers to accept lower wages than he requires for his comfortable maintainance . . . Neither has this state any tendency to correct itself. Whatever point populations may attain, it can with equal ease at least maintain itself there" (pp. 3–4).

However, in 1846 Thornton felt compelled to couch his assault on the Malthusian consensus in terms which left the orthodox concepts of supply and demand unquestioned. This is revealed in passing in his commentary on the Poor Laws: "It cannot be denied that in this instance the rate of wages was in part determined by the price of provisions, but this can only happen where the circumstances which naturally regulate the price of labour are arbitrarily interfered with. When the money price of labour is suffered to adjust itself according to the proportions between the supply and the demand, it will remain unaffected by any variations in the price of provisions or of other commodities" (p. 227). Initially closer to Malthus than to Ricardo on questions of price theory, Thornton was situated somewhere in that large second group identified in the previous section of those who were inclined to elevate supply and demand to pride of place in political economy, but with the proviso that there was plenty of room for concerted action on the part of the state and of the actors to lift the poorest members of society out of penury. In this regard, he resembled no major contemporary figure so much in the British context as John Stuart Mill.

This raises the very important issue, perversely avoided by most historians of economic thought but openly acknowledged by general historians (Packe, 1954, p. 387), of the close and prolonged personal relationship between William Thomas and Mill Jr. As he relates in his memoir, Thornton knew Mill by sight at the India House, but had no occasion to have a conversation with him until he sent him a copy of his *Over-population* in 1846. As he told it,

> A day or two afterwards he came into my room to thank me for it; and during the half-hour's conversation that thereupon ensued, sprang up, full grown at birth, an intimate friendship, of which I feel that I am not unduly boasting in declaring it to have been equally sincere and fervent on both sides. From that time for the next ten or twelve years, a day seldom passed without, if I did not go into his room, his coming into mine, often telling me as he entered that he had nothing particular to

say; but that, having a few minutes to spare, he thought we might as well have a little talk (1873, pp. 34–5).

This working relationship developed into a close friendship which was enriched by discussions of many philosophical, intellectual and economic issues, described below primarily in Thornton's eulogy to Mill. Indeed, in many ways Thornton owed his elevation in intellectual stature to his friendship with Mill. As Mill once wrote to Cairnes, "Thornton is a person I particularly respect and like. In perfect candour, sincerity and singleness of mind few men come near him" (in O'Brien, 1943, p. 274). As Mill proceeded to vouch for him, others began to take him more seriously. In 1856, when Mill was promoted to examiner at the India Office, he made it a condition of his acceptance that Thornton be appointed his assistant. Yet, as time wore on, much more than mere intellectual issues bound them together. In times of personal crisis or distress, it was often the other member of the duo to whom the stricken party would turn for assistance. In Thornton's case, his perennial ill-health was periodically the cause for alarm. Once when Thornton suffered from nervous exhaustion which kept him away from his position for over a year in 1857, Mill carried his workload at the India Office so that Thornton would not lose his position (Thornton 1873, p. 35). This action secured the position of first secretary for public works at the India Office for Thornton in 1858. An example of the reverse dependence is that J. S. Mill, immobilised by his bereavement over the death of his wife, entrusted Thornton with the task of placing Harriet Taylor's obituary in London newspapers.[8]

Hotel d'Europe, Avignon
Nov. 9, 1858

My Dear Thornton — The hopes which I commenced this journey have been fatally frustrated. My wife, the companion of all my feelings, the prompter of all my best thoughts, the guide of all my actions, is gone! She was taken ill at this place with a violent attack of bronchitis or pulmonary conjestion-the medical men here could do nothing for her, & before the physician at Nice who saved her life once could arrive, all was over.

It is doubtful if I shall ever be fit for anything public or private, again. The spring of my life is broken. But I shall best fulfil her wishes by not giving up the attempt to do something useful, and I am not quite alone. I have with me her daughter, the one person besides myself who most loved her & whom she most loved, & we help each other to bear what is inevitable. I am sure of your sympathy, but if you knew what she was you would feel how little sympathy can do.

We return straight to England but shall be detained here for some days longer & I beg of you the kind office of inserting the inclosed notice twice in the Times & once in the Post, Herald & Daily News & in the principal weekly papers. Believe me my dear Thornton, very sincerely yours, J. S. Mill

Thornton was the right person for this particular job, given that he was an intimate of Harriet Taylor's circle as well as Mill's. For instance, it was he, along with Arthur Ley, who served as the trustees of John Taylor's estate, the long-suffering first husband of Harriet Taylor (Packe, 1954, p. 382).

If anything, after Mill bought a cottage in Avignon to be near his wife's grave, Thornton and Mill grew closer. Although Mill retired from the India Office in 1858, and was frequently absent from London, Thornton was always treated as a welcome guest. It was Thornton who was entreated to visit Mill and Harriet's daughter, Helen Taylor in Avignon, and Thornton who provided others in the early 1860s with reports on Mill's emotional status (Elliot, 1910, vol. I, pp. 261–2). Mill, when writing to Thornton from Avignon as late as 1869, makes reference to "your room" as being refurbished (Mill, *Collected Works*, 1967, vol. 16, letter 1380).

It is our view that much of Thornton's subsequent literary output, from 1848 until roughly 1870, in the field of political economy (but most emphatically *not* his poetic or philosophical writings!) should be regarded as the product of a prolonged discussion, shading imperceptibly over into collaboration, with Mill. Mill had few friends; and fewer still whom he regarded comfortably as intellectual equals. This alone should stand as motivation to prompt a substantial re-evaluation of Thornton's writings. One of the early fruits of this long relationship was the 1848 tract A *Plea for Peasant Proprietors*. As mentioned in his first edition of *Principles*, Mill was greatly concerned over the plight of the labouring peasantry in England and Ireland. Thornton's *Over-Population* had argued that the settlement of "wastelands" by small peasant proprietors would constitute one plausible remedy for the Irish famine, and Mill praised this analysis in his *Principles* (1965, 997–9), calling it "honourably distinguished from most others which have recently been published [this in 1849], by its rational treatment of the great questions affecting the economical condition of the labouring classes." Sharp criticism by others of the thesis that small landholdings would be economically viable (e.g., Anon., 1847), and that population growth would simply wipe out any temporary gains, prompted Thornton to redouble his efforts to come up with a programme for Irish resettlement, and a vindication of the social and economic consequences of a wide distribution of smallholders. Mill read the proofs for this second book, and there is reason to think much of his stamp is imprinted upon it.[9]

Nevertheless, the *Plea* is Thornton's least satisfactory economic work. There is a penchant for excessive minutiae and the retail of anecdote as a replacement for concerted marshalling of evidence in all of Thornton's writings; yet here, these vices tend to overwhelm his other virtues. For instance, the fact that certain forms of smallholdings seemed to flourish on the Channel Islands would seem to bear little relevance for the larger agricultural infrastructures of Ireland or England, a point which appears to have eluded Thornton. Likewise, isolated national statistics of average pounds of agricultural produce per acre did not begin to confront the issue of the truth or falsity of widespread impressions of the pervasiveness of scale economies in agriculture. Furthermore, he did indulge a weakness for writing "conjectural history", a tendency already noted by Brentano, and in the *Plea* it was given free rein in the treatment of Irish history as well as ancient Greece. It is worthwhile to note however, that an entire chapter was given over to the effects of peasant proprietorship in France. It seems that Thornton was here for the first time forced to confront the vexing French problem of explaining why the freely operating grain markets there were not able to stem the tide of subsistence crises; by construction, Thornton could not accept the conventional wisdom that the problem could be traced to the absence of large-scale capitalist agriculture and the atavism of *morcellement.*

Outside Mill and his small circle of confidants in the 1850s, it would seem that Thornton was not deemed a major thinker or accorded much respect amongst the literati of the day. The *Plea* was essentially ignored in the periodical press; and there followed a notable hiatus in Thornton's output in political economy, lasting roughly a decade from about 1854. Some of this might have been attributable to the illness mentioned above; but part of the explanation must lie in his advocacy of what were regarded as lost causes, while another moity should be laid at the doorstep of his own personality. To put it bluntly, there were very few others like Mill who treasured his tenaciousness in argument and his deficiency in the civilities associated with a certain strata of the leisure classes in Victorian Britain. Our primary evidence of this latter character trait comes from the minutes and records of the Political Economy Club.

From 1847 until his death, Thornton was an active member in the Political Economy Club of England. This was a monthly conclave of influential scholars and business people, originally founded by David Ricardo and sustained by his followers, to address the major issues affecting the new science of Political Economy. The meetings consisted of an evening of supper and an after-port discussion of a question posed by one of the members. Thornton's entrée into this rather august conclave undoubtedly was owed to Mill's intervention. In the thirty-three years that Thornton was a member of the club, he formally presented questions on fifteen occasions. These questions give us a very good indicator of Thornton's enthusiasms; but they also provide us a fair calendar of the years in which Thornton was actively engaged in political economy. We reproduce the full schedule of these questions below, divided into three discrete phases.

Questions Posed by Thornton at the Meetings of the Political Economy Club

**February 3, 1848.*
Is the system of letting small pieces of land to agricultural labourers, commonly called the allotment system, open to any valid objection, as a means of improving the condition of those labourers?

**June 6, 1850.*
What reason is there for believing that the recent approximations towards Free Trade in food, have affected the ability of the country to bear the burthen of the National Debt?

**May 1, 1851.*
Is not the Ricardo theory of Rent unnecessarily artificial, and might not another be devised less complicated, yet equally accurate and more comprehensive?

**June 5, 1851.*
Instead of being true, as is frequently asserted, that taxation presses with disproportionate weight on the poor, would it not rather appear that no taxes, other than Protective duties, can permanently diminish the income of the labouring classes?

**February 1, 1852.*
Can it, in any circumstances whatever, be advantageous to raise the money required for public expenditure, by means of a loan, instead of immediate taxation?

**June 2, 1853.*
What is the most correct definition of Capital?

**May 4, 1854.*
Are Copy-right and Patent-right founded on justice, or merely on sufferance, and are not those terms really misnomers?

**December 7, 1854.*
What is the foundation of the Tenant Right of Ulster?

***June 5, 1862.*
Can any Income Tax, and, a *fortiori*, an uniform Income Tax, be otherwise than at variance with the just principals of Taxation?

***July 1, 1864.*
What would be the effect on Literary Produce and Literary Producers of a total abolition of Copyright?

***December 7, 1866.*
What is the meaning of Supply, and what of Demand? Is it correct to say that supply and demand determine price? If not, in what manner is it that supply and demand affect price?

****February 6, 1874.*
Is it possible for the construction of a Railway, the purposes for which are purely commercial, and which cannot by the most judicious management be made to yield profit at the current average rate on its cost, to have been other than a bad investment of a portion of the National Capital?

****May 7, 1875.*
Political Economy being commonly regarded as the Science which treats of National Wealth, in what sense should the word Wealth be understood when used in politco-economical discussions?

****June 7, 1878.*
Is there really such a thing as Economic Law? If so, how far should Economic Law be defined, and what specimens of it can be adduced?

****July 4, 1879.*
Is it possible, and if possible, would it be desirable, to establish and maintain Bimetallism in India, without regard to the monetary arrangements of any other country?

(Source: Political Economy Club (1921))

From the materials surviving from the Political Economy Club, it seems safe to infer that Thornton was not one of the social favourites at these gatherings. Leslie Stephen was one of the least tolerant, reporting, "I am suffering the torments of the damned from that god-forgotton Thornton, who is boring on about supply and demand . . . He is not a bad fellow, but just now I hate him like poison." [10] Another of Thornton's frequent sparring partners was William Newmarch.[11] An extract of a letter from L. H. Courtney to Sir Louis Mallet describes the setting of one such argument.

> Dear Mallet,
> I share your regrets at the apparent decline of decorum at the Political Economy Club. Last Friday the breaches of manners were sadly conspicuous. One officer must not find fault with another, but the truth is that our treasurer is habitually too contemptuous of views other than his own – not infrequently wider than his own – and this characteristic does not abate as the years pass. With his rough disdain and Thornton's tendency to querulous irritability there must be occasional splutterings, and the only way of keeping them down is for you and other members to attend as often as convenient to discountenance them by quietly maintaining the rules of debate.[12]

On another occasion, Sir J. Macdonnel tagged Thornton a "disruptive revolutionary influence", but nevertheless a "useful solvent [who] had the art of putting questions disconcerting to the dogmatic spirit, and he had a vision, temperate of a world that was to come – more questions than he himself could answer" (ibid., p. 344).

It is difficult to imagine that such a cantankerous fellow with his unseemly enthusiasms would have been suffered so stoically by the members of the club without the obvious and repeated endorsement of Mill. In the first phase of his career, his questions reveal a concern with agricultural issues which assumed an essentially anti-Ricardian stance, well in line with his earliest publications. This would not have tended to endear him to the members of the club; and moreover, there is no evidence that he succeeded in winning any of them over to his position. In 1853–4 his interests appeared to begin to branch out into issues of capital theory and intellectual property rights, although these latter subjects never prompted any specific further texts authored by Thornton. Instead, it is hard to escape the impression that he grew rather disappointed with political economy; for instance, his participation in the Political Economy Club experiences a hiatus of eight years beginning in 1855. In its place, in the mid-1850s he turned to composition of poetry, publishing "The Siege of Silestria" in 1854; *Zohràb and Other Poems* in 1854; and *Modern Manicheism, Labour's Utopia and Other Poems* in 1857. One of these poems, written in 1854 in the form of an epistle to Mill, confesses his disaffection from political economy:

> Dear Mill, whose friendship's kindly emphasis
> Approved my first work, and encouraged this.
> Scarce will you ask, why, from old studies turned,
> My name unknown, a pension yet unearned.
> Problems abstruse and tough, no more I try,
> Of dark Political Economy.
> Digging no more in serious dissertation
> To trace the source of "Over-population,"
> Nor publishing what hidden treasure lies
> Deep in the soil of "Peasant Properties."

Unfortunately, Thornton's Muse fared no better with poesy, even given the rather special Victorian predilections for iambic pentameter, heroic couplets, and deliciously awkward rhymes like "try" and "Economy". (We include a few sample poems in this anthology so that readers may exercise their own literary judgment. One of us particularly relishes Thornton's habit of footnoting his poems in order to "explain" his egregiously obscure allusions. Here we can savour the trademark practices of modernists such as T. S. Eliot *avant la lettre.*) One reviewer of his later translations from Horace accused him of a deficient ear and a want of metrical grasp, while tendering the backhanded compliment that they displayed a species of seventeenth-century quaintness (Ellis, 1878). It seems safe to observe that these works would not have cemented his intellectual reputation for future generations. Hence, at age 40, that fearsome watershed in many lives, there was very little to indicate that Thornton would ever amount to anything more than a competent bureaucrat in government service.

The situation changed dramatically in the mid-1860s, for reasons that we have been unable to fully divine. While we know of no particular landmarks in Thornton's personal life, there is reason to suspect the hand of Mill in encouraging Thornton in his return to political economy. He resumed attendance at the Political Economy Club in 1862, and a stream of publications on wages, unions and the treatment of labour in political economy commenced in 1864. In part, this was a response to British political initiatives of the 1860s to gain the suffrage for working men and legal legitimacy for trades unions (see the next section); and in equal part it must have been sparked by Thornton's conviction that there was something fundamentally flawed about the conventional wisdom concerning price theory, a wisdom, it must be noted, best exemplified by his good friend's own *Principles of Political Economy*. In that text, Mill's abstract treatment of demand and supply did not correspond very well to the newly added passages, such as the following from the 1862 edition, where he intended to signal a much more favorable inclination towards certain forms of union organisation:

> [D]emand and supply are not physical agencies, which thrust a fixed amount of wages into a labourer's hand without the participation of his own will and actions. The market rate is not fixed for him by some self-acting instrument, but is the result of bargaining between human beings . . . those who do not "higgle" will long continue to pay more than the market prices for their purchases. Still more might poor labourers who have to do with rich employers, remain long without the amount of wages which the demand for their labour would justify, unless, in the vernacular phrase, they stood out for it; and how can they stand out for terms without organized concert? What chance would any labourer have who struck singly for an advance of wages? . . . . I do not hesitate to say that associations of labourers, of a nature similar to trades unions, far from being a hindrance to the free market of labour, are the necessary instrumentality of that free market" (Mill, 1965, p. 932).

Here in a nutshell was the position which Thornton chose to elaborate upon in the *Fortnightly Review* over the course of the 1860s, and then republish together as the first edition of his epoch-making book, *On Labour* (1869). Since 1844, Mill had been desirous of repudiating the "hard, abstract mode" of treating the "labour question" (Mill, *Collected Works*, 1967, vol. 13, p. 645); by the early 1860s he was endorsing a pamphlet by Thomas Dunning on *Trades Unions and Strikes* which argued that only by combination could workmen be situated on a basis of equality for negotiation with employers. Essentially, Thornton set out to expound Mill's position vis-a-vis the benefits of union organization in greater detail, but fairly quickly came to the conclusion that if this doctrine were to hold, revision of the "laws" of supply and demand would be required to restore a semblance of consistency to Mill's position. In 1866, both in the *Fortnightly Review* and in the meetings of the Political Economy Club, Thornton first aired this conclusion.[13] It was the pained reactions to his presentation in 1866 which provoked the disparaging comments from other clubmen about the deficiencies in Thornton's character which we quoted above. Nevertheless, at least among the cognoscenti, and the readers of Mill's preferred outlet the *Fortnightly*, Thornton's heresies were familiar, dating at least from 1866.

Let us be quite clear about this. Thornton's positions vis-a-vis supply and demand and the legitimacy of trades unions were known to Mill at least from 1866, and perhaps before, largely because he helped thrash them out in concert with his friend Thornton. Both Mill and Cairnes gave Thornton comments on the manuscript before the actual book was published. Presumably, Mill facilitated this early exposure to other prominent political economists to assay their reactions, and it took his intervention to pave the way for immediate reviews in the *Fortnightly* and other publications. But there is more: research at the British Library has also uncovered evidence that Mill had some involvement in the actual publication of *On Labour.* Mill was indeed more sensitive than Thornton to the politics of changing economic opinion, as revealed by his comment in a letter to Cairnes in 1869, "It is very amusing in this and other cases to see how the tyros in Political Economy think themselves bound to give no quarter to heresies, being afraid to make any concessions which their masters make" (Mill, *Collected Works,* 1967, vol. 16, letter 1418). As the following review notes of a Macmillan editor indicates, Mill was fully aware that the book was being positioned to provoke a controversy.

> I have thought about the Thornton Book. The following considerations sum to the point.
>
> Mill's testimonial could not very well be made known on the surface of the book. Even if it could, just now it would not be so very effective, though it might become so. Thornton's book is not of the size or calibre to be a standard work or a text-book. It has already been published in the F[ortnightly].R[eview]., and the students of economic questions who would otherwise have bought it are now familiar with it.
>
> On the other hand is the very weighty fact that the subject will shortly be the subject of the day – and will probably continue so for a considerable time to come; and everything bearing on it will be brought. And Thornton is an authority in economics, as the author of the "Plea for Peasant Proprietors". It will be a risk, decidedly, I think – though the book is one which would look well in your list.[14]

We shall describe the intellectual content of *On Labour* below; for now we restrict ourself to how this situation has been treated in the historical literature. It is our contention that historians, following the lead of some subsequent commentators such as Cairnes, have reified the appearance of *On Labour* and J. S. Mill's review in the 1869 *Fortnightly Review* as the "Recantation of the wages fund doctrine". In this construct, Thornton is relegated to the marginal status of Rosencrantz (or is it Guildenstern?), passive observer of Hamlet's solo deconstruction of Denmark.[15] To their credit, Evelyn Forget (1992) and Mark Donoghue (1997) have smelled something rotten, and have suggested alternative (Copenhagen?) intepretations. Forget asserts "Mill's recantation was not motivated by internal inconsistencies, but was a calculated political act" (p. 32). Donoghue goes further, suggesting that Mill never regarded himself as recanting something so grand as "the wages-fund doctrine". We shall propose an interpretation, buttressed by our new evidence, which restores Thornton to his role as independent and active agent, combining Forget and Donoghue in something resembling a convex combination.

In fact, neither Mill nor Thornton initially regarded the theses of *On Labour* (*OL*) as being anything other than tangentially concerned with "the wages fund".

Indeed, in the first edition of *OL*, it was mentioned only in a footnote.[16] Instead, the objective was to flesh out the argument broached in Mill's 1862 edition of the *Principles*: supply and demand for labour was neither mechanical nor inevitable in wage determination; the steadfastness of will and bargaining behavior of masters and men mattered; unions could help offset an asymmetry of bargaining power in the wage relationship; and unions could serve longer-term goals of education and social improvement of the lot of the working class. On each and every point, Mill and Thornton were in full concert. Both also thought that working men were vulnerable to pernicious and wrong-headed analysis of their predicament provided by socialists, although here they might differ with regard to the place of various real-life socialists in their rogue's gallery of error. Both saw the need for a text which would codify what they both anticipated would be the orthodox case that unions were a necessary complement to the operation of the market, once a society reached a certain level of development. When Mill was in London, they regularly discussed these issues personally; when he was in Avignon, his letters reveal that these were the overriding shared concerns.

Nevertheless, Thornton was no martinet, no mere stalking horse for Mill. The fact that he was his own man is what endeared him to Mill – let us not forget, the author of *On Liberty* as well as *Principles of Political Economy*. The author of the former text argued that truth was not found in consensus, but derived from the process of individual dissent. So Thornton was encouraged to set out on his own path in order to determine what exactly would have to be given up to prosecute the case outlined in the previous paragraph. Mill thought that a revised understanding of supply and demand would suffice to make the case; Thornton, notoriously, believed rather that the laws of supply and demand would have to be given up. Mill, the serene proponent of common sense, believed "that what is true in the abstract, is always true in the concrete with proper *allowances*" (Mill, *Collected Works*, 1967, vol. 14, p. 326). Thornton the iconoclast sought rather to base the case for unions on the bare minimum of theoretical presumptions: in effect, just the axiom of self-interest and a few symmetry principles.[17] In contrast with Mill, he signalled an unwillingness to have to depend upon Mill's or any other version of utilitarianism to ground his account. The fact that Mill was fully aware of this well before the appearance of *OL* can be gleaned from a letter to Thornton dated 19 October 1867:

> I have just finished reading your Chapter in the Fortnightly & I put down my observations while my mind is full of its contents. In execution I think it excellent & of good augury for the success of the book . . . I expect that the subsequent chapters will be equally well executed & that I shall agree with all or most of your practical conclusions. But in its principles the chapter does not carry me with it. I find in it what I always find where a standard is assumed of so-called justice distinct from general utility . . . Not only do I not admit any standard of right which does not derive its sole authority from utility, but I remark that in such cases an adversary could always find some other maxim of justice equal in authority but leading to

> opposite conclusions . . . . I have stated strongly the fault I find with your Chapter. It would take me a considerable space to set out all the good I find in it. To mention only one thing, the book will be very serviceable in carrying on what may be called the emancipation of pol. economy – its liberation from the kind of doctrines of the old school (now taken up by well to do people) which treat what they call economical laws, demand and supply for instance, as if they were laws of inanimate matter, not amenable to the will of the human beings from whose feelings, interests, & principles of action they proceed. This is one of the queer mental confusions which will be wondered at by & by & you are helping very much in the good work of clearing it up. (Mill, *Collected Works*, 1967, vol. 16, letter 1150)

This explains why, in a seeming paradox, both Forget and Donoghue could actually be right. Mill could orchestrate an endorsement of Thornton's *OL* both behind the scenes and in print, because he thought the political objectives were fundamentally sound and the need for a synoptic text treating the theory of unionism was imminent. Yet simultaneously, he could disagree with Thornton's rejection of his price theory and his utilitarianism, and still cheerfully endorse the book, because he himself did not think he was "renouncing" much of anything – it was those epigones, those "tyros of Political Economy" who had turned the doctrine of supply and demand into a wicked device, a "hard, abstract" object to prod and torment the working classes with its dismal prognostications. Of course, no one, including his most loyal follower Cairnes, was impelled to share his view; and by and large, the self-identified orthodoxy did not.[18] Instead, Mill's endorsement of Thornton was treated initially as a gracious but somewhat inexplicable gesture to an old friend; and then later, a moment of deplorable weakness which brought the whole jerry-built structure of British classical political economy crashing down into ruin in a few decades. Mill did not live to experience the latter defalcation, but he did manage to enter a demurrer regarding one of its main protagonists.[19] The very idea that there was something so dramatic as a "recantation of the wages fund" was a construct of those who came after, such as Cairnes, Taussig, and Jacob Hollander. It was these late classicals who feared the world was turned upside-down; it was the fledgling neoclassicals like Jevons who donned their white hats and put it right again, thus supporting the narrative. These ruptures are important for the student to remember, especially after Marshall sought to impose a bland facade of continuity over the whole episode by inventing a history of price theory out of whole cloth.

Having insisted upon a proper understanding of the motives and role of Mill, we now return to the life of Thornton. *On Labour* and the subsequent furore provoked by its bold theses rendered Thornton a celebrity in political economy circles. The book was rapidly translated into Russian, German and Italian; his *Plea* was reprinted in 1874; now not only the *Fortnightly Review* but the *Cornhill* and the *Contemporary Review* were happy to publish his occasional pieces; and Macmillan even sanctioned a second edition of *On Labour* (prodigiously expanded, as the reader will note from our concordance) a year later in 1870. In

1873, Thornton was presented with a C.B., upon the recommendation of the Duke of Argyll. More importantly, in the critical decade of the 1870s, Thornton was the writer one just had to confront if one had any hope of gaining one's spurs in English political economy. J. E. Cairnes's 1874 book *Some Leading Principles of Political Economy* was one long wrangle with Thornton. Fleeming Jenkin's classic papers on supply and demand were intended primarily to upbraid Thornton. Jevons, with Jenkin serving as intermediary, was also responding to Thornton in his own *Theory of Political Economy.* Francis Edgeworth's *Mathematical Psychics* was the ultimate utilitarian riposte to Thornton's disdain for utilitarianism. And last but not least, Marshall without Thornton is like the Prince . . . well, one readily gets the drift.

It is instructive to gauge whom Thornton deems worthy to answer in the last decade before his death. Cairnes here holds pride of place, precisely because he was so very close to Mill; and that does help explain why they both accorded each other such ample courtesy and attention. Longe was acknowledged after the fact, only to be written off as irrelevant. Mill is repeatedly revisited as a font of authority and source of dissention, even after his death. The new breed of utilitarians, by contrast, did not warrant individual confrontation; instead, Thornton sought to deal with them *en masse* in his 1870 broadside "Anti-utilitarianism", republished in 1873 in his *Old-fashioned Ethics.* And that exhausts his reference set within political economy. This was not due to lack of acquaintance or opportunity; indeed, Thornton became very active in the Political Economy Club in the mid-1870s, proposing such impertinent questions as, "Is there really such a thing as Economic Law? If so, how far should Economic Law be defined, and what specimens of it can be adduced?" However, as interlocutors, it just seems he did not regard them as rising to the standard of discussion he had grown accustomed to with Mill. He would rather turn his critical attention as an author to someone like Thomas Huxley, whose "naturalism" was the most diametrically opposed to his own position.[20]

In the mid-1870s he returned to what was clearly his first love, the specifics of land tenure systems, irrigation works and other artifacts of the bureaucratic levers of control and economic development. In his last substantial book, *Indian Public Works* (1875), he put on display much of the economic specifics which had absorbed much of his working life; in this respect he diverged from Mill, who kept explicit acknowledgment of much of the context of his India House work out of his publications (Zastoupil, 1994). The book tracked the controversies over Indian railroads, ship canals, telegraph wires and educational establishments as the nitty-gritty of the provision of infrastructure for markets to operate, something which underlies much of Thornton's theoretical approach to markets. Among its virtues, it surveys the late-classical case for the legitimate undertaking of public works, suggesting that market rates of return may be an inadequate guide for choice of projects in poorer or less developed countries; there, the second-round effects of drawing out "idle capital" might more than offset what initially appear to be unpromising projects. Thornton was very critical of the "Dalhousie plan" which sought to draw private investment into railway construction through investor guarantees: the result, he claimed, was a cost per mile far above that experienced in direct government construction. The work was not entirely disengaged from his previous preoccupations, however; for instance, he recommended therein that the Indian government consider various cooperative schemes to deal with problems of labour motivation and supervision (1875b, p. 90).

By all accounts, William Thornton lived out the last years of his life in Cadogan Place near Sloane Street in London enjoying the respect of his India House colleagues and the joys of classical Latin literature, publishing a volume of *Word for Word from Horace* in 1878. Judging from his personal estate of roughly eight thousand pounds, he also enjoyed the modest prosperity of a colonial bureaucrat of a middling rank.

William Thomas Thornton died on 17 June 1880 and in accordance with his wishes, was buried in a wicker coffin in an unbricked grave. He was survived by his wife, Elizabeth Evelyn Thornton, and a son, Edward Zohrab Thornton. While some of his heirs shared in his penchant for classical literature, none served to perpetuate or preserve his views on political economy.

The British Trades Unions Movement as a Context for the Rupture in British Political Economy

While historians of economic thought have been busy rooting about asking who should be charged with having killed the wages fund, it seems that they have overlooked a phenomenon much more relevant to the evolution of political economy in the 1870s, namely, the political movements which served to legitimate trades unions in Britain. Sir John Hicks once wrote: "The sixty years from 1870 to 1930 were in Britain the time of the rise of the Labour Movement; thus it was not surprising that the British post-classics (Marshall, Edgeworth and Pigou in particular) should have had labour problems very much on their minds" (1983, p. 71). Yet, far from passively reacting to a new empirical development - "I say, don't you think it's high time we looked at these union chappies!" – it is far more correct to inquire about the extent to which the British neoclassical movement was itself provoked by the prior appearance of the political problem of trades-unionism; and to see that Hicks's timing was off, at least by a decade.

The saga of the demise of Chartism, the rise of the new models unions and the foundation of the International Working Men's Association and the Trades Unions Congress has been often told. A number of fine histories of this development exist, and we direct the interested reader to them in order to better appreciate the context for the rise of neoclassical economics in the 1870s.[21] Some have asserted that "political economy suffered a sharp decline in prestige and influence in Britain after 1870" (Mason, 1980, p. 565); and that one of the most compelling reasons for the slide was that numerous representatives of classical political economy persisted in their mantra that unions could not "permanently" alter wages nor benefit society, all the while that unions were growing in strength and numbers as a political force to be reckoned with. The demise of classical political economy in Britain was intimately bound up with the various political and economic reform movements of the 1860s and 1870s, something overlooked by those doggedly intent on operating only in the rarified realm of pure ideas.

After the failure of the Owenite and Chartist movements in the 1830s and 1840s, a number of "new model" unions began to be formed in the later 1850s, at first limited to particular trades, and favouring the better paid and educated strata of the labour hierarchy. Foremost among these were the Amalgamated Society of Engineers (ASE) and the Amalgamated Society of Joiners and Carpenters, two unions which would provide much of Thornton's stock of exemplars. The ASE experienced rather stunning expansion, from 11,000 members and an annual income of £22,000 in 1851 to 20,000 members and £52,000 in 1860 and by the time of Thornton's attention, 33,000 members and £83,000 by 1866 (Howell, 1890). This occurred during a period of pronounced expansion of employment of engineers, growing from 75,000 in 1841 to 130,000 in 1851 and 198,000 in 1861 (Lee, 1979). More importantly, it had become apparent to those closest to the industry that the ASE had managed to raise the average wage of the engineers. Even after a generation or more of cliometrics, there exists very little solid quantitative data which allows us to get specifically at this issue; however, the earlier work of Arthur Bowley did allow some generalisations to be made (Bowley & Wood, 1905; 1906). Although the data really only commences in 1860, it appears that the ASE managed to persistently raise the standard wage rates in a number of areas in England, and this in an era of falling prices. Bowley and Wood also provide some evidence that wages paid to non-unionised trades in unionised firms tended to rise in tandem with elevated standard union rates. At least prior to 1873, the period most germane to Thornton's claims, it was difficult to argue that the ASE had produced deleterious effects upon the growth of the firms where unionisation had taken hold. Therefore, the first and most immediate challenge to the time-honoured laws of political economy derived from the success of the new model unions.

The unions, while often claiming to restrict themselves to parochial bread-and-butter concerns, were in fact in the vanguard of various broader-based political movements to redress political inequities. The most salient example was the relationship of union agitation to the Reform League in the early 1860s, which culminated in the Reform Act of 1867, extending male suffrage and doubling the electorate. The fact that the extension of the suffrage and the legitimisation of unions were often regarded as a single conspiracy from the vantage point of the British Right is best instantiated by the dyspeptic writings of that favourite of the first generation of neoclassicals, Herbert Spencer: "And if there needs a demonstration that representative equality is an insufficient safeguard for freedom, we have it in the trades' unions already referred to; which, purely democratic as is their organization, yet exercise over their members a tyranny that is almost Neapolitan in its rigour and unscrupulousness . . . Hence the great mass of the new borough-electors must be expected to act simultaneously, on the word of command being issued from a central council of united trades" (1872, pp. 378–9). A seismometer of the hairline fractures which such middle-class reform movements were inflicting on political economy was the fact that John Stuart Mill, the great self-proclaimed "socialist", declined to join the League, whereas his follower Cairnes did lend his name to the organisation. Margot Finn makes the argument that the mobilisation around the extension of suffrage acted to move the goalposts for other middle-class reform initiatives. "Determined both to pre-empt the escalation of class sentiment incited by the Reform League speakers and to seize the initiative of reform from the Tory government, bourgeois liberals now offered working-class radicals new varieties of liberal argument that conceded, albeit reluctantly, the very legitimacy of abstract political rights . . . [and] the efficacy of trade unions as political agents . . . the escalation of class-consciousness under the aegis of the Reform League encouraged an efflorescence of bourgeois radical agitation in which left-wing liberals endorsed lines of political argument that they had earlier denounced as socialist delusions of the working class" (1993, pp. 249, 253). This interplay of political reform and trades union legitimation is a necessary backdrop for the publication of *On Labour.*

The perceived link between unions and reform agitation conjured the prospect of a state backlash right on the threshold of the successful extension of the franchise. Using as a pretext the "Sheffield outrages" of 1866, and the case of Hornby vs. Close in 1867 – a Queen's Bench ruling which suggested that unions could not prosecute for their stolen funds since they organized strikes in restraint of trade, which violated common law – the government announced in 1867 the constitution of a Royal Commission to look into all aspects of trades unions. The outcome of the inquiry was by no means a foregone conclusion, inducing both sides to sharpen their nibs and occupy strategic positions in the *Quarterlies* and the *Reviews,* which should signal that the dispute over legal and economic legitimacy of unionism had been pumped up to a fever pitch precisely in the period in which Thornton composed *On Labour.*

At this juncture, classical political economy was extracted from the realm of mere apologetics to become a bludgeon to be used to strip trades unions of all legal protection. The language of the "immutable laws of political economy" took on an especially ominous heft and virulent tone in the mid-1860s; and most of the heavy lifting was carried out by the particular "laws" of supply and demand. For example, *The Times* of 27 November 1867 regarded the effulgence of labour activism as an effort to subvert the laws of political economy (Finn, 1993, p. 245). Henry Fawcett wrote: "If trades unions are permitted to prevent this free passage of labour from one employment to another, wages may permanently maintain an artificial advance; but trades unions can only exert such an influence by resorting to a social tyranny, which is in every sense illegal and unjustifiable." In a comparison which would shortly assume deeper significance, one P. H. Rathbone wrote in 1867, "let it be understood that labour is only a commodity (like fish); that employer and employed stand in relation to each other merely as buyer and seller of the commodity; and that the laws of political economy, rightly understood, are as much the laws of Providence as the laws of gravitation" (in Clements, 1961, p. 96). Frederic Harrison, a Comtist and a member of the 1867 Royal Commission, captured some of the frustrations of the time when he complained about those who "even suggest an Act of Parliament to suppress all [union] associations whatever. It is like the Vatican raving at newspapers and railways" (1908, p. 299). For their part, some unionists were quite fed up in constantly being chided about these supposedly ironclad "laws". While they were rarely direct participants in the debates amongst the high theorists, it was commonplace to hear reports of their exasperated disdain for the imperious laws. As David Chadwick reported in 1860, he "much regretted to find that some of the leading members of Trades Unions, attempted to deny the existence and operation of the *law* of political economy in regard to Supply and Demand governing the *price* of labour" (p. 22).

We also tend to forget that this antagonism was the context for the composition of Karl Marx's *Capital* in the early 1860s. Marx's first public statement of his theory of wages came in an address before the General Council of the First International Working Men's Association in June 1865, published posthumously as *Value, Price and Profit.* The objects of Marx's scorn on that occasion were figures within the International who had made use of Mill's wages fund doctrines to argue that unions who achieved wage increases merely hurt other segments of the working class. Marx, good Ricardian that he was, felt he could wave away supply and demand as mere accessory to a theory of value: "You would be altogether mistaken in fancying that the value of labour or of any other commodity whatever is ultimately fixed by demand and supply. Supply and demand regulate nothing but the temporary *fluctuations* of market prices. They will explain to you why the market price of a commodity rises above or below its *value*, but they can never account for that *value* itself" (1935, p. 26).[22] Of course, his innovation was to deny that "labour" (as opposed to labour power) was a commodity at all.

There is a literature which debates the relative consequence of Thornton and Mill in this agonistic field of labour mobilisation and political proselytisation of the 1860s and 70s (Clements, 1961; Biagini, 1987; Pelling, 1963, p. 63); this is neither the place nor the time to try and intervene in this debate. Nevertheless, there are two things to note about the immediate aftermath to the publication of *On Labour.* First, subsequent to the report of the Royal Commission in 1869, Parliament passed the Trades Unions Act of 1871 and the Conspiracy and the Protection of Property Act of 1875 and the Trade Union Amendment Act of

1876, the upshot of which was to provide legal acknowledgement of the full legitimacy of trades union organisations. This clearly placed classical political economy in the awkward situation of condemning as an unnatural abomination a political entity and economic framework which was clearly here to stay, and moreover, one which enjoyed the support of a large proportion of the voting polity as having salutary benefits. This untenable situation could not persist indefinitely. Second, by roughly 1880, conventional wisdom among the literati had performed an about-face, wherefore it became commonplace to deride those supposedly inviolate laws of supply and demand as defunct. Trades unions' sympathisers did it: "To-day the old orthodox Economy – the Gospel, or Sophism, of Supply and Demand, absolute freedom for Individual Exertion – all this is ancient history . . . [Socialist unionism] has killed that old Targum about Supply and Demand – the plain English of which was – 'May the devil take the weakest!'" (Harrison, [1889] 1908, p. 410). But pillars of the establishment, such as presidents of Section F of the British Association for the Advancement of Science, also did it: " 'The recognized principles of political economy' or 'the immutable laws of supply and demand' were phrases that occurred as readily to a journalist in the sixties as 'the exploded doctrine of laissez faire' does to the leader writer of today" (in Smyth, 1962, p. 127).

In our view, Thornton's *On Labour* brought to a head the contradictions inherent in the classical theory of value and distribution when juxtaposed with the political realities of escalation of worker organisation across Europe. The effect of this wake-up call was to induce a brief and concentrated period of theoretical innovation in political economy unmatched by almost any other period in British history. While much of this efflorescence would be couched in the language of supply and demand, it is important to acknowledge that the two decades up until 1890 experienced multiple alternative resolutions to the conundrum, which only were collapsed in Marshallian retrospect to a single orthodoxy of the newly coined neologism "neoclassical economics". These alternatives can be arrayed according to their relationship to the prior multiple interpretations of supply and demand outlined above in the section 'British Treatments of Supply and Demand Prior to Thornton.

To begin, there was the hardcore Ricardian response, best exemplified in Marx's *Capital.* Here supply and demand was allowed no fundamental role, and the doctrine that lasting wage increases by trades unions were economically possible was reified in the treatment of the "labour"/ "labour power" dichotomy. For Marx, trades unions were not an end in themselves, but merely a necessary way-station for the political organisation of the proletariat to usurp political power from the bourgeoisie (Marx, 1974). By contrast, the "engineering" group derived from the Whewell orientation assumed the technocratic position that supply and demand constituted the sum total of economic theory applicable to this controversy; yet a suitably disinterested perspective would admit the proposition that unions violated no particular "natural" equilibrium, since the interests of capital and labour were naturally antagonistic. This position had its own special piquancy, since it was the British labour aristocracy of engineers who had pioneered the structure of the new model unions. Fleeming Jenkin ventured this interpretation in his 1868 article "Trade-Unions: How Far Legitimate?", written, it should be noted, *before* the more widely known "Graphic Representation of the Laws of Supply and Demand". In the former article, he wrote, "simple restriction of the extension of trade is not *per se* an evil, and none of the pleas against trade-unions founded upon it will hold water" (1931, p. 33). Combination for the purposes of bargaining could permanently raise wages, but only at a cost to the larger community. "Admitting that total abolition [of unions] is out of the question as impolitic, undeserved and impossible, we must insist that the great power granted to bodies of workmen shall be administered upon stringent regulations" (1931, p. 67). From an Olympian height, unions performed no necessary or logical function; they were simply a fact of existence, rather like the mechanical imperfections of steel beams or chemical imperfections of copper wire which every engineer had to take into account (Smith & Wise, 1989, chs 19, 20). Supply and demand theory could incorporate them just as well as any other relevant structural parameter – once supply and demand were adequately formalised, an unfortunate detail awaiting rectification.

If these two positions constitute the polar extremes of the repertoire of approaches to supply and demand, it was the great muddled middle – the forced alliance of the classical and demand/supply perspectives – which dominated the controversy. It may seem odd to lump together such figures as J. E. Cairnes and W. S. Jevons in this group, but their similarities do tend to dominate their standard distinctions as, respectively, the last orthodox champion of British classicism and the parvenu herald of the nascent neoclassical position. The reason they belong together is that they wished to have their cake and eat it too: they strove to preserve something very like the wages fund story, but also insist that wages were natural phenomena set by supply and demand; they wanted to accord a certain grudging legitimacy to trades unions, and allow that they had effectively raised wages, but that this legitimacy and efficacy had nothing to do with economic laws, which were still being violated and besmirched by their existence; they felt that Thornton was onto something in focusing on the structure of the bargaining situation and previous inadequacies in demand theory, but that when all was adequately explained it would be seen that what Thornton had done was exaggerate some minor special cases way out of proportion to their importance. Of course, they did differ in important specifics – for instance, Jevons was more concerned to deny that unions could raise real wage rates, and his use of the terminology of "supply and demand" was very idiosyncratic. Yet for both, their dicta concerning supply and demand and trades unions ended up being a terrible hotchpotch, distinguished primarily by their desire to upbraid and discipline the reprobate Thornton.[23]

We shall merely indicate what a vertiginous experience it must have been for a stalwart trades unionist to read the prognostications of the sober representatives of political economy in the 1870s and 1880s. After denying that the content of political economy sufficiently underpins the prescription of *laissez faire* (1871), Cairnes proceeded to assert that "there is a law of market price, as there is a law of normal price, as there is a law of wages, of profit, of rent, as there are laws of the winds and tides and seasons, and of the phenomena of external nature" (1874, p. 98). Although no sane economist is thought to ever have believed in the doctrine of the wages fund (p. 182), trades unions were deemed utterly incapable of enlarging the wages fund (p. 218). Finally, "combination, whether employed by capitalists or by labourers, may succeed in controlling for a time the price of labour, is utterly powerless in the hands of either, to effect a permanent alteration in the market rate of wages as determined by supply and demand" (p. 235). Likewise, for Jevons, the wages fund was transparently false, and "Practically, the whole question resolves itself into a complex case of the laws of supply and demand" (1894, p. 95). However, when Jevons got down to the task of specifying the details of his price theory, an explicit description of these laws of supply and demand were notable predominantly by their absence (White, 1989). As for unions, they were a curse and a fraud, since "whosoever tries to raise his own wages . . . attempts to levy contributions from other people. It is simply a case of private taxation" (Jevons, 1894, p. 106). Contrary to all contemporary belief, "the supposed conflict of labour with capital is a delusion. The real conflict is between producers and consumers" (p. 101). Nevertheless, "Even when we can clearly perceive that the action of a "corner" or trade union is pernicious, it does not necessary follow that the State would do well to intervene. In some cases evils are best left to work their own remedy" (p. 32). In a bizarre variant on Marx, it seems that Jevons believed that union organization would simply degenerate and wither away (p. 129). Mill's belief in the civilizing effects of union organisation upon the workers was derided as just so much rank ignorance of the teachings of science. "Human nature is one of the last things which can be called 'pliable'. Granite rocks may be more easily moulded than the poor savages which hide among them" (Jevons, 1890, p. 290).

The decades of the 1860s and 1870s were the silly season of the political economy of British labour, with hysterical denial of palpable political realities rife and logical analysis at a definite premium – analysts managed to avoid discussing actual unions and their actual functions, regarding them either as little better than abstract spanners in the clockwork market, or alternatively, as concrete embodiments of Christian charity. This had as much to do with the diminished reputation of political economy in Britain as did its dreaded dismal demeanour. An appreciation of this fact will help to explain why it was Thornton's *On Labour* which came for many of his contemporaries to represent the locus of calm dispassionate economic analysis of unions, the central tendency of political realism, the Golden Mean in the muddled centre of divergent vectors of rival value theories, incommensurate pretensions to scientific status, diverse attitudes towards empiricism, and lurking threats of socialism. Thornton's book garnered the attention it did because it appeared to occupy the elusive centre: that is, at least until Marshall's *Principles* burst upon the scene.

Hence, we perhaps now possess some inkling of the context in which John Hicks's heroes – Jenkin, Marshall, Edgeworth, Pigou – were all so very exercised to repeatedly address the problem of the "indeterminacy of wages" and the "correct" understanding of demand and supply. Their convergence upon this issue was no mere coincidence.

What Did Thornton Do?

As broached earlier, Thornton's purpose in writing *On Labour* was to elaborate upon Mill's mature position that wages were the product of intentional activity and bargaining, that unions levelled the field in this respect for workers, and that far from hobbling the operation of a free market, this was a fine example of the means by which the evolution of markets encouraged civilized improvement over time. Where Thornton parted from Mill is that he regarded the doctrine of supply and demand as hopelessly confused, and worse, a major hindrance to making Mill's political brief in favour of the legitimacy of trades unions. Thornton's contemporaries certainly found this his most compelling theme, for although it accounted for a very small proportion of the text in the first edition – basically, Book II Chapter I – it drew more criticism and commentary than the whole rest of the text combined. In response to the hitting of this obviously exposed nerve, Thornton expanded that chapter to twice its original length in his second edition. For long afterward, Thornton's overarching position regarding the virtues and vices of unions was neglected in favor of his strictures regarding supply and demand. In order to avoid repetition of this habit, let us first survey the architecture of the volume, and then return to the problem of supply and demand in greater detail.

The purpose of the first book is to argue that, due to a flawed theory of pricing, political economists had misapprehended the fundamental function of trades unions. Labour was appreciably different from any other commodity because – under the conditions of rules of bargaining and closure specific to British practice – it was offered unreservedly in the market, whereas other commodities were not. If shoes went unsold, or if buyers made unsatisfactory bids, the shoes could be put aside by the seller for another day. If the commodity was perishable, like fish, special kinds of auctions could be arranged to move the product with dispatch and thus address the bargaining imbalance. But labour, by its very nature could not be reserved – labour unsold simply evaporates, never again to be put on the market. Combined with the fact that it is predominantly the poor who labour and the rich who provide capital, there is a systematic handicap which hinders the purveyors of labour from resorting to the most important device available to any other participant in the marketplace for higgling the terms of trade in their own favour. Moreover, due to the class interests of the buyers of labour, no special kinds of market institutions had developed to redress this handicap. Without some form of concerted intervention, this asymmetry between buyers and sellers would persist indefinitely. The economic functions of trades unions were primarily two: (1) to restore symmetry to the commodity labour by allowing labour to be reserved in effect (if not in fact) when buyers made unsatisfactory bids; and (2) to elevate labour to a plane of bargaining equality with the more powerful and already locally coordinated body of employers.

There were a number of minor additional functions which trades unions might also perform, although Thornton was rather less sanguine about their abilities to do so: unions might administer pensions, disability insurance and strike funds; they might actively seek to alter the market institutions and practices which coordinated the pricing of labour (after the style of the fish merchants); they might help legislate the conditions of work on the shop floor and arbitrate individual disputes between masters and men; they just might help bring about self-improvement through the encouragement of education and the bracing experience of self-government and self-reliance. But Thornton should never be confused with some starry-eyed apologist for unions; indeed his contemporaries recognised this as one of his chief virtues. For instance, he opined that most of these latter auxiliary functions might be better performed by the state. He allowed that specific unions were often corrupt; that the costs of union organisation might be burdensome to those within and without the union; that strikes often hurt the workers concerned more than they helped, at least in the short-run; that they might throw up obstacles to the mobility of resources. Unions, in his view, were a "necessary evil", at best an intermediate expedient on the road to some better future format of work organisation. Indeed, "the great object of this treatise is to show, that whatever unionism may be able to do for working men, industrial co-operation can do still more" (*p. 170[24]). In this regard he was not so very different from Mill, Cairnes and many of his contemporaries, putting their millenarian faith in cooperatives, profit-sharing and some vague form of industrial democracy to address the larger questions of the future of the troubled adversarial relationship between labour and capital.[25]

The most striking novelty of Thornton's work is, whereas he openly accepted the principle of universal selfishness as the starting point for analysis, he abjured any and all appeals to "Nature" and "natural law" to ground his theory. Whereas he tended to agree with Mill in practical political economy and politics, Thornton found himself at odds with his friend over philosophy, and tended to reject Mill's paternalistic approach to the responsibilities of the social theorist. The ambition of the construction of a natural science of society was a chimera for Thornton. He applied this dictum symmetrically to his patron and friend Mill, to the old-fashioned detractors of unions, and to the socialists. It begins, of course, with the theory of price, but it does not stop there. To the political economists he throws down the gauntlet:

> Price is scarcely ever mentioned without provoking a reference to the "inexorable", the "immutable," the "eternal" laws by which it is governed; the laws which, according to my friend Professor Fawcett, are "as certain in their operation as those which control physical nature." It is no small gain to have discovered that no such despotic laws do or can exist; that, inasmuch as the sole function of scientific law is to predict the invariable recurrence of the same effects from the same causes, and as there can be no invariablity where – as in the case of price – one of the most efficient causes is that ever-changing chameleon, human character or disposition, price cannot possibly be subject to law (*pp. 40–1).

Yet the socialists were warned they also must take their medicine unsugared. There are no abstract principles upon which workers might base their claims for improvement, he warned. No one has a right to a job, or a "living wage," or claims upon the means of production, or "original rights" to the fruits of their labour, or realisation of their God-given potential for happiness. John Locke and David Hume were painted as part of the problem, not part of the solution. There is nothing "natural" which serves to allocate "responsibility" to labour and capital: "Your employer's profits are not the product of your labour in any sense in which your wages are not equally the product of his capital"[26] There exist no principles of justice which insist that employers not combine against the interests of their workers, said Thornton; they owe no economic obligation to society for having been born with the proverbial silver spoon. Thornton was a theorist of the symmetry imposed upon market process, not of equality of status or opportunity or original position. To Mill's discomfort, he became an anti-Millian; but it has escaped attention that he also was an anti-Marxist before the fact. Thus he would also be unsympathetic to late century theorists of egalitarianism, such as Rawls, Roemer and Sen.

It is interesting to speculate on the extent to which Thornton can be read in retrospect as a representative of a "Darwinian" approach to political economy antithetical to that innovated by Herbert Spencer and others. Thornton certainly devoted more than passing consideration to the arguments for and against Darwinian evolution.[27] Whereas Spencer was the theorist of a *telos* of development, a Victorian scientism which sought to reduce utilitarianism to a few physical laws, Thornton was the prophet of irreducible diversity of human ingenuity: of market forms, of legal forms of property, of human motives, of economic outcomes. In this, he felt he was seconding Mill's opinion that there existed different categories of markets (in Mill's case, wholesale vs. retail) which would in principle require differing explanatory strategies. Thornton described a world where structures cobbled together initially to meet one purpose might end up serving another, entirely unforeseen function. He privileged competition as a causal principle, but warned that the outcome is never unique. "There is never any such 'stable equilibrium' as that of which the teachers of political economy dream" (*p. 290). Spencer regarded man as a machine, a conflation which underwrites the ambitions of a unified science of man; whereas Thornton regarded this to be a delusion prevalent among those who aimed to turn Darwinism into just another version of Cartesian philosophy: "Professor Huxley . . . goes on to avow his belief that the human body, like every other living body, is a machine, all the operations of which will sooner or later be explained by physical principles, insomuch as we shall eventually arrive at a mechanical equivalent of consciousness, even as we have already arrived at a mechanical equivalent of heat" (1873b, p. 169). This, perhaps to a greater degree than any other consideration, explains why Thornton was impervious to the charms of the new model mechanical version of utilitarianism which was being taken up by Jevons, Edgeworth (Mirowski, 1994), and the younger Marshall (1994).

Indeed, the extent to which the dispute over supply and demand and the legitimacy of trades unions was reinforced by and overlapped the controversy over the meaning of Darwinism is noteworthy. Here we refer not to any simplistic and erroneous conflation of the ideology of rapacious capitalism with "Social Darwinism" (Bowler, 1988, pp. 156–65), but rather the more specific point that the major players in the union controversy were understood to also have substantial intellectual stakes in the interpretation of theories of evolution. Herbert Spencer of course popularised the term "evolution" as a biological analogue to utilitarian self-improvement, giving it a very Lamarckian cast (Bowler, 1988, pp. 39–40). Fleeming Jenkin is well known in the literature of the history of biology as an early critic of Darwinian selection.[28] Cairnes sought to explain Thornton's attack on what he considered to the the "demand" side of orthodox explanations of the wage as motivated by the fact that the "supply" side, by which he meant the population principle, had been situated beyond the pale of dispute by Darwin: Malthus's theory "has of late been powerfully helped forward by the influence of Mr. Darwin's work, in which the obnoxious principle . . . was shown to be merely a particular instance of a law pervading all organic existence" (1874, p. 157). Jevons believed that one of Mill's most grievous faults was that, "the whole tone of Mill's moral and political writings is totally opposed to the teaching of Darwin and Spencer . . . He might be defined as the last great philosophic writer conspicuous for his ignorance of the principles of evolution" (1890, pp. 289, 290). One would surmise Thornton's somewhat similar anti-Spencerian stance would have equally earned his contempt. Alfred Marshall, notoriously, sought to relocate the Mecca of the economist into biology, but what this meant in practice was a warmed-over Spencerianism (Groenewegen, 1995, p. 167); for instance, he proved incapable of grasping the significance of Weissman's disconfirmation of the inheritance of acquired characters (p. 484).

Whatever Thornton's exact relationship to Victorian biology, he did make one statement of principle in the second edition of *OL* which earned him the obloquy of future generations, as well as loss of a modicum of Mill's favour. In Mill's famous review essay on Thornton's book in the *Fortnightly* of May and June 1869, he took exception to the attack on the theory of supply and demand, insisting that if one conceded there might be special cases where the analysis did not apply (as Mill had repeatedly done previously), then Thornton's strictures should only have counselled amendment, and not full scale repudiation. Inexplicably, Thornton, an intemperate debater at the best of times, felt impelled to strike back, and added a passage in the second edition of *OL* which stated, "a scientific law admits of no exception whatever, one single exception sufficing completely as a thousand to deprive it of all legal character. If one single instance could be found, or conceived, in which water failed to seek its own level, that water seeks its own level would cease to be a scientific law" (*p. 32). How any reader of Mill's *Logic* with its elaborate defence of tendency laws, with the proviso of special application therein to political economy, would ever think he could make such a bald statement and hope to get away with it, is beyond the ken of mere mortals. Whatever prompted Thornton to make such a rash and fundamentally false statement, it certainly gave welcome hostage to the clutch of younger economists straining at their leads to reprimand the older generation on its weak understanding of the nature of science, and diverted the controversy back in a direction which Thornton had originally tried to avoid.

Thus the real significance of Thornton's *chef d'oeuvre* was the attempt to rid political economy of its dependence upon natural law, and yet simultaneously produce a theoretically grounded economics that could make strong and controversial policy prescriptions about one of the most politically charged issues of the day. In that light, contemporaries were correct to focus their attentions upon Book II Chapter I, which serves as the pivot of this argument. Since everyone from Jenkin to Negishi who seeks to indict Thornton of various "confusions" begins by denying this very first premise, it is important to register his rhetorical question: "what is it that determines price? Assuredly neither inherent utility nor cost of production has the smallest effect on it" (*p. 71). In the question of isolating the causes of realised price, "Our best chance of finding this out is by considering carefully all that happens when a sale takes place" (*p. 38). To that end, Thornton proposes a series of examples of specific markets: Dutch vs. English auction for herring (*p. 28); two horse fairs with face-to-face negotiations (*p. 29); a shopkeeper selling gloves at various posted prices (*p. 30). The point of each of these differing bargaining situations is to suggest that some generic law of supply and demand cannot adequately explain how it could be that, under essentially the same circumstances, with the "same" goods and the "same" transactors, realised prices *may* turn out to be different, depending upon the sequence of bargaining and the nature of the closing rules. Some imprecision does haunt the discussion, given that Thornton both challenges Mill's "definitions" of supply and demand, but then posits in his examples that "demand" is greater or less than "supply" for purposes of exposition.

It is this close proximity of Thornton's denials of the existence of laws of supply and demand with his use of the terminology of supply and demand to discuss specific cases which, probably more than any other aspect, provokes later readers to accuse him of inconsistency and muddle. Therefore, it behoves us to try and clarify what Thornton believed about price theory. First, when engaging with other theorists, but mainly Mill, Thornton tries to use their conceptions of supply and demand in order to demonstrate that standard conclusions need not be drawn from their premises. This is the rhetorical device of temporarily entertaining your opponent's premises and respecting their preferred terminology. Secondly, when venturing this first device, Thornton reluctantly sanctions the use of the terminology of supply and demand to respectively refer to specific quantities of goods formally offered in a well-defined spot market, and explicit bids tendered in the same market. However, in Thornton's view, *these quantities do not regulate price.* This is because in most well-organised markets – and, following Mill, this probably excludes most retail markets – dealers continually privately harbour estimates of magnitudes of bids or quantities which might be tendered in the near but nonspecific future. Because all markets exhibit the phenomenon of "reservation" to a greater or lesser extent, the relationship between flow bids and asks and order backlogs/inventories is inescapable. All actual behaviour is predicated upon these beliefs, which he calls "prospective demand and supply". However, in his view there is no fixed mathematical relationship between the solid quantities which appear in a spot market and the psychological estimates which constitute prospective supply and demand.

> The competition which [a dealer] apprehends is that of a variety of men anxious to sell, or believing themselves under the necessity of selling, very different proportions of their actual stocks, and that within very different periods of time – a competition of men of every gradation of experience, shrewdness, and neediness; who, in the first place, estimate the future probabilities of the market for very different periods; in the second, would form very different estimates, even for the same period; and in the third, would be influenced very differently by the same estimate. Surely such competition can in no intelligible sense be said to *depend* upon prospective supply and demand (*p. 39).

The irreducible diversity of the participants, as made manifest in their widely divergent linkage of observable quantities to their own private expectations and their resulting behaviour of reserving some portion of their stocks from immediate bid or offer, prevents "supply and demand" from dictating a single price/quantity outcome in any given market. Furthermore, resort to the "long period" does not constitue an adequate resolution of this problem.

This, then, constitutes the core of Thornton's theory of price. "Plainly, then, it is competition, and competition alone, that regulates price; but what regulates competition? . . . if by regulating be meant the laying down of rules or prescribing a course which competition in any given circumstances must follow, the simple answer is Nothing. There is no regularity about competition – competition is not regulated at all" (*p. 39). Was this nihilism, or the abdication of all pretence to scientific explanation, as modern commentators moan? No indeed, although it must be said that Thornton leaves off his analysis of commodities in general in order to concentrate his attention upon labour right at this exact juncture, thus abandoning the analysis suspended right where it ought to push home its final advantage. From the remainder of the book, it is easy to extrapolate that Thornton was not left paralysed, unable to propose anything further about the nature of competition and its bounding of realised price. If that had been the case, then nothing he said about the effects of unions would have followed. Instead, the next obvious thesis concerning price theory for Thornton was that, although competition was not regulated by any natural laws of psychology or cost, competition could be hemmed in and regulated by the specific market structures which came over time to be associated with particular commodities in certain cultural settings. Patently, if trades unions could raise wages, then something about the market had been altered to regulate competition.

It is only in the late twentieth century that each of Thornton's theses on price theory have been vindicated, ironically enough through the prosecution of a research tradition which was initially generated to reprimand Thornton for his heresy. Although this is not the place to make the case in detail, we can briefly indicate how the argument would run. First, utilitarian psychology is incapable of underwriting deterministic laws of supply and demand. This is the lesson of the Sonnenschein/Mantel/Debreu (SMD) proofs of the indeterminacy of excess demand functions in a full system of neoclassical general equilibrium.[29] This point can be made in a much less technical fashion: if Walrasian general equilibrium cannot guarantee uniqueness and stability of equilibrium except under wildly unrealistic circumstances, then even with a supposedly generic market mechanism, economic "laws" do not operate in general the way their advocates suggest. Thornton said supply and demand does not lead to unique price/quantity pairs; and Hugo Sonnenschein agrees. Secondly, a generation of research on decision theory has produced one very pronounced empirical generalisation: people don't generally conform to the so-called "laws" of probability in their formation of expectations. The utter bankruptcy of the Bayesian tradition in finding itself asserting that everyone must form identical probability assignments in order to be "rational" only reveals the fundamental soundness of Thornton's insistence upon the irreducible diversity of traders' cognitive capacities and economic expectations. Third, suppose for the moment we abandon the pure modern neoclassical approach, but instead preserve the idea that there still exists some kind of function relating demand price to quantity demanded of some suitable aggregation of market traders. Even in this relatively unprepossessing case, Thornton was still correct in asserting that the "equation" of a supply and a demand function will not themselves determine price. Since this last point may be unfamiliar to most economists, it may be worthwhile to sketch the argument in some detail.

The postwar rise of "experimental economics" has had two salutary effects on the community of economic theorists: one, it has driven home the point that individuals do not conform to the neoclassical characterisation of rational choice in controlled laboratory circumstances; and two, that formats of market institutions matter, and while some kinds of structures (primarily double-sided auctions) do nonetheless conform to neoclassical predicted price and quantity equilibria when costs and reservation prices (that is, "preset" supply and demand curves) are given exogenously, other alternative sorts of market structures do not (Holt in Kagel and Roth, 1995, p. 371 *et seq.*). For some economists, such as Vernon Smith, this has suggested that the profession should seek solace in something he calls the "Hayek hypothesis": namely, that markets somehow "work" independently of the cognitive states of the agents (1991, p. 221 *et seq.*). For Smith the avowed Marshallian, "working" means converging to equilibrium identified by the pregiven supply and demand curves; he neglects to highlight that success in experiments is restricted to a small subset of possible market formations. The situation has been better clarified by the recent papers of Gode and Sunder (1993, 1997), wherein it is demonstrated that *it is the market rules alone* which explain eventual convergence or nonconvergence to preidentified price/quantity pairs, since this will happen even with brainless automata making random bids. In other words, if for the sake of argument, stable Marshallian curves are presumed to exist a *priori*, then it is solely the institutional format of market rules such as choice of auction set up, closing rules, bid-improvement rules, ability to withdraw posted offers, enforcement of budget constraints and the like, which result in any predictable regularities which eventuate. *Markets are not an expression of individual rationality.* In general, price/quantity pairs fall within a probabalistic range rather than collapse to a single point, unless this condition is itself imposed by some sort of clearing house mechanism. Among other interesting corollaries, in many formats the supposed "law of one price" fails to hold even within a single market period, if recontracting is disallowed. All of this can be found in Thornton more than a century ago.

We might venture further to suggest that there is no longer any good reason, other than irrational sentimental attachment to a hallowed analytical tradition which has rather inconveniently been altogether cut adrift from its erstwhile moorings in utilitarianism, to believe that platonic supply and demand curves really exist somehow independent of the contingencies of time, chance and price distributions transmitted from other, similarly constituted markets. Rather, those nostalgic curves are little more than cultural vestiges of the nineteenth century, a period in which hard sciences like physics were thought to uncover rock-solid deterministic functions which could be readily subjected to the differential calculus for purposes of manipulation and control. This, too, can be gleaned from Thornton.

This constitutes the case for entertaining Thornton as a serious economic thinker, one that differs from those previously made in his favour. Thornton should not be understood as being concerned with the stability or multiplicity of equilibria in any neoclassical sense. Since judicious criticism begins at home, we should admit that Mirowski (1990) is vulnerable to this charge of inadequate understanding, especially in the assertion that the "overarching theme of [Thornton's] remarks is that no real market transactor is stupid enough or passive enough to acquiesce in abstract market-clearing price". This comment fundamentally misplaced the stress upon the cognitive states of the agent in opting to reserve sales in the architecture of Thornton's argument. Or, to take to task an author who has otherwise provided the most insightful overview of the impact of Thornton's book, Michael White's assertion that Thornton's price theory was really concerned with "path-dependent adjustment processes" (1994, p. 157) does not sufficiently get to the heart of the matter. Fleeming Jenkin did allow that with what a later Walrasian might call "false trading", the demand and supply curves would shift: but this was not the gist of Thornton's insight. Thornton was not a partisan of hysteresis phenomena, nor was he Brian Arthur without the urn model (although White did not intend to suggest this). The problem faced by these and other authors who seek to recast Thornton's claims in more modern language is the fact that the neoclassical framework is not only awkward, but thoroughly antithetical to the ideas Thornton was striving to express. This incompatibility is no mere accident, given that much of the Marshallian variant of the neoclassical programme was generated expressly for the purpose of denying the cogency and legitimacy of Thornton's claims. Econ 101 is an artifact of the original reprimand of Thornton's impudence, as explained in White, 1994 and Mirowski, 1990. The language required to capture his intentions is one where the portrait of active agents and passive economic environments consisting of generic markets undergoes a gestalt reversal; instead one must envision a multiplicity of diverse market institutions providing some boundaries for the essentially lawless or random actions of the economic agents.[30]

Philip Mirowski
with the assistance of
Stephen Tradewell

NOTES

1 For those who need a skeleton key to decode the parallels, here we are referring to the fact that William Thomas Thornton has been sometimes confused with Henry Thornton (1760–1815), a leading authority on early British monetary economics. On these confusions, see Peake, 1994. Of course, the Danish prince without which our drama would have no protagonist is none other than John Stuart Mill.

2 These statements refer to the set of arguments often referred to as the Sonnenscheim/Mantel/Debreu theorems. For the technical discussions, see Sonnenschein, 1972; Mantel, 1976; Hildenbrand, 1994. A good non-technical introduction is provided by Rizvi, 1994;1998.

3 Unless our readers think this a bootless caricature, we bid them to consult the first chapter of Niehans, 1990.

4 We should note that precision in language matters here, a precision lacking in Cournot's English translator. *Débit* has the connotation of retail sales, as from a shop. This is significant, since it was precisely in this era that retail stores with fixed posted prices were becoming prevalent in urban contexts (Alexander, 1970; Fairchilds, 1993). It is true that in this chapter Cournot states that he regards *débit* and *demande* as synonyms, but the reason is important: "we do not see for what reason theory need take account of any demand which does not result in a sale" (p. 46). Already we are far from the world of neoclassical economics.

5 The need to make these distinctions is provoked by the ubiquitous unreliable accounts found in the modern secondary literature on the history of economic thought. Most textbooks simply take any mention of "supply and demand" as making reference to the Marshallian apparatus *avant la lettre*, no matter whom the author. Some, such as Samuel Hollander, venture much further beyond the pale in insisting upon a profound continuity between classical and neoclassical writers by spinning interpretations which construct each individual as a more or less conscious Marshallian. This practice was criticised by Neil de Marchi (Thweatt, 1988, p. 146). Elsewhere, one is often confronted by such factually false statements as: "The chief adversary of the labour theory of value in the nineteenth century was always the supply-and-demand theory" (Ekelund & Hebert, 1990, p. 160).

6 "Mill's theory of value shifted the emphasis to the equilibrium of demand and supply" (Niehans, 1990, p. 128). "Mill clearly analyzed supply and demand in terms of schedules, thus clearing up much of the confusion present in earlier controversies" (Backhouse, 1985, p. 40).

7 British Library, Manuscripts Room.

8 Mill, *Collected Works*, 1967, vol. 15, pp. 574–5.

9 See, for instance, the footnote on p. 123: "In these masterly papers, Mr. Mill will be found to have anticipated many of the remarks in the text, and he has, moreover, discussed, at considerable length, some matters to which my plan required only a slight reference."

10 Comment at the Political Economy Club, December 1866, quoted in White, 1994, p. 149.

11 While the exact nature of discussions of the Political Economy Club are not reported in the minutes, they are clear about who held the various positions in the club. Both were

officers and Newmarch eventually succeeded Thornton as treasurer of the club.

12 Source: Political Economy Club, 1921.

13 Both the timing of Thornton's publications and the fact that in 1866 he identified supply and demand as the theoretical crux of the problem of wages give the lie to ridiculous attempts by Jacob Hollander, following the lead of Wilson (1871) and others to smear Thornton by suggesting he derived his ideas from Francis Longe's *Refutation of the Wages Fund Theory* (1866). Likewise, the attempt by Forget (1991) to sympathetically link Mill and Longe while treating Thornton as somehow external to the Millian tradition will also be shown to be inconsistent with the evidence.

There are some further tantalizing bits of evidence that Thornton had been pressing Mill on weaknesses in his account of demand and supply even before the papers on wages and unions. On this, see Mill, *Collected Works*, 1967, vol. 3, p. 608.

14 Macmillan Archives, British Library, Manuscripts Room. Original emphasis.

15 Examples of this interpretation can be found in (Ekelund, 1976, 1985; Hollander, 1985, pp. 409–17; Schwartz, 1972; Vint, 1994; Backhouse, 1990; Niehans, 1990, p. 129). Hollander's statement can serve as the epitome of this error: "Thornton's book merely provided an opportunity to express publicly the reservations against formulations of the wages fund doctrine such as Fawcett's which Mill already had in mind for several years" (1985, p. 418n).

16 The footnote is found in the first edition of *On Labour* (1869, pp. 84–5n). This also explains why Longe's 1866 *Refutation* was essentially irrelevant for both Mill and Thornton, contrary to Forget (1991).

17 For a discussion of the central importance of symmetry principles in economic theory, see Mirowski, 1989; Sent, 1998.

18 This assessment is shared by the modern proponents of a Whig history of the neoclassical ascendancy. See, for instance, the assessment of Nobelist John Hicks: "The evidence surely is that after 1848 [Mill] again turned away from economics. There is very little about economics in his correspondence, until we come to his last years (he died in 1873). Then there are letters directed to his friend W. T. Thornton, who had written a book entitled *On Labour.* But it seems to me that these letters show only that by that date he had got so far away from economics that he had lost the grip he had once possessed" (1983, p. 61).

19 See Mill's comments on William Stanley Jevons in his letter to Cairnes dated 5 December 1871, in O'Brien, 1943, p. 274. The contempt was mutual. On the latter, see Jevons, 1878 and his famous complaint in the *Theory of Political Economy*, that "that able but wrong-headed man, David Ricardo, shunted the car of economic science on to a wrong line – a line, however, on which it was further urged towards confusion by his equally able and wrong-headed admirer, John Stuart Mill" (1970, p. 72)

20 A very readable summary of Huxley's career is to be found in Desmond, 1994. The bearing of the doctrine of Darwinism upon many of the key figures in our narrative, including Cairnes, Fleeming Jenkin and Jevons, is briefly assayed below in the section "What Did Thornton Do?".

21 See, for instance, Pelling, 1963; Finn, 1993; Howell, 1890; Webb, 1907; Clements, 1961; Biagini, 1987.

22 There remains the interesting issue of what Marx thought of Thornton, although one might construct a preliminary conspectus from his scattered remarks on Mill. I have been unable to find any commentary, unusual in one so comprehensive in his critique of political economy.

23 Cairnes: "if this style of reasoning be legitimate, the whole structure of economic doctrine must inevitably go down" (1874, p. 184). Jevons: "Though Mr. Thornton's objections are mostly beside the question, his remarks have served to show that the actions of the law of supply and demand were inadequately explained by previous economists" (1970, p. 149).

24 This, and all subsequent starred (*p. xxx) references are to this edition of *On Labour*, in vol. 4.

25 The widespread faith in "Cooperation" as economic panacea was subjected to scathing critique by Frederic Harrison in his 1865 "Industrial Cooperation" (reprinted in 1908, pp. 323–65). Although Thornton repeatedly refers to this article, it seems to us that he never adequately addressed Harrison's fundamental point, that cooperatives have never been successful outside retail activities, and the reason for this is that they do not change any aspect of the employment relationship in any substantial manner.

26 The nearest modern thinker to this position is David Ellerman (1995). He is one of the few to try and develop some positive economic theory out of the ashes of the pyrrhic Cambridge capital controversy of the 1960s.

27 These are discussed in his essay "Recent Phases of Scientific Atheism" in his *Old Fashioned Ethics*, especially (1873b, pp. 217–23). Thornton's primary difference from those he calls the "Darwinians" is his attempt to preserve some compatible version of creationism.

28 See the articles by Bowler and Hull in Kohn, 1985 and Bowler, 1988. Jenkin's review appeared as 1867, that is, almost contemporaneous with his work on unions.

29 See note 2 above. The significance of the SMD proofs for the historical attempts to marry Walrasian theory to supply and demand explanations is explored by the author elsewhere (Mirowski & Hands, 1998).

30 One can peruse a formal statement of a more faithful "Thorntonian" approach to price theory in Mirowski & Somefun, 1998.

REFERENCES

[Anon.], 1847, "Overpopulation and its Remedy by William Thomas Thornton", *Westminster Review*, January (46): 161–77

[Anon.], 1869a, "Thornton on labour", *The Athenaeum*, 20 February no. 2156: 275

[Anon.], 1869b, "Labour & Capital", *Westminster Review*, July (92): 36–56

[Anon.] 1869c, "On Labour by W. T. Thornton" *British Quarterly Review*, October (50): 448–74

Alexander, David, 1970, *Retailing in England in the Industrial Revolution* (London: Athlone)

Backhouse, Roger, 1985, A *History of Modern Economic Analysis* (Oxford: Blackwell)

Bagehot, Walter, 1905, *Economic Studies* (London: Longmans Green)

Bain, Alexander, 1882, *James Mill:* A *Biography* (London: Longmans Green)

Barnes, Donald, 1930, A *History of the English Corn Laws* (London: Routledge)

Becher, Harvey, 1971, *William Whewell and Cambridge Mathematics* (PhD thesis, History, University of Missouri)

Becher, Harvey, 1992, "The Whewell Story", *Annals of Science*, (49): 377–84

Bharadwaj, Krishna, 1978a, "The Subversion of Classical Analysis", *Cambridge Journal of Economics*, (2): 253–71

Bharadwaj, Krishna, 1978b, *Classical Political Economy and the Rise to Dominance of Supply and Demand Theories* (New Delhi: Orient Longmans)

Biagini, Eugenio, 1987, "British Trade Unions and Popular Political Economy, 1860–80", *Historical Journal*, (30): 811–40

Blaug, Mark, 1992, *The Methodology of Economics*, 2nd edn (Cambridge: Cambridge University Press)

Blaug, Mark, 1996, *Economic Theory in Retrospect*, 5th edn (Cambridge: Cambridge University Press)

Bowler, Peter, 1988, *The Non-Darwinian Revolution* (Baltimore: Johns Hopkins Press)

Bowley, A. & Wood, G., 1905, "The Statistics of Wages in the UK during the last hundred years: Engineering and Shipbuilding, a trade union standard rate", *Journal of the Royal Statistical Society*, (68): 104–37; 373–91

Bowley, A. & Wood, G., 1906, "The Statistics of Wages in the UK during the last hundred years: Engineering and Shipbilding, general results", *Journal of the Royal Statistical Society*, (69): 148–92

Breit, William, 1967, "The Wages Fund Controversy Revisited", *Canadian Journal of Economics and Political Science*, (23): 509–28

Brentano, Lujo, 1870, "On the History and Development of Gilds", in*English Gilds*, ed. Toulmin Smith (London:Trubner)

Cairnes, J. E., 1866, "The Law of Demand and Supply", *Economist*, 20 October, 3 November, with letters by T. E. Cairnes, 1 December, and W. T. Thornton, 15 December

Cairnes, J. E., 1871, "Political Economy and Laissez Faire", *Fortnightly Review*, (10): 80–97

Cairnes, J. E., 1874, *Some Leading Principles of Political Economy Newly Expounded* (New York: Harper & Bros)

Cairnes, J. E., 1875, *The Character and Logical Method of Political Economy* (London: Macmillan)

Canard, Nicolas-François, 1969 [1801], *Principes d'Économie Politique* (Rome: Bizzarri)

Chadwick, David, 1860, "The Rate of Wages in Manchester and Salford", *Journal of the Royal Statistical Society*, (23)

Chipman, John, 1965, "A Survey of the Theory of International Trade: Part I", *Econometrica*, (13): 477–519

Clements, R.V., 1961, "British trade Unions and Popular political Economy 1850–75", *Economic History Review*, (14): 93–104

Cliffe Leslie, T. E., 1868, "Political Economy and the Rate of Wages", *Fraser's Magazine*, (78): 81–95

Cliffe Leslie, T. E., 1969 [1888], *Essays in Political Economy* (New York: Kelley)

Cournot, Antoine-Augustin, 1971 [1838], *Researches into the Mathematical Principles of the Theory of Wealth* (New York: Kelly)

Creedy, John, 1992, *Demand and Exchange in Economic Analysis* (Aldershot: Edward Elgar)

Daston, Lorraine, 1986, "The Physicalist Tradition in Early 19th Century French Geometry", *Studies in the History and Philosophy of Science*, (17): 269–95

De Marchi, Neil, 1974, "The Success of Mill's Principles", *History of Political Economy*, (6): 119–57

Dennis, Kenneth, 1977, *Competition in the History of Economic Thought* (New York: Arno)

De Quincey, Thomas, 1877, *The Works of Thomas De Quincey, Riverside Edition* (Boston: Houghton Mifflin)

De Quincey, Thomas, 1897, *Collected Writings*, vol. IX (London: Black)

Desmond, Adrian, 1994, *Huxley: the Devil's Disciple* (London: Michael Joseph)

De Ville, P. & Menard, C., 1989, "An Insolent Founding Father?", *European Economic Review*, (33): 494–502

Dewey, Clive, 1974, "The Rehabilitation of the Peasant Proprietor in 19th Century Economic Thought", *History of Political Economy*, (6): 17–47

Dickens, Charles, 1961, *Hard Times* (New York: Signet)

Dimand, Robert, 1993, "Alfred Marshall and the Whewell Group", *Manchester School*, (61): 439–41

Dmitriev, V. K., 1974 [1902], *Economic Essays on Value, Competition and Utility* (Cambridge: Cambridge University Press)

Donoghue, Mark, 1995, "The Wages-and-profits Fund: classical remnants in Marshall's early theory of distribution", *European Journal of the History of Economic Thought*, (2): 355–74

Donoghue, Mark, 1997, "Mill's Affirmation of the Classical Wage Fund Doctrine", *Scottish Journal of Political Economy*, (44): 82–99

Dunning, T. J., 1860, *Trades Unions and Strikes* (London: T. J. Dunning)

Dupuit, Jules, 1952 [1844], "On the Measurement of Utility of Public Works", *International Economic Papers*, (2): 83–110
Ekelund, Robert, 1985, "Mill's Recantation once again: a reply to Professor Negishi", *Oxford Economic Papers*, (37): 152-3
Ekelund, Robert, 1997, "W. T. Thornton: savant, idiot, or idiot-savant?", *Journal of the History of Economic Thought*, (19): 1–23
Ekelund, R. & Hebert, R., 1990, A *History of Economic Theory and Method*, 3rd edn (New York: McGraw Hill)
Ekelund, R. & Kordsheimer, W., 1981, "J. S. Mill, unions and the wages fund doctrine", *Quarterly Journal of Economics*, (96): 531–41
Ekelund, R. & Thommesen, S., 1989, "Disequilibrium Theory and Thornton's Assault on the Laws of Supply and Demand", *History of Political Economy*, (21): 567–92
Ekelund, R. & Thornton, M., 1991, "Geometric Analogies and Market Demand Estimation", *History of Political Economy*, (23): 397–416
Ellerman, David, 1995, *Intellectual Trespassing as* a *Way of Life* (Lanham: Rowman & Littlefield)
Ellis, Robinson, 1878, *Academy*, 29 June
Etner, Francois, 1987, *Histoire du Calcul Économique en France*, (Paris: Economica)
Fairchilds, Cissie, 1993, "The Production and Marketing of Populuxe Goods in 18th Century Paris", in *Consumption and the World of Goods*, eds J. Brewer & R. Porter (London: Routledge)
Fawcett, Henry, 1860, "Strikes: their tendencies and remedies", *Westminster Review*, (18): 1–23
Fawcett, Henry, 1865, *Economic Position of the British Labourer* (London: Macmillan)
Fetter, Frank, 1980, *The Economist in Parliament: 1780-1868* (Durham: Duke University Press)
Finn, Margot, 1993, *After Chartism* (Cambridge: Cambridge University Press)
Fontana, Biancamaria, 1985, *Rethinking the Politics of Commercial Society* (Cambridge: Cambridge University Press)
Forget, Evelyn, 1991, "John Stuart Mill, Francis Longe, and William Thornton on Demand and Supply", *Journal of the History of Economic Thought*, (13): 205–21
Forget, Evelyn, 1992, "J. S. Mill and the Tory School", *History of Political Economy*, (24): 31–59
Forget, Evelyn, 1993, "J. B. Say and Adam Smith", *Canadian Journal of Economics*, (26): 121–33
Forget, Evelyn, 1994, "Disequilibrium Trade as a Metaphor for Social Disorder in J.-B. Say", in *Higgling*, eds N. de Marchi & M. Morgan, supplement to vol. 26 of *History of Political Economy* (Durham: Duke University Press)
Garnier, Germain, 1796, *Abrège des Principes de l'économie politique* (Paris: Agasse)
Gherity, James, 1988, "Mill's Friendly Critic – Thornton or Whewell?", *Manchester School*, (56): 282–5
Gode, D. & Sunder, S., 1993, "Allocative Efficiency of Markets with Zero-Intelligence Traders", *Journal of Political Economy*, (101): 119–37
Gode, D. & Sunder, S., 1997, "What Makes Markets Allocatively Efficient?", *Quarterly Journal of Economics*, (112): 603–30

Grattan-Guinness, Ivor, 1990, *Convolutions in French Mathematics* (Boston: Birkhauser)
Groenewegen, Peter, 1973, "A Note on the Origin of the Phrase Demand and Supply", *Economic Journal*, (83): 505–9
Groenewegen, Peter, 1995, A *Soaring Eagle* (Cheltenham: Edward Elgar)
Hadden, Richard, 1994, *On the Shoulders of Merchants* (Albany: State University of New York Press)
Halevy, Elie, 1972, *The Growth of Philosophical Radicalism* (London: Faber)
Harrison, Frederic, 1865, "The Limits of Political Economy", *Fortnightly Review*, (1): 356–76
Harrison, Frederic, 1889, "Socialist Unionism", *Nineteenth Century*, (26): 721–32
Harrison, Frederic, 1908, *National and Social Problems* (New York: Macmillan)
Hayek, F., 1951, *John Stuart Mill and Harriet Taylor* (London: Routledge Kegan Paul)
Hearn, William, 1863, *Plutology* (Melbourne: G. Robertson)
Henderson, James, 1996, *Early British Mathematical Economics* (Totawa: Rowman & Littlefield)
Hicks, John, 1983, *Classics and Moderns* (Oxford: Basil Blackwell)
Hildenbrand, Werner, 1994, *Market Demand* (Princeton: Princeton University Press)
Hollander, Samuel, 1985, *The Economics of John Stuart Mill* (Oxford: Basil Blackwell)
Howell, G., 1890, *The Conflicts of Labour and Capital historically and economically considered* (London: Macmillan)
Jeffreys, J., 1945, *The Story of the Engineers, 1800–1945* (London: Lawrence and Wishart)
Jenkin, Fleeming, 1867, "The Origin of Species", *North British Review*, (46): 149–71
Jenkin, Fleeming, 1931 [1887], *The Graphic Representation of Supply and Demand, and other essays* (London: LSE Reprint no. 9)
Jevons, William Stanley, 1868, *Trade Societies: their objects and policy* (Manchester)
Jevons, William Stanley, 1878, "John Stuart Mill's Philosophy Tested", *Contemporary Review*, (32): 88–99
Jevons, William Stanley, 1890, *Pure Logic and Other Minor Works*, ed. Robert Adamson (London: Macmillan)
Jevons, William Stanley, 1894 [1st edn 1882], *The State in Relation to Labour* (London: Macmillan)
Jevons, William Stanley, 1905, *Principles of Economics*, ed. Henry Higgs (London: Macmillan)
Jevons, William Stanley, 1970, *Theory of Political Economy* (Baltimore: Penguin)
Kagel, John & Roth, Alvin, 1995, *Handbook of Experimental Economics* (Princeton: Princeton University Press)
Kaplan, Stephen, 1976, *Bread, Politics and Political Economy in the Reign of Louis XVI* (Hague: Nijhoff)
Kaplan, Stephen, 1984, *Provisioning Paris* (Ithaca: Cornell University Press)
Keynes, John Neville, 1917, *The Scope and Method of Political Economy*, 4th edn (London: Macmillan)
Kohn, David, ed., 1985, *The Darwinian Heritage* (Princeton: Princeton University Press)
Kula, Witold, 1986, *Measures and Men* (Princeton: Princeton University Press)
Lee, C., 1979, *British Regional Employment Statistics 1841–1971* (Cambridge: Cambridge University Press)

Levy, David, 1998, "The Premature Death of Path Dependence", paper presented to History of Economics Society meetings, June, Montréal, Canada
Longe, Francis, 1903 [1866], A *Refutation of the Wage-Fund Theory* (Baltimore: Johns Hopkins Press)
Longfield, Mountifort, 1834, *Lectures on Political Economy* (Dublin: Milliken)
Malthus, Thomas, 1827, *Definitions in Political Economy* (London: John Murray)
Malthus, Thomas, 1966 [1820], *Principles of Political Economy* in vol. II of David Ricardo's *Collected Works*, ed. Piero Sraffa (Cambridge: Cambridge University Press)
Malthus, Thomas, 1986, *Essays on Political Economy*, vol. 6 of *The Works of T. R. Malthus*, eds E. Wrigley & David Souden (London: Pickering & Chatto)
Mantel, Rolf, 1976, "Homothetic Preferences and Community Excess Demand Functions", *Journal of Economic Theory*, (12): 197–201
Marcet, Jane, 1827, *Conversations on political Economy* (London: John Murray)
Marshall, Alfred, 1947 [1920], *Principles of Economics*, 8th edn (London: Macmillan)
Marshall, Alfred, 1975, *Early Economic Writings*, 2 vols, ed. J. Whittaker (New York: Free Press)
Marshall, Alfred, 1994, "Ye Machine", *Research in the History of Economic Thought and Method, Archival Supplement* No. 4: 116–32
Marx, Karl, 1935, *Value, Price and Profit* (New York: International)
Marx, Karl, 1974, *The First International and After*, ed. David Fernbach (New York: Vintage)
Mason, John, 1980, "Political Economy and the Response to Socialism in Britain, 1870–1914", *Historical Journal*, (23): 565–87
Mason, Roger, 1989, *Robert Giffen and the Giffen Paradox* (Totawa: Barnes & Noble)
Menard, Claude, 1978, *La Formation d'une Rationalité Économique* (Paris: Flammarion)
Mill, Anna, 1960, *John Mill's Boyhood Visit to France* (Toronto: University of Toronto Press)
Mill, James, 1966, *Selected Economic Writings*, ed. D. Winch (Chicago: University of Chicago Press)
Mill, John Stuart, 1897, *Early Essays* (London: Bell)
Mill, John Stuart, 1965, *Principles of Political Economy* in *Collected Works*, vols 2 & 3 (Toronto: University of Toronto Press)
Mill, John Stuart, 1967, *Collected Works* (Toronto: University of Toronto Press)
Mirowski, Philip, 1989, *More Heat than Light* (New York: Cambridge University Press)
Mirowski, Philip, 1990, "Smooth Operator", in *Alfred Marshall in Retrospect*, ed. Rita Tullberg (Aldershot: Edward Elgar)
Mirowski, Philip, ed., 1994, *Edgeworth on Chance, Economic Hazard and Statistics* (Savage, MD: Rowman & Littlefield)
Mirowski, Philip & Somefun, Koye, 1998, "Markets as Evolving Computational Entities", *Journal of Evolutionary Economics*, (8): 329–56
Mueller, Iris, 1955, *J. S. Mill and French Thought* (Urbana: University of Illinois Press)
Musson, A., 1974, *Trades Unions and Social History* (London: Frank Cass)
Negishi, T., 1985, "Comments on Ekelund", *Oxford Economic Papers*, (37): 148–51
Negishi, T., 1986, "Thornton's Criticism of Equilibrium Theory and Mill", *History of Political Economy*, (18): 567–77

Negishi, T., 1989, "On Equilibrium and Disequilibrium: reply to Ekelund and Thommesen", *History of Political Economy*, (21): 593–600

Niehans, Jurg, 1990, A *History of Economic Theory* (Baltimore: Johns Hopkins University Press)

Norgate, Gerald le Grys, 1937, "William Thomas Thornton", in *Dictionary of National Biography*, vol. XIX, eds Stephen & Lee, pp. 790–1

O'Brien, G., 1943, "J. S. Mill and J. E. Cairnes", *Economica*, (10): 273–85

Packe, Michael, 1954, *Life of J. S. Mill* (London: Secker & Warburg)

Peake, Charles, 1994, "A Note on John Stuart Mill, William Thornton, and William Whewell", *Manchester School*, (62): 319–23

Pelling, Henry, 1963, A *History of British Trades Unionism* (London: Macmillan)

Pigou, A., ed., 1956, *Memorials of Alfred Marshall* (New York: Kelley & Millman)

Polanyi, Karl, 1957 [1944], *The Great Transformation* (Boston: Beacon Press)

Political Economy Club, 1921, *Political Economy Club Centenary Volume* (London: Macmillan)

Raffaelli, Tiziano, 1994, "Marshall's Analysis of the Human Mind", *Research in the History of Economic Thought and Method, Archival Supplement* No. 4: 57–93

Richards, Joan, 1988, *Mathematical Visions* (New York: Academic)

[Rickards, G. K.], 1869, "Thornton On Labour", *Edinburgh Review*, October (130): 198-212

Rizvi, Abu, 1994, "The Microfoundations Project in General Equilibrium Theory", *Cambridge Journal of Economics*, (18): 357–77

Rizvi, Abu, 1998, "Responses to Arbitrariness in Contemporary Economics", in *New Economics and its History*, ed. John Davis (Durham: Duke University Press)

[Rogers, Edward], 1822, *An Essay on Some General Principles of Political Economy* (London: H. Butterworth)

Say, Jean-Baptiste, 1830, *Treatise on Political Economy*, trans. C. Princep, 4th edn (Philadelphia: Grigg)

Say, Jean-Baptiste, 1852, *Cours Complet d'Economie Politique Practique, Tome II* (Paris: Guillaumin)

Schumpeter, Joseph, 1954, A *History of Economic Analysis* (New York: Oxford University Press)

Schwartz, Pedro, 1972, *The New Political Economy of J. S. Mill* (London: Weidenfeld & Nicolson)

Scrope, G. Poulett, 1969 [1833], *Principles of Political Economy* (New York: Kelley)

Senior, Nassau, 1965 [1836], *An Outline of the Science of Political Economy* (New York: Kelley)

Sent, Esther-Mirjam, 1998, *The Evolving Rationality of Rational Expectations Theory* (New York: Cambridge University Press)

Sidgwick, Henry, 1879, "The Wages Fund Theory", *Fortnightly Review*, n.s. (153)

Smith, Adam, 1976 [1776], *An Inquiry into . . . the Wealth of Nations* (Chicago: University of Chicago Press)

Smith, Crosbie & Wise, Norton, 1989, *Energy and Empire* (Cambridge: Cambridge University Press)

Smith, Vernon, 1951, "The Classicists' Use of Demand", *Journal of Political Economy*, (59): 242–57

Smith, Vernon, 1956, "Malthus' Theory of Demand", *Scottish Journal of Political Economy*, (3): 205–20

Smith, Vernon, 1991, *Papers in Experimental Economics* (New York: Cambridge University Press)

Smyth, R., ed., 1962, *Essays in Economic Method* (London: Duckworth)

Sonnenschein, Hugo, 1972, "Market Excess Demand Functions", *Econometrica*, (40): 549–63

Spencer, Herbert, 1872, *Essays: Moral, Policial and Aesthetic* (New York: Appleton)

Stephen, Leslie & Lee, Sydney, eds, 1937, *Dictionary of National Biography*, vol. XIX (London: Oxford University Press)

Stigler, George, 1965, *Essays in the History of Economics* (Chicago: University of Chicago Press)

Stoppard, Tom, 1967, *Rosencrantz and Guildenstern are Dead* (New York: Grove Press)

Taussig, Frank, 1897, *Wages and Capital* (New York: Appleton)

Theocharis, Reghinos, 1983, *Early Developments in Mathematical Economics*, 2nd edn (London: Macmillan)

Thompson, E. P., 1993, *Customs in Common* (New York: New Press)

Thweatt, William, 1983, "Origins of the terminology of supply and demand", *Scottish Journal of Political Economy*, (30): 287–94

Thweatt, William, ed., 1988, *Classical Political Economy* (Boston: Kluwer)

Thornton, Thomas, 1807, *The Present State of Turkey; or*, A *Description of the political, civil and religious constitution, government and laws of the Ottoman Empire* (London: Joseph Mawman)

Thornton, William, 1846, *Over-population and its remedy* (London: Longman, Brown, Green and Longmans)

Thornton, William, 1848, A *Plea for Peasant Proprietors* (London: John Murray)

Thornton, William, 1850, "Equity Reform", *Westminster Review*, April (53): 100-12

Thornton, William, 1854, *Zohràb; Or, a Midsummer's Day's Dream: and other poems* (London: Longman, Brown, Green and Longmans)

Thornton, William, 1857, *Modern Manicheism, Labour's Utopia, and Other Poems* (London: John Parker and Sons)

Thornton, William, 1862, "On the Income Tax", *British Association for the Advancement of Science Report*

Thornton, William, 1863, "Maritime Rights of Belligerents and Neutrals", *MacMillans Magazine*, January (7): 231–40

Thornton, William, 1864, "Strikes and Industrial Cooperation", *Westminster Review*, (25): 349–83

Thornton, William, 1866, "A New Theory of Supply and Demand", *Fortnightly Review*, (6): 420–34

Thornton, William, 1867, "What Determines the Price of Labour or the Rate of Wages?", *Fortnightly Review*, (7): 551–66

Thornton, William. 1869a, *On Labour* (London: Macmillan)

Thornton, William, 1869b, "Indian Railway Reform", *Westminster Review*, July (92): 1–17

Thornton, William, 1870a, *On Labour*, 2nd edn (London: Macmillan)

Thornton, William, 1870b, "Anti-Utilitarianism", *Fortnightly Review*, September n.s. (8): 314–37

Thornton, William, 1871a, "National Education in India", *Cornhill Magazine*, March (23): 282–95

Thornton, William, 1871b, "Natural Rights, Abstract Justice", *Fortnightly Review*, September n.s. (10): 359–76

Thornton, William, 1871c, "Technical Education in England", *Cornhill Magazine*, September (24): 323–41

Thornton, William, 1871d, "Neutrality for Neutrals", *Contemporary Review*, November (18): 489–505

Thornton, William, 1872, "Huxleyism", *Contemporary Review*, October (20): 666–91

Thornton, William, 1873a, "His Career in the India House", in *John Stuart Mill: His Life and Works* (Boston: James Osgood)

Thornton, William, 1873b, *Old-fashioned Ethics and Commonsense Metaphysics* (London: Macmillan)

Thornton, William, 1875a, "Economic Definition of Wealth", *Fortnightly Review*, April (23): 566–74

Thornton, William, 1875b, *Indian Public Works; and cognate Indian topics* (London: Macmillan)

Thornton, William, 1876, "Professor Cairnes on Value", *Contemporary Review*, October (28): 813–35

Thornton, William, 1878, *Word for Word from Horace: the odes literally versified* (London: Macmillan)

Thornton, William, 1879a, "The Wages Fund", *Nineteenth Century*, August (6): 293–307

Thornton, William, 1879b, "The Bright Clauses of the Irish Land Act", *Fortnightly Review*, April (25): 608–26

Thornton, William, 1880a, "Parliament without Parties", *MacMillans Magazine*, January (41): 259–66

Thornton, William, 1880b, "Indian Exchange Difficulty", *Westminster Review*, July (114): 173–92

Thweatt, William, 1983, "Origins of the Terminology of Supply and Demand", *Scottish Journal of Political Economy*, (30): 287–94

Tiling, Laura, 1975, "Early Experimental Graphs", *British Journal for the History of Science*, (8): 193–213

Uemiya, S., 1981, "Jevons and Fleeming Jenkin", *Kobe University Economic Review*, (27): 45–57

Vatin, François, 1998, *Économie Politique et économie naturelle chez A. A. Cournot* (Paris: Presses Universitaires de France)

Vint, John, 1994, *Capital and Wages:* A *Lakatosian History of the Wages Fund Doctrine* (Aldershot: Edward Elgar)

Walras, Léon, 1965, *Correspondence*, ed. W. Jaffee (Amsterdam: North Holland)

Waterman, Anthony, 1998, "Reappraisal of Malthus the Economist", *History of Political Economy*, (30): 293–334

Webb, Sydney & Beatrice, 1904, "The Assize of Bread", *Economic Journal*, (14): 196–218

West, E. G. & Hafer, R. W., 1978, "J. S. Mill, unions and the wages fund recantation", *Quarterly Journal of Economics*, (92): 603–19

Whewell, William, 1967 [1862], *Six Lectures on Political Economy* (New York: Kelley)

Whewell, William, 1971, *Mathematical Exposition of Some Doctrines of Political Economy* (New York: Kelley)

White, Michael, 1989, "Why are there no demand and supply curves in Jevons?", *History of Political Economy*, (21): 425–56

White, Michael, 1994, "That God-Forgotton Thornton: Exorcising Higgling after *On Labour*", in *Higgling*, eds N. de Marchi & M. Morgan, supplement to vol. 26 of *History of Political Economy* (Durham: Duke University Press)

White, Michael, 1998, "Obscure Objects of Desire?", Paper presented to Duke Conference on Economics of Art

[Wilson, John], 1871, "Economic Fallacies and Labour's Utopias", *London Quarterly Review*, July (131): 121–39

Wise, M. N., 1993, "Mediations: Enlightenment Balancing Acts", in *World Changes*, ed. Paul Horwich (Cambridge: MIT Press)

Wise, M. N. & Smith, C., 1989, "Work and Waste", *History of Science*, (27): 263–301

Zastoupil, Lynn, 1994, *John Stuart Mill and India* (Stanford: Stanford University Press)

LETTERS TO THE *ECONOMIST* BY AND CONCERNING THORNTON

Cairnes, John Elliott, "The 'Law' of Demand and Supply",
Letter to the *Economist*, 20 October, 1866.

Cairnes, John Elliott, "The 'Law' of Demand and Supply",
Letter to the *Economist*, 3 November, 1866.

Leslie, Thomas Cliffe, "Demand and Supply",
Letter to the *Economist*, 1 December, 1866.

Thornton, William, "Supply and Demand",
Letter to the *Economist*, 15 December, 1866.

The first three letters are reviews of Thornton's provocative 1886 essay, "A New Theory of Supply and Demand". In the last letter, Thornton mainly replied to Leslie's critique. On 7 December 1886, the meaning of supply and demand was discussed at the Political Economy Club.

20 October 1866: John Elliott Cairnes, letter to the Economist

THE "LAW" OF DEMAND AND SUPPLY.

By not a few persons who take an interest in the problems of political economy "the law of demand and supply" would probably be pronounced the most fundamental principle of that science, if not in itself containing potentially all its conclusions. The prices of commodities, the rates of wages, the rent of land, the interest of money – in short, all the leading phenomena of wealth – are thought by those to whom we refer – that is to say, by the majority of public writers and speakers – to find in this maxim their plenary explanation. Whence once the magical phrase has been spoken, enough, it is thought, has been done: to push elucidation further is pedantic, almost impertinent. Do we wish to know, for example, what have been the effects of the gold discoveries on prices, we are sapiently told that the whole occurrence resolves itself into a question of demand and supply: the utterer of this form of words being fully under the impression that he has said enough to satisfy all legitimate curiosity. Nor is the faith in the efficacy of this "law" confined to the theory. Some years ago Mr. Hutt argued gravely in the House of Commons against the policy of maintaining the African squadron, because it was an interference with "the law of demand and supply." "You might as well," said Mr. Hutt, not without considerable sympathy from his audience, "arm a fleet or denounce penalties "against the flow of tides, or the revolutions of the seasons, "as an attempt to stop by similar means the operation of that great "law – the law of demand and supply." In connection with the wages problem, the sort of worship paid to this dogma has become a serious evil; the "inexorable law" being not unfrequently used as a sort of bugbear to scare away free inquiry from precisely those points of our social economy into which the most fearless and searching investigation is needed. Such being the prevelent feeling regarding this notion, how will not a few of our popular expositors if economic doctrine be startled from their propriety, when they find in a recent number of the *Fortnightly Review* an elaborate essay in which the very existence of the universal postulate is called in question! The writer who has been bold enough to publish this challenge is Mr. W. T. Thornton. "The object of the paper," says Mr. Thornton, "is to show that the knowledge which every one supposes himself to possess {respecting the doctrine of demand and supply} is really possessed by no one, for that, firstly, no definition of supply and demand have ever been given which do not require more or less of correction or amplification; and secondly, no definition of them can be given consistently with which it is possible for them to determine price;" or, we may add (for Mr. Thornton's reasoning need not be limited to the particular case to which he happens in his essay to confine it), most of those phenomena of wealth which demand and supply are commonly adduced to explain. Mr. Thornton not merely undertakes to prove this, but, as we think will be the opinion of most unprejudiced readers of his essay, goes a long way towards accomplishing his purpose. It will be seen, therefore, that the doctrine of demand and supply, as popularly understood, is just now seriously endangered; and those persons whose notions of economic science are summed up in that phrase will need to look to it, or they may find themselves ere long in the painful position so touchingly depicted in George Eliot's latest novel – the position of men "deprived of their formula."

The essay which Mr. Thornton has adventured on this daring enterprise deserves study, as an example of economic analysis even apart from the important bearings of his conclusions on many accepted portions of economic science. It is an exhaustive examination of the possible meanings attached, to the expression "demand and supply," accompanied by an exhibition by means of hypothetical cases of the inability of the doctrine in any of its received, or of conceivable, senses, to solve the most ordinary phenomena of price. To appreciate the full force of Mr. Thornton's argument, it must be followed through all its stops; but a statement of that portion of it which deals with what is of course the most formidable form of the doctrine he opposes – that in which it is held by Mr. Mill – will give an idea of the thoroughness of his method, and prepare us for an estimate of the value of his criticism as a contribution to political economy.

It would of course be apparent to any one who regards an explanation in political economy as something beyond the repetition of certain hackneyed phrases, that to serve as an explanation of the phenomenon of price, demand and supply must be understood in some sense more determinate than that in which the words are employed in ordinary conversation. Adam Smith attempted to furnish the necessary limitation by defining "supply" as "the quantity of a commodity actually brought to market," and qualifying "demand" by the epithet "effectual;" "effectual demand" being in his language "the demand of those who are willing to pay the natural price of the commodity." In this explanation, or one nearly tantamount, to it, political economists acquiesced down to Mr. Mill, who in his *Principles of Political Economy* pointed out the inadequacy of Smith's definition. The senses in which the terms were defined precluded a comparison such as the doctrine supposed. "What ratio could there be between a quantity and a desire, or even a desire combined with a power?" To evade this difficulty Mr. Mill proposed to substitute for "effectual demand" the idea of "quantity demanded," pointing out at the same time that "this was not a fixed quantity, but in general varies according to the value." A conception was thus attached to "demand" which rendered its comparison with "supply" possible; and, having thus fixed the meaning of his terms, Mr. Mill laid it down, as the law of market values, that they were such, or tended to become such, as to produce an equality between supply and demand. "Demand and supply, the quantity demanded, and the quantity supplied, will be made equal. If unequal at any moment, competition equalises them, and the manner in which this is done is by an adjustment of the value. If the demand increases, the value rises; if the demand diminishes, the value falls; again if the supply falls off the value rises, and falls if the supply is increased. The rise or the fall continues until the demand and the supply are again equal to one another: and the value which a commodity will bring in any market is no other than the value which in that market gives a demand just sufficient to carry off the existing or expected supply."

Such is Mr. Mill's doctrine of "the law of demand and supply." It will be obvious that it presupposes several conditions, and more particularly these – an open market, free competition, and that the commodities are offered unreservedly for sale, any of these failing, the play of interests, described in the above passage, will evidently be brought at once to a hitch. Accepting these qualifications, Mr. Thornton contends – or rather, as we propose to state his argument in a form somewhat different from that in which he has put it, let us say his data seem to us to justify him in contending – first, that the principle stated does not *determine* price, inasmuch, consistently with satisfying the "law" – the equalisation of demand and supply – many different prices may be obtained for the same commodity in the same market; secondly, that the price which finally prevails in a given market does not always or even generally fulfil the required conditions, that is to say does not equalise demand and supply; and not only so, but that there is not any necessary or constant tendency to this result; and thirdly, that even if the doctrine were true, even if the price, ultimately resulting from competition were always such as to produce an equality between supply and demand, the truth would be one of small significance.

In support of these positions, Mr. Thornton puts amongst others the following case: – "When a herring or mackerel boat has discharged on the beach at Hastings or Dover last nights take of fish, the boatmen, in order to dispose of their cargo, commonly resort to a process called 'Dutch auction.' The fish are divided into lots, each of which is set up at a higher price than the salesman expects to get for it, and he then gradually lowers his terms, until he comes to a price which some bystander is willing to pay rather than not have the lot, and to which he accordingly agrees. Suppose on one occasion the lot to have been a hundredweight, and the price agreed to twenty shillings. If, on the same occasion, instead of the Dutch form of auction, the ordinary English mode had been adopted, the result might have been different. The operation would then have commenced by some bystander making a bid, which others might have successively exceeded, until a sum was arrived at beyond which no one but the actual bidder could afford or was disposed to go. That sum would not necessarily be twenty shillings; very possibly it might be only eighteen shillings. The person who was prepared to pay the former price might very possibly be the only person present prepared to pay even so much as the latter price; and if so, he might get by English auction for eighteen shillings the fish for which at Dutch auction he would have paid twenty. In the same market, with the same quantity of fish for sale, and with customers in number and every other respect the same, the same lot of fish might fetch two very different prices."

It is obviously quite possible that in either of the supposed cases, the condition required by Mr. Mill's principle may have been equally satisfied. There may have been but one person who was prepared to pay either 18*s*. or 20*s*. for the quantity actually put up for sale; and this quantity may have been as much as he was disposed to buy either of those prices. Whether he gave one or the other depended, not upon any difference in demand or supply, but upon the form in which the auction was conducted. Of course had the purchaser known precisely how matters stood he would have taken care to have given only the lower price; but he has no means of knowing this; and therefore his giving one or the other varies with the mode of sale. In other words, in an open market, with free competition and a commodity offered unreservedly for sale, demand and supply – the quantity demanded and the quantity supplied – have been brought in equilibrium, not by one certain price, but by two, or (since the hypothesis might be varied indefinitely we may say) by any one of several, distinct prices – that is to say, the "law" is satisfied while price is not determined.

This is one possible, and not very improbable, contingency. But the case might have been different. Suppose the purchaser of the fish had been willing to take a larger quantity at one of the prices stated, say at 20*s*. though not disposed to exceed this; or again, that amongst the bidders there were others who would also have been disposed to purchase the quantity in the market or a larger quantity at the current price, though also as in the former case, unwilling to exceed this sum, – on either hypothesis, the price would have been precisely the same as if there had been one purchaser requiring exactly the quantity in the market. No one would have been disposed to give a higher price than that actually paid, while many would have been willing to give that price for a much larger supply. Price would thus have stood at a given point without any tendency to rise above it, while the quantity demanded was largely in excess of the quantity supplied. The former illustration showed that the law of demand and supply as conceived by Mr. Mill, even when realised in fact, does not determine price; the present shows that price may be determined, while the "law" is not realised; and this, be it observed, while all the conditions required by Mr. Mill are in existence, while competition is free, and commodities are offered for sale without reserve.

We own that to our minds these considerations appear decisive as against the strictly "legal" character of the principle in question. The cases put – and those which we have are but a sample of a great many more equally striking furnished by Mr. Thornton – are manifestly possible cases; and manifestly the "law" in such cases does not hold. But it will be said – indeed , we observe it has already been said – that the cases on which the question has been argued are exceptional cases and, however, readily conceivable, represent transactions of so limited a sort, and having so little analogy with the mass of commercial dealings, that Mr.

Thornton's conclusion, founded as they are upon these, may be admitted without derogation from the substantial truth of the doctrine of demand and supply as propounded by Mr. Mill. The truths of political economy, we are told, are truths in the rough; and a few exceptions to a "law" more or less does not render it less a "law," or the less valuable as a light in theory or a guide in practice. Such language, however, we hold, implies a misconception of a rather fundamental kind as to the nature of a "law" in political economy, and falls besides to do justice to Mr. Thornton's exposition, in which the objection as to the cases being exceptional is met by anticipation. But we reserve our examination of these points for a future paper.

3 November 1866: John Elliott Cairnes, letter to the Economist

THE "LAW" OF DEMAND AND SUPPLY

Mr. Thornton's imaginary case of the fish sold by Dutch and English auction established, as we pointed out in our former notice of his essay, the two following points: – 1. that the equalisation of demand and supply does not necessarily determine price; and 2. that price may be determined – *i.e.*, may settle for a time at some given point – while demand and supply are not equal, and have no tendency to become so. Mr. Thornton puts many other cases in corroboration of the same conclusions. For example, a man has a horse to sell which he values at 50*l.*, there may be several purchasers prepared to give that sum, but none disposed to exceed it; in such case the price at which the horse would sell is 50*l.*, notwithstanding that the demand for horses at this price might be to any conceivable extent greater than the supply. Or, again, "a glover in a country town on the eve of an assize ball, having only a dozen pair of white gloves in store, might possibly be able to get ten shillings a pair for them. He would be able to get this if twelve persons were willing to pay that price rather than not go to the ball or go ungloved. But he could not get more than this even though, while we was still higgling with his first batch of customers, a second batch, equally numerous and neither more nor less eager, should enter his shop and offer to pay the same but not a higher price. The demand for gloves, which had at first been just equal to the supply, would now be exactly doubled, yet the price would not rise above ten shillings a pair."

Such instances, which might easily be multiplied, establish beyond controversy that there are conceivable conditions of the market in which Mr. Mill's doctrine of demand and supply will not hold good. This much at least will be admitted by every fair opponent. But it is contended that they establish no more than this; the instances being – so Mr. Thornton's critics maintain – of a purely exceptional kind. They show, it is said, "some inaccuracies in the ordinary 'statement of the law'," while they leave untouched its substantial truth. It is added that occasional failures are in the nature of economic laws, and that we should not therefore be surprised if we find evidence of this sort of imperfection in the law of demand and supply.

The latter observation suggests a question in the philosophy of political economy, which we would gladly follow up did our space permit it; but for the present it will perhaps be better to confine ourselves to the more precise allegation as to the exceptional nature of Mr. Thornton's illustrations. To us, it appears that not only is this charge not well founded, but that it may be justly retorted on the supporters of the received doctrine; – that is to say, we think it may be shown that the cases in which Mr. Mill's doctrine would not hold good, are such as rarely or never occur in real life; while Mr. Thornton's examples, purely hypothetical as they are, appear to us to represent pretty accurately the conditions of an ordinary market, and to be, as he maintains, fairly "typical of commercial transactions in general."

If the reader will turn to the passage in Mr. Mill's *Political Economy*, which we give below,* in which the doctrine of demand and supply is expounded, he will find that the two following assumptions underlie the reasoning: – 1. that the supply of commodities is a supply without reserve; and 2. that the demand is also in a certain sense without reserve. For example, Mr. Mill says "if the demand increases the value rises," but the necessity for this entirely depends on the new demand being of such a kind that it will advance on the current price, *whatever that price may be:* short of this the demand might increase without producing the slightest tendency to a rise of value. Again, "if the supply diminishes, the value rises;" where we have a similar assumption as to the existing demand, viz., that some portion of it, large enough to absorb the reduced supply, possess the character of indefinite intensity. And so of the other factor of the problem. "If the demand diminishes, the value falls;" which requires for its truth the analogous supposition with regard to the holders of the commodity, viz., that they are prepared to sell at any sacrifice rather than withdraw their goods from market. Where both these conditions are fulfilled, where demand and supply are both without reserve, where purchasers, numerous enough to absorb the existing supply, and sellers are each determined at any cost the one to obtain, the other to dispose of, the commodity – goods will doubtless sell or tend to sell in conformity with the principle, which Mr. Mill lays down; but surely it will not be pretended that cases satisfying these conditions are such as frequently occur; or that a law regulating prices only when they are present, can be regarded as giving

* "Demand and supply, the quantity demanded and the quantity supplied, will be made equal. If unequal at any moment, competition equalises them, and the manner in which this is done is by an adjustment of the value. If the demand increases, the value rises; if the demand diminishes, the value falls; again, if the supply falls off, the value rises; and falls if the supply in increased. The rise or the fall continues until the demand and supply are again equal to one another: and the value to which a commodity will bring in any market, is no other than the value which, in that market, gives a demand just sufficient to carry off the existing or expected supply." (Vol. I, pp. 541–2, Fifth Edition.)

the solution of the phenomena presented by the ordinary fluctuations of the markets.

"With one notable exception," says Mr. Thornton, "that of labour, commodities are almost never offered unreservedly for sale: scarcely ever does a dealer allow his goods to go for what they will immediately fetch - scarcely ever does he agree to the price for which would result from the actual state of supply and demand, or, in other words, to the price at which he could immediately sell the whole of his stock. Imagine the situation of a merchant who could not afford to wait for customers, but was obliged to accept for a cargo of corn, or sugar, or sundries, the best offer he could get from the customers who first presented themselves; or imagine a jeweller, or mercer, or draper, or grocer, obliged to clear out his shop within twenty-four hours. The nearest approach ever made to such a predicament is that of a bankrupt's creditors selling off their debtor's effects at a proverbially 'tremendous sacrifice;' and even they are comparatively speaking, able to take their time. But the behaviour of a dealer under ordinary pressure is quite different from that of a bankrupt's assignees." And it is perhaps, still more obviously true, that neither is demand in actual commercial dealings of that indefinitely elastic character which is not less essential than the converse condition in regard to supply to the truth of Mr. Mill's theory.

Let us endeavour to present to ourselves the state of mind in which buyers and sellers enter an ordinary wholesale market, – we say wholesale market, as it is there that competition comes most freely into play. The great majority of dealers have probably already formed some notion, more or less precise, of the price at which the commodity which is to be the subject of their bargaining ought to sell. This they take as their guide in their subsequent operations, allowing themselves, however to be drawn from it in one direction or the other by what they find in the market. If the purchaser finds the demand greater than he expected, he will be prepared to advance a little upon his ideal standard; while the holder of the commodity, in the opposite condition of the case, will on his side be prepared to make some concession in a decline of price. In general, we imagine the limits within which either will feel inclined to move in a direction opposed to his interest as buyer or seller will not be very great, though cases will occasionably happen when the market itself will reveal conditions of which both were before in ignorance, and which may induce either to deviate widely from his original judgement. The point, however, on which we wish to insist is this, that under all circumstances – whether the market prove such as dealers expect to find it, or whether it discloses new circumstances which they had not before taken account of – as a general rule, the data on which all, whether purchasers or sellers, form their opinion as to legitimate price – the price, we mean, at which in the actual state of the markets it is considered safe to trade – are pretty nearly the same. These data are what they know of the state of consumptive demand on the one hand, and of the supplies coming forward or expected to come forward to the other. At times, no doubt, it would happen that particular traders would be in possession of special intelligence; but this would be comparatively rare occurrence, and the general rule would be, as we have said, that the great majority of dealers would form their opinion upon nearly identical grounds. Now, this being so, and considering further that the object of their dealing is in general the same – to obtain the current profit on their transactions – we think it must be admitted as highly probable that in ordinary cases the great majority would arrive at nearly identical conclusions. Instead of the indefinite elasticity of demand on the one side, and the equally indefinite urgency to sell on the other, which Mr. Mill's theory assumes, we should have intending purchasers and sellers conducting their operations within very definite limits – limits which for the great majority on either side would not lie very widely apart. In other words, we are brought to this result, that, in ordinary markets, those conditions of mind amongst dealers which are the proximate causes of price are in general extremely analogous to those imagined by Mr. Thornton in his hypothetical cases, where in one instance the seller of a horse fixes upon some price for it which is also the highest that several intending purchasers are prepared to pay; or where, in another, a glover taking advantage of the demand created for gloves by the utmost point, finds the limit of the squeezability of his customers occur about the same point.

It seems to us, then, that Mr. Thornton's illustrations represent the rule; while any that would suit Mr. Mill's theory would represent the rare exception; and we, therefore, hold that Mr. Thornton's argument does much more than his critic in the *Saturday Review* is disposed to concede to it. Mr. Thornton not merely "points out some inaccuracies in the ordinary statement of the law," but, as it seems to us, proves that no "law" of demand and supply, in any sense which has yet been assigned to these words, exists; – that neither in fact, nor in tendency, do market prices conform to the rule which is commonly supposed to govern them.

We will not undertake to say that it might not be possible, by framing new definitions of demand and supply, to save the received theory, – though we are unable just now to imagine any that would be quite equal to this feat. But supposing this were possible, unless it could be also shown that the modified doctrine really threw light on the phenomena, really gave us the principle which governed market prices, we hold that such a mode of meeting Mr. Thornton's arguments would be essentially unphilosophical. To illustrate our meaning, suppose "supply were defined to mean 'the quantity of a commodity offered *unreservedly* for sale'," it being agreed to consider all supply no so offered as non-existing, and suppose further (what is far from being true) that, thus qualified, the received doctrine were rendered susceptible of logical defence, – what would be the gain of this to economic science? Simply, we conceive, none at all. The doctrine (as we concede for the sake of illustration) would no longer be in conflict with facts, but it would be as far as ever from covering the facts, as far as ever from furnishing an explanation of market prices. Nay, we conceive it would be farther from this than if "supply" were understood in its ordinary sense, even though this should involve the vulnerability of the doctrine; for so long as this is embraced as a condition affecting price the whole supply in the market, it would embrace that which is a veritable condition in the case – a true element in determining price: whereas by excluding supply in this sense it would exclude a veritable condition; the new form of the doctrine, therefore, though more defensible, would be further than ever from expressing the law of the phenomena. What a theory of market prices ought to give us is a statement of the conditions which determine market prices; what such a theory would give us would be a proposition which it would be difficult to refute. The ends of the science would be sacrificed to the credit of the doctrine.

And now, accepting as we do, Mr. Thornton's main position as proved, let us consider briefly the relation in which it stands to the body of economic doctrine as it is to be found in the best treatises – we will say in the volumes of Mr. Mill. In our opinion that position does not affect any doctrine of political economy that can be properly called fundamental. The laws of the production of wealth, for example, are obviously entirely untouched by a criticism of the doctrine of demand and supply. So (as we are sure Mr. Thornton himself would allow) are the theories of rents and profits as well as the general doctrines regarding taxation. It is not till we come to the theory of value that Mr. Thornton's speculation impinges on existing views: and even as regard the theory of value, it is a portion of it only, and that not the most important, that is challenged. For, it must be remembered, that all the phenomena of value which are not of a strictly temporary character – to give a few examples of our meaning, such phenomena as are presented by established differences of value in particular commodities existing in different times and countries, or by the steady fall which occurs with the progress of civilisation in the value of manufactured goods as contrasted with the rise in the value of raw products, or, again, by such permanent disturbances of price as are caused by increased production of the precious metals – all such cases of value (and they compromise the most important) are referred by the existing doctrines of political economy, not to demand and supply, but to the principle of cost – that principle no doubt acting through demand and supply. It is only in connection with "market values," as contradistinguished from what Adam Smith calls "natural values" – with those changes of value which occur from day to day, and from hour to hour, – that "demand and supply" claims the place of a "law" in modern political economy; and what Mr. Thornton has done is to show that to this place it is not entitled. Not that Mr. Thornton would eliminate these terms altogether from economic reasoning; not that he would not allow that they may be usefully employed to assist our comprehension of the phenomenon of price; – Mr. Thornton's point, as we understand it, is not this, but that the modes and conditions under which demand and supply affect prices are so numerous and complicated that they do not admit being brought into a precise formula, but can only be set forth in a number of distinct propositions more or less unconnected. "Supply and demand are commonly spoken of as if they together formed some nicely-fitting, well-balanced, self-adjusting machinery, whose component parts could not alter their mutual relations, without evolving as the product of every change; a price exactly corresponding with that particular change," this is the view of the demand and supply which Mr. Thornton combats, and combats, as it seems to us, with success. Rough generalisations are perfectly allowable in economic as in other reasoning, where more exact expressions cannot be obtained, or are not needed; but to style every such rough generalisation a "law" does serious mischief; it checks freedom if inquiry; it brings upon the branch of inquiry, in connection with which this language is used, the discredit of advancing scientific pretensions which it cannot sustain; and in general it encourages sciolism and cant.

We must qualify our general concurrence with Mr. Thornton by a single observation. He has apparently engaged in this investigation as preliminary to the discussion of the labour question; and, as we gather from his concluding remarks, he conceives that his negative conclusions apply to that problem. We are far from saying that they are without bearing on it. But we are, for our part, disposed to regard the labour question as standing in some degree on grounds of its own. Mr. Thornton has himself remarked that labour "forms a notable exception to the rule, the commodities are almost never offered unreservedly for sale." We think he will find that the "demand for labour" forms equally an exception to the rule regulating other demand, in this circumstance, that it is in a certain intelligible sense a demand without reserve, since it is the means by which the desire for profit – an insatiable desire – seeks to satisfy itself. It would carry us too far to pursue this speculation further here. We only suggest this consideration as one which, if followed up, might remove the phenomenon of wages from the general scope of Mr. Thornton's criticisms. In short, we are disposed to believe in a law of demand and supply in the case of labour, – not, indeed, that "inexorable," "immutable" principle independent of, and dominating the human will, which is the common notion of a law of demand and supply, but a tendency deducible form the known character of the human will, in connection with the relations of men as buyers and sellers of labour – a law in the only sense in which laws exist in political economy. With this remark we leave the subject for the present, awaiting with interest the results of Mr. Thornton's further speculations in a department of inquiry on which he has already thrown so much new and useful light.

1 December 1866: Thomas Cliffe Leslie, letter to the Economist

DEMAND AND SUPPLY

Sir, – Apart from the light thrown by Mr. Thornton's acute and ingenious criticism upon a part of the theory of demand and supply, hitherto involved in some obscurity and error (not so great, however, I hope to show as Mr. Thornton supposes, so far as Mr. Mill is concerned), he has, I conceive, rendered a service to political economy by the mere fact of challenging one of its doctrines, and interrogating it with regard to its meaning, foundation, and limits. For, in the first place, a number of doctrines have been in circulation for some years past, purporting to issue from a standard economic mint, but really without the stamp of any respectable authority. Mr. Senior mentions in his journal a conversation four years ago with Archbishop Whately, in which they "talked of the falsehood of commonly received maxims;" and he would have done well to add that these two eminent political economists were agreed that among the falsest maxims going were some commonly passed off as maxims of political economy. As an instance of the extent to which this has been carried, I may refer to the notions which became current after the crisis of 1847 and 1857, that a decennial crisis in racing, after the Two Thousand Guineas and the Derby had been won by the same horse, Cotherstone, in 1843; and again by West Australian in 1853; and again, after another ten years, by Macaroni, in 1863. Yet the theory of a decennial commercial crisis obtained the recognition even of the *Saturday Review.* More commonly it happens that a really well-founded and genuine economic doctrine becomes the foundation of a superstructure of fallacies, and such has been the especial misfortune of the doctrine of demand and supply.

The part of that doctrine which is generally in view when a law of demand and supply is spoken of, is not I think the equation described by Mr. Mill and criticised by Mr. Thornton, but merely that demand regulates supply, and supply accords with demand, through the competition of producers; so that there is on the average just such a supply of things as consumers want and can pay the cost of. Within just limits, that is to say in its true meaning, this view of the play of demand and supply has a substantial truth; and I see no great harm in terming it, sometimes for brevity, a "law" of the market. But the sort of abuse which is made of this law was very well exemplified sometime ago by Lord Shaftesbury, when speaking in the House of Lords of the destruction of the dwellings of the poor by metropolitan railways. "The question is, what is to be done with respect to those great displacements? The answer generally is, that that the supply will be equal to the demand. But those who give that answer seem to have very little notion what the demand and supply are. The demand is for something immediate, and something near the places of employment." It would be easy to cite a number of similar perversions of economic doctrine, by means of which political economy itself becomes practically little better than the logic of established abuses.

It is not, however, only on account of such distortions that political economy is served by a vigilant scrutiny of maxims and theories claiming its authority; the doctrine of its most eminent professors ought not to escape criticism and controversy. An able writer, in a previous number of the same review, which has published Mr. Thornton's critique, makes the amount of controversy among political economists a reason for questioning the pretensions of their science altogether. Some of the controversies he refers to really turn, not upon economical principles, but upon the facts to which they are applied; as for instance, the question he cites – "whether large or small farms succeed best!" – can receive no general answer, and is very much a question as to the soil, climate, agricultural art, institutions, and customs of each particular country. But it is, moreover, really a necessary condition of science, being progressive on the one hand, and of its most eminent teachers not being infallible on the other, that what they do teach should be open to question, and should sometimes be convicted of inaccuracy or error; nor has any other living writer done so much as Mr. Mill towards enabling his successors to discover any inaccuracies or errors in his own pages. I may add my belief that there is really more divergence of opinion among political economists than is ever made known to the public, and when Mr. Thornton speaks of a "doctrine preached by the first "teachers" being "unanimously accepted as axiomatic by their successors," and seeming acquiescence in some cases, *carent quia vate sacro*, – because they find neither editor nor publisher; or in other words, because the demand for political economy is not equal to the supply. On the other hand, and apparent difference of opinion among economists sometimes arises from a misunderstanding of each other's actual doctrine, and such, I think, is partly the case with respect to Mr. Thornton's recent criticism of Mr. Mill's theory of demand and supply, the defect in which extends over a much smaller corner of the field of prices than that criticism appears to assume. Mr. Thornton applies the theory to prices in general; Mr. Mill expressly limits its application to certain exceptional cases.

For the purpose of describing the class of cases in which price is determined by the equation of demand and supply, he supposes Mr. Mill divides commodities into three classes, which, changing his order for convenience, are as follows: –

First, the things of which the supply is limited only by their cost of production, "embracing the majority of all things that are bought and sold." To this immense class Mr. Mill does not apply his theory of demand and supply, at least not in a manner open to Mr. Thornton's objections. "The value of things which can be increased in quantity at pleasure does not depend (except accidentally, and during the time necessary for production to adjust itself) upon demand and supply; on the contrary, demand and supply depend upon it." – Book iii., chap. iii. Even in the accidental cases in which the value of some of this great majority of things may be determined by supply and demand, Mr. Mill does not say more than that their value in such cases "is that which is necessary to create a market for the existing "supply;" a statement which does not seem open to the objections Mr. Thornton very properly makes, to the sort of equation described in the chapter on "Demand and Supply." – Book iii., chap. ii.

Secondly, Mr. Mill's division embraces a class of commodities, the supply of which can be increased, but generally not without increased proportionate cost. "To this class belong agricultural produce, and generally all the rude produce of the earth"; and the price of things in this class is also, accordingly to Mr. Mill, determined, unless in exceptional cases, by a principle different from that of the equation of supply and demand.

Thirdly, comes a class of cases where there is "an absolute limitation of the supply"; for example, rare wines, ancient pictures and coins, the best sites and spaces in towns, and in a country where the supply of food cannot be increased until next harvest, the food of the year. It is of this limited and exceptional class of things alone that Mr. Mill treats in his chapter on demand and supply, and he does not even apply to all things of this class the part of his theory which Mr. Thornton shows to be inaccurate. The case, for example, which Mr. Thornton puts of a single glover with a small supply of white gloves in a country town on the eve of an assize ball, is not one where, according to Mr. Mill, the market price is that which equates the demand to the supply, through the competition of buyers. This case would come under the principle of Mr. De Quincey's musical snuff box on Lake Superior, because there is no competition of sellers; and the competition which really determines price is that which goes on in the buyer's own mind between his desire for the snuff-box, or the gloves, and his other desires. The case of the gloves and the ball-goers does not fall within the principal Mr. Mill sets forth, for another reason, namely, that ball-goers are not actuated by purely commercial calculations and notices in the prices they give; for which reason he excepts retail prices altogether from his theory of competitive prices. It is only when the limited supply of things is held by different dealers, among whom there is competition, and where buyers also are dealers, or, at least, have the knowledge and pecuniary objects of dealers, that Mr. Mill says "the price is that which cuts off the extra from the demand; or brings forward additional sellers to supply it." There can be no question that Mr. Mill has here committed an oversight, and has forgotten that the very fact of the absolute limitation of the supply he supposes may render it physically impossible to supply the whole demand at any price whatever. When a Bethell, a Cairns, and a Palmer monopolise an eminence at the bar, there may be thirty suitors, all men of business, and for business reasons wanting their advocacy at the same time, and willing to give the same price for it, but they cannot supply more than three at a time. The chief physicians in London, in like manner, are perhaps sent for every hour by many times the number of patients, they can visit. It is evident that only one-half of Mr. Mill's theory can here be sustained – namely, that where the supply at a given price exceeds the demand, the price falls until the demand equals the supply; while the demand at this price may not only equal, but also largely exceed the supply.

Mr. Mill's theory thus stands in need of emendation; but the chief part of his whole exposition of prices is quite unaffected by the error which Mr. Thornton has drawn to light. And there is one point where I think Mr. Thornton is himself in error respecting the conditions of Mr. Mill's equation, in those few exceptional cases where prices according to the latter are determined by it. According to Mr. Thornton, Mr. Mill's equation necessarily assumes that dealers offer their whole stock of commodities unreservedly and immediately for sale; which, as he says very justly, is scarcely ever the case; but which Mr. Mill certainly does not assume. On the contrary, speaking of the year's stock of food in a particular country, Mr. Mill says that when the supply after a good harvest exceeds the demand at a given price, a fall in price must take place; "and the fall is practically arrested only when the farmers withdraw their corn, and hold it back in hopes of a higher price, or by the operations of speculators who buy corn when it is cheap, and store it up to be brought out when more urgently wanted." Mr. Mill's equation of supply and demand is a theory of market prices, and therefore of the prices obtained by the things actually supplied to the market, not of the things which are withheld from it.

It is right to add that although in his chapter on "Demand and Supply," Mr. Mill expressly limits his exposition to the prices of a limited and exceptional class of things, be remarks at the end that the principle extends to two cases of great breadth and importance, namely, international values and the value of labour. In the case of international values, Mr. Mill's exposition is, therefore, not altogether free from imperfection. Nevertheless, Mr. Thornton will be one of the first to concede that, as a whole, it forms a substantial and valuable addition to the literature of economical science. With regard to labour, I shall feel myself in much better position to estimate all the conditions of the question when enlightened by the luminous discussion which we have reason to expect from Mr. Thornton. But I will venture to make one observation now with respect to a part of the question of wages in the form it is beginning to assume on a large scale, namely, in Mr. Thornton's concluding words, "Whether it be possible to raise the price of labour artificially and irrespectively of supply and demand?" – that if, by a general combination, labourers offer to employers only the alternative between paying a stipulated price or getting no supply of labour at all, the case is no longer within the limits set by Mr. Mill to his discussion when he gives warning that the cases he contemplates are "those in which values and prices are determined by competition alone." It becomes, ultimately, in the event of such a combination, a question simply whether labourers can do without employees longer than employers can do without labourers. – I am, Sir, your faithful servant,

T. E. C. Leslie
Lincoln's inn, Nov. 28

15 December 1866: W. T. Thornton, letter to the Economist

SUPPLY AND DEMAND

Sir, – Last Saturday week's impression of the Economist contained a letter by my friend Professor Leslie, on a recent article of mine on "Supply and Demand," in the *Fortnightly Review*, on which I should be glad, with your permission, to make a few observations.

On the main question I am happy to perceive that I have Mr. Leslie's entire concurrence. He quite agrees with me that price does not depend either, as commonly supposed, on the *proportion* or *ratio* between supply and demand, or, as represented by Mr. Mill, on the *equation* of supply and demand; but he considers that I have greatly exaggerated the error which both he and I conceive our great master to have committed. Mr. Mill, he says, expressly limits the application of his equation theory to certain exceptional cases, whereas I describe him as applying it to prices in general. Mr. Mill, he proceeds to explain, divides commodities into three classes – 1. Those which can be increased indefinitely at the pleasure of any one willing to incur the requisite labour and expense – this class embracing the majority of things that can be bought and sold. 2. Those which can also be increased indefinitely, but only at increased cost, such, for instance, as agricultural produce. 3. Those which are absolutely limited, and of which the supply cannot be increased at all, such as ancient sculptures, pictures by old masters, rare books or coins, and choice sites in districts of limited extent. And he adds that it is to this last limited and exceptional class of things alone that Mr. Mill applies his equation theory.

If this were so, I should clearly have overstated my case. Mr. Mill's error, supposing him to have committed one, would not be less real, but it would be so small in extent, and of so little practical moment, that, unless for the sake of and almost pedantic precision, it might perhaps be scarcely worth while correcting. Now I cannot deny that Mr. Leslie has considerable warrant for this statement. Both in opening and in closing the exposition of his equation theory, Mr. Mill, no doubt, expressly confines it within very narrow bounds. He begins by saying that what he is about to consider are "things absolutely limited in quantity, such as ancient sculptures or pictures;" and he ends by saying that the law of value which he has laid down respects only such exceptional commodities as are "not susceptible of being multiplied at pleasure;" adding, "that there is another law for that much larger class of things which admit of indefinite multiplication." Language can scarcely be more distinct, and if Mr. Mill had said nothing in a contrary sense, it would be difficult for me to repel the charge of having exaggerated his meaning.

Fortunately for my credit, however, he uses language equally distinct of a directly opposite signification. He does so even in the midst of the exposition just referred to. Even while promulgating a law purporting to be applicable only to a class of commodities so exceptional as ancient sculptures and paintings, he does actually apply that law to all classes of commodities whatever; "from those peculiar luxuries the taste for which is confined to a few," to "absolute necessaries," such as food, which no one can do without. Then, when he comes to speak specially of "that larger class of things which can be increased in quantity at pleasure," and which he says are governed by a separate law, although he does certainly state that the value of such things does not depend on supply and demand, he yet accompanies this negative proposition by an exception which completely nullifies its meaning. He says that the value of the things in question does not depend on supply and demand, "*except* during the time necessary for production to adjust itself" – that is, until production has had time to augment supply. Evidently he considers that *until* production has had time to do this, price depends on present supply and demand; but this is also all that is ever meant by the statement that price depends on supply and demand. Whoever says so, merely means that there can be no variation in price which is not preceded by a corresponding variation in the ratio between supply and demand; he does not mean that price will remain unchanged after supply has been augmented either by increased production or otherwise. To say, then, that the price of commodities in general does not depend on supply and demand, except in the only sense in which it can be conceived to be so dependent, is merely another way of recognising the general dependence of prices on supply and demand .

And what Mr. Mill here appears to say by implication, he elsewhere affirms in express terms in the following passage:– "though there are few commodities which are at all times and for ever unsusceptible of increase of supply, and commodities whatever may be temporarily so, and with some commodities this is habitually the case, Agricultural produce, for example, cannot be increased in quantity before the next harvest; the quantity of corn existing in the would is all that can be had for sometimes a year to come. During that interval, corn is practically assimilated to things of which the quantity, and if the demand increases, then, until a corresponding supply can be brought forward, that is, until the supply can accommodate itself to the demand, the value will so rise as to accommodate the demand to the supply." Here we are in effect told, as plainly as words can speak, that in the case of "most" commodities – of all commodities, indeed, the quantity of which can be increased but cannot be increased without the lapse of a certain interval – value (or price) depends on the equation of supply and demand. We are told that during the time which must elapse before supply can be so augmented as to become equal to demand, price will rise so as to make demand equal to supply, as according to parity of reasoning, if supply exceeded demand, price would fall until supply and demand became equal.

Finally, as if to prevent the possibility of doubt on this subject, Mr. Mill, still speaking of "things which can be increased in quantity at pleasure," sums up as follows:– "The real law of demand and supply, the equation between them, holds good in all cases: if demand equal to the supply, the market value will deviate from the natural value"; the supposed reason for the deviation being obviously the supposed necessity for a selling price at which demand and supply would be equal. Mr. Mill had begun by saying that the price of things which *cannot* be increased in quantity depends on the equation of supply and demand. He now says that the price of things which *can* be increased depends on the same equation. I think, then, that Mr. Leslie must own that I was not wrong in saying that Mr. Mill applies his equation theory to all commodities whatever.

According to the above account, Mr. Mill has not always been quite consistent with himself; but I believe that his inconsistencies are more apparent than real, or at any rate that they exist more in words than in substance. They appear to me to be owing to his having used the same word in different senses. When he says that price depends upon supply and demand, he is thinking of selling or market price; when he says that it does not so depend, he is referring to what – not very happily in my opinion – he calls "necessary price." This price he defines to be "cost of production" plus "ordinary profit." It is a price towards which the market price is continually gravitating, but from which it is continually varying, and with which it never *necessarily* coincides. This necessary price certainly does not depend on supply and demand, but neither, as Mr. Mill himself has conclusively shown, does market price depend upon it. What Mr. Mill desires to prove, appears to me to be that market or selling price depends upon supply and demand, and that supply and demand depend upon cost of production. With the second clause of this proposition, in the limited sense in which I understand it, I am prepared to concur. From the first, I am compelled, though with all possible deference, to dissent.

I trust no one will think – I am quite sure my friend Mr. Mill will not – that in so freely criticising one of his opinions, I am at all wanting in respect to his pre-eminent authority. The photographer who in his portraiture of the sun exhibits here and there a spot on the surface of that grand luminary, is not suspected in consequence of wishing to disparage the sun. Mr. De la Rue does not require to be told that it is the sun's own surpassing brilliance alone which reveals to him the solar spots, and I, for my part, most gladly and gratefully acknowledge that, if I have pointed out any imperfections in Mr. Mill's doctrine, it is only the light which he has himself furnished that has enabled me to see them. – I remain, Sir, your obedient servant,

W. T. Thornton
London, 11 Dec. 1866

ON THE INCOME TAX

Thornton, William, "On the Income Tax", *British Association for the Advancement of Science Report*, (1862).

Thornton's long hiatus in the realm of political economy came to an end with this severe critique of income tax. He posed the same question at the Political Economy Club on 5 June 1862.

On the Income Tax

[Summary]

THE object of this paper was to show, first, that every income-tax whatsoever must necessarily violate the just principles of taxation; and, secondly, that a uniform income-tax does so to a greater extent than there is any necessity for. Taking as the principles of taxation those laid down as such by Adam Smith, and adopted by Ricardo and John Stuart Mill, the writer undertook to prove that the least objectionable income-tax must needs infringe three of Adam Smith's four maxims. Instead of being levied at the time and in the manner most convenient to the contributor, an income-tax is levied at the most inconvenient time and in the most offensive manner. A man pays his customs or excise dues a little at a time, and chooses his own time for paying, – never, of course, volunteering to pay, except when he has wherewithal to pay. But the income-tax comes upon him both all at once and just at the very time when he is beset with his half-yearly bills, levying a pitiless percentage on his means of meeting them. It lays him, too, on the rack, endeavours to extort a confession from him, and leaves him no alternative but to criminate or to perjure himself. Then, the income-tax is levied most unequally. It is assessed, not, as Adam Smith says it should be, in proportion to a man's ability, but in proportion to his honesty. An income-tax must often be, to a certain extent, a matter of conscience. Those who have no conscience may partially evade it by lying; and thus it acts as a bounty upon lying, and a tax upon truth. The honest man bears the full burden; the dishonest goes comparatively free. This is a vice inherent in and inseparable from every income-tax whatsoever. There must always be this to counterbalance any virtues it may possess. True, it has the merit of raising a revenue more effectually than any other expedient, but at what cost does it do so? The mere pecuniary cost of its collection may perhaps be moderate as compared with that of the customs or excise, but money is not the sole element of cost. The income-tax is collected at the expense of the national honesty. It offers a powerful temptation to every commercial and every professional man to tell one deliberate falsehood, to commit one gross act of fraud, every year, and it is certain that a large majority of commercial and professional men yield to the temptation; for, from the last returns, it appears that there are, in Great Britain, only 6066 persons in trades or professions honest enough to confess that they make more than £500 and less than £600 a year; only 6020 who confess to more than £1000 and less than £2000 a year; only 997 persons who confess to £5000 and less than £10,000. Since it cannot be supposed that people who cheat regularly once a year will cheat only once a year, or that, beginning with cheating government, they will end without cheating their customers, it is plain that the income-tax is undermining the national honesty, and consequently that commercial prosperity may possibly not *take* out of people's pockets a great deal more than is paid into the exchequer, it is calculated to *keep* out a great deal that would otherwise have entered.

Considering it to be thus apparent that every income-tax must necessarily be at variance with just principles, Mr. Thornton proceeded to argue that a uniform income-tax violates them to a needless extent. It does so by superadding to the inequality and injustice inseperable from every income-tax an inequality and injustice peculiar to itself. This is implied by its very name – a uniform income-tax, *i.e.* a tax levied at the same rate on all incomes. But, says Adam Smith, every one should pay taxes in proportion to his ability. His ability to do what? Obviously in proportion to his ability to pay taxes. But such ability by no means corresponds with income. To illustrate this point, Mr. Thornton supposed two persons, each with £1000 a year, but the one a bachelor, and the other a man with a family. Both have the same income, but their ability to bear taxation is very different; or, to use Ricardo's application of Adam Smith's principle, equal taxation requires from them very unequal sacrifices. Consequently, a tax assessed at the same rate on all incomes, without reference to the varying amount of claims on those incomes, is not assessed "in proportion to the respective abilities of the several contributors." Moreover the income-tax is the only tax at present in use amongst us which does not affect incomes without regard to other claims upon them. A prudent family man, by living in a cheaper situation, by keeping only female servants, by walking on foot or riding only in cabs or omnibuses, by eschewing cigars, and drinking beer or spirits instead of wine, may always manage to pay a smaller percentage of his income, in the shape of assessed taxes, customs, and excise duties, than an unencumbered bachelor of equal income. It is the income-tax alone which falls with indiscriminating weight upon both, and which, regarding not the ability to pay taxes, but simply the amount of income, makes the same deduction from the £1000 by which a persons are to be supported, as from the £1000 appropriated to the exclusive use of a single individual.

Here is one inequality incidental to a uniform income-tax. Another arises from the equal assessment of permanent and precarious incomes. Two persons, each of £1000 a year, but derived in the one case from landed, funded, or otherwise realized property, and in the other, from the profits of trade, the gains of a profession, or the salary of an office, have not the same means of paying taxes. The one may spend the whole of his £1000 a year for fifty years together and at the end of that period his means of spending £1000 a year will be found undiminished. But if a merchant, or tradesman, or doctor, or lawyer or railway secretary be silly enough to spend the whole of his £1000 a year, then if health fail, or business fail, he may suddenly find himself without a penny. Accordingly, he commonly puts by part of his income, and spends only the remainder; and the amount of that remainder is the measure of his ability to pay taxes, the amount therefore on which he ought to be taxed. In support of his view on this point, the writer quoted an expression of Adam Smith, to the effect that "every subject of a state should contribute to the support of the government in proportion to the revenue which he enjoys under the protection of the state;" from which he inferred that Smith intended to distinguish between the income which a man possesses and enjoys and that which possesses and does not enjoy, remarking that a man enjoys only that part of his income which he spends, and that he no more enjoys what he saves for the benefit of his heirs than he enjoys the wine which is ripening in his cellar, and which it spoils and may never be drank at all, just as money that is invested may not be accumulating for the benefit of the actual owner, and perhaps may not be accumulating at all, but may be dwindling away to in the shape of railway shares. Mr. Thornton proceeded to remark that, among the many faults of an income-tax, there is only one which can be remedied. The tax is in most respects incurably bad. Nothing can prevent its being a discouragement to honesty and a bounty upon fraud, or from being collected at the expense of probity, or from pressing with equal weight on single and married men of the same income, notwithstanding their unequal ability to bear the weight. One of its iniquities, however, is partially remediable. It might be prevented from pressing equally on permanent and precarious incomes, in the manner proposed by Mr. Mill, viz. by exempting from taxation that proportion of a precarious income which, taking the average of cases, its recipient would be bound in prudence to save.

The remainder of the paper was occupied with an examination of objections to Mr. Mill's suggestion. It has been urged that there is often a great difference between what a man ought to save and what he does save; and it has been asked, what could be more monstrous than to extend exemption to a spendthrift, who, being bound in prudence to lay by say, a fourth of his income, thinks proper to spend all, and to save nothing? What could be more monstrous than to confer the reward assigned for the performance of a particular duty to one who had culpably neglected to perform that duty? In Mr. Thornton's opinion it is more monstrous still to withhold the reward from those who have performed the duty. In a country in which economists must be spendthrifts as 100 to 1, it would, he thinks, be better that one spendthrift should obtain an exemption which he does not deserve rather than that a hundred economists should be denied the exemption they do deserve.

Again, it has been urged that to assess precarious at a lower rate than permanent incomes, on the avowed ground, too, that the former belong to a poorer class of men, would be to tax the poor at a lower rate than the rich – a measure subversive of security and property. If, however, a reduced rate has been proposed for precarious incomes, it has been on the supposition that whatever rate were adopted would be assessed on the whole income. But to assess the whole of a precarious and the whole of a permanent income at the same rate would be to disregard their relative ability to bear taxation. If only that part of an income be taxed on which depends ability to pay, no one will object to the same rate being applied to all incomes. It is only because injustice is committed by taxing the whole income that an attempt is made to repair the injustice by demanding that a lower rate be imposed than would be proper if only part were taxed.

A third objection to Mr. Mill's suggestion is the opposite of the second. It has been said that to exempt savings would be to favour the rich at the expense of the poor, insamuch as it is by the comparatively rich that the greater part of savings are made. To this Mr. Thornton answers, that if the rich pay on all they spend, and are exempted only on what they save, they obtain the exemption only on that part of their income with respect to which they abdicate the advantage of riches, not consuming it themselves, but making it over to be consumed by the poor. Moreover, if they pay on all they spend, they pay on all they enjoy; and the principle that every man should pay on what he enjoys, whether the sum be great or small is fully carried out.

ENGLAND AND IRELAND

Thornton, William, "Mill's *England and Ireland*", *Fortnightly Review*, January/June, 1868, pp. 472–4.

This is Thornton's review of *England and Ireland*, John Stuart Mill's forty-four page pamphlet. Not only did Thornton defend Mill's argument against his contemporaries' severe condemnation, but he also presented his own slightly different view of the situation

England and Ireland

Mr. Mill has in his time written and said a good many startling and unpopular things, but nothing that he ever before said or wrote gave such general offence as the forty-four pages which he has just issued under the above title. By the bulk of the reading public they have been received with feelings little short of indignation and disgust. The author's reputation as availed little to bear up the pamphlet; rather the pamphlet seems calculated to bear down the author. Most critics by profession fall foul of it without mercy. The *Times*, forgetting its accustomed staidness of demeanour, flares up into something like Billingsgate in abuse of it. The Rhadamanthus-like *Saturday Review* condemns it with more than Rhadamanthine sterness. The gentler *Pall Mall Gazette*, confessing to one of those touches of infirmity that make the whole world kin, intimates that, like the Athenian who tired of hearing Aristides called the Just, it is glad of so good an excuse for doubting whether Mr. Mill really deserves to be thought wise. Even the *Economist* turns Judas, and insinuates heresy against the acknowledged master of its own peculiar sect. The example of the professionals emboldens amateurs. Scarcely any one speaks to you of the pamphlet without contemptuous pity or contemptuous exultation, while in the House of Commons even one of the minor Whiglings ventures on an ignorant sneer at the philosopher who would neutralise the effects of three land-confiscations by institution a fourth. When a man is hardest pressed then does it most become what friends he has left to press forward to the rescue; and being myself one of the minority of Englishmen who regard the doctrine of "England and Ireland" as substantially sound, and as increasing the claims of the teacher on the gratitude of his country and of mankind, I am not going to shrink from speaking out my thought.

That the proposals which the pamphlet embodies have been so ill received affords no presumption against them. At least as well, on the contrary, might this be taken as a proof of their processing some peculiar merit. In order to have met with immediate acceptance they ought to have been less original, less bold, less apposite. Other writers ought to have gone before with suggestions more or less like Mr. Mill's in order to have prepared the way for his. But those who have gone farthest in the same direction have gone little farther than timidly to inquire what might possibly be done for the Irish tenant. He is the first to show that the true matter for consideration is, what is to be done with the Irish landlord? How can those who have never had the true blot pointed out to them be expected to see immediately that the blot has been fairly hit? How, while still mistaking the character of the disease, can they recognise the appropriate remedy? And, because

Mr. Mill tells his readers that their not seeing, and not recognising, is the real essence of the Irish difficulty, the *Times*, getting into a passion, charges him with calling his readers fools or knaves. But is not this very anger of the *Times* a proof of the very blindness against the imputation of which the *Times* protests? No mirror could more faithfully reflect the average English mind than the *Times* does, and does the Times itself affect to be able to see what Mr. Mill points out?

Now, what is it in the tract before us that, on the one hand, bids fair to deprive the author of half the honour in which – prophet as he is – he has hitherto been held by the mass of his countrymen; and, on the other, causes here and there one of them to regard him with, if possible, increased respect? One and the same reply will serve for both branches of the two fold question. What Mr. Mill proposes to do for Ireland is, with no greater difference than the difference of circumstances renders imperative, the very same thing as that, by doing which for Prussia, Stein and Hardenberg have gained universal and undying renown as the regenerators of their country. The Prussian legislators found the peasant bound to the soil, but connected with it by no ties but those of feudal bondage. Of these ties they made as short work as men of kindred genius always do of Gordian knots. By one stroke of the pen they transformed abject serfs into independent peasant proprietors of land purchased from its previous lords at its full value in perpetual annuities. The English statesman finds the Irish peasant in a state, not indeed of serfdom, but in one for which the old Prussian serfdom would be a blessed exchange, and he seeds to raise him to the level of the emancipated Prussian serf at no more expense to the Irish landlord than that to which the Prussian landlord was subjected. For the sake of regenerating a whole people he proposes less interference with vested interests than the legislature every year sanctions for the sake of furthering some dirty job of railway speculators. Here is the whole head and front of Mr. Mill's offending. This it is for which the bulk of his audience hiss and a few exceptional eccentrics cheer him. Of course the Prussian landlords, although paid in full for every acre taken from them, raised a furious outcry about "spoilation;" and of course perfervid Irish landlords and their sympathisers, at the mere idea of similar treatment, raise an outcry more furious still. *Celà va sans dire.* And it is equally plain why exceptional Englishmen, untainted by landlordism, who, when travelling through north-eastern and central Germany, have sighed despairingly over the contrast between the smiling homestead of a German boor and the half-hut half-pigsty of an Irish cottier, look with admiration on a scheme which shows how the inmates of the one can be placed in all social respects on a par with those of the other, not only without injustice, but without detriment to any one. That which was Stein and Hardenberg's condemnation in the eyes of large classes of their contemporaries has become their glory in the eyes of all classes of posterity, as it would be Mr. Mill's glory likewise if his case, instead of being judged by compatriot contemporaries, were referred to contemporary posterity in the shape of a jury of aliens.

The allegiance due from a disciple to his master must not, however, prevent my here observing that an alien jury in the case supposed would probably go farther in eulogy of Mr. Mill than I should myself be prepared to follow. Since, instead of being, as I fancy would be more in accordance with my deserts, placed in the same dock with Mr. Mill to be tried on the same charge as an accessory before and after the fact, I find the greatness thrust on me of a seat on the critical bench before which he is arraigned, I must needs say that I hesitate a little to pass upon his latest outpouring a sentence of absolutely unqualified approval. The remedy prescribed by him for the woes of Ireland does certainly seem to me by far the best that has been suggested; but I am not equally convinced that nothing short of it might serve the turn. He himself admits it to be revolutionary, and he would scarcely deny that it is both very delicate and very violent. It is, in truth, so delicate, that, unless very skilfully applied, it might very possibly prove fatal; and it is violent in this sense, and to this extent, that it interferes with property inland in a way which I, at least, consider that no necessity, however great, would justify, were it not for certain essential differences between property in land and all other kinds of property. What those differences are cannot here be explained, for to do so adequately would require more pages than I should be allowed lines for the purpose. I can only spare room to say that they are such as even to one with my own almost superstitious reverence for property in general, seem sufficient to justify the public in resuming property in land whenever the public good may appear to render such a steep expedient. The violence of Mr. Mill's specific is not necessarily, therefore, any objection to it, and still less is its delicacy; for Mr. Mill, like every other practitioner, of course assumes that the operation he prescribes will be performed with all proper precautions, and will not be intrusted to such botchers and bunglers as have for the last half-century been wrangling over Ireland's sick body – wrangling alternately with their patient and with each other.

But though there be nothing about Mr. Mill's plan to prevent its being the most efficacious that can be adopted, there may be good reasons for scrupling to adopt it except as a last resource. Lithotomy is the most effectual cure for the stone, yet is only resorted to in extreme cases. If the millstone that hangs round Ireland's neck can be got rid of in no other way, let it by all means be cut away. But I am loath to believe that there are no other ways, and Mr. Mill himself once certainly thought there were. There was a time when he would have been content with the abolition of the Irish church establishment, the enactment of such a Tenant Right or Tenants' Improvements Bill as Lord Kimberley could frame and Lord Dufferin would not disapprove, and such an application of Irish waste lands as was recommended in a certain "Plea" which was put forward by myself twenty years ago, and which, if the legislature would condescend to listen to it now, they might possibly regret not having listened to somewhat earlier. To these measures I would venture to add the partition of Irish Church revenues rateably among the clergy of the three chief denominations, and the equalisation in dignity as well as emoluments of Protestant and Catholic Bishops, either by their impartial exclusion from, or by their equal admission into, the House of Peers and the Privy Council. By these measures, together with those previously enumerated, and coupled with a vigorous enforcement of governmental authority, and the instant suppression of both the practice and the preaching of treason by whatever severities might be required for their suppression, I conceive it to be still possible that Ireland's traditional hatred of England might be gradually extinguished, and complete reconciliation between the two sisters effected, without which there can be no well-grounded hope for Ireland's future. Of some of my recommendations, however, Mr. Mill would certainly not approve; and with regard to the rest he would probably say that the time for half-measures has gone by. I should be unwilling to think that in this he is right, but where he doubts it is not for others to dogmatise.

TECHNICAL EDUCATION IN ENGLAND

Thornton, William, "Technical Education in England",
Cornhill Magazine, September (24), 1871, pp. 323–41.

Arguing the necessity of educational reform in order for England to recommence its industrial growth, Thornton put forward his view on the educational policy relevant to England in the 1870s.

Technical Education in England

EIGHTEEN hundred and fifty-one, the year of the first International Exhibition, was a grand time for Great Britain. She had challenged the whole world to meet her in the lists, and she held her ground victoriously against all comers. In the Palace of the Crystal which the genius of Paxton had conjured up for the reception of her visitors, she bore herself in state like a feudal sovereign accepting the homage of her vassals. Some compliments she was graciously pleased to bestow on the achievements of one or other of her neighbours – praising highly the silks and porcelain of this, and the glass-ware of that, but so she could well afford to do, for in all those more substantial fabrics which constitute the mainstay of commercial prosperity, she stood apart in unapproached supremacy.

Yet "let him who thinketh he standeth, take heed lest he fall," specially if standing on a giddy and intoxicating height. In the midst of Britain's industrial triumph, plots were being laid for her industrial discomfiture. The admiration she excited was of the imitative sort; and her foreign guests, after remaining for a season in appreciative and discriminating examination, returned home pensively emulous, pondering how best to undermine the pre-eminence they had been contemplating. In 1855 they made bold to return the challenge they had received four years previously, bidding British craftsmen to come to Paris to see what progress had been made by Continentals along paths parallel to their own; when those who responded to the call were not over pleased to find how great that progress was. John Bull, however, though readily startled, soon recovers his composure, and though somewhat taken aback at first at the sight of a huge French annexe full of gigantic steam-machines and other metal products, he presently bethought himself how and with what result a frog is fabled to have once before tried to swell itself out to bovine dimensions, and consoled himself accordingly.

It was without any misgiving, therefore, that after a short pause, England for the second time defied the world to a comparative display of wares. At the Exhibition held, consequently, in London, in 1862, a host of well-equipped rivals attended. Switzerland was there, with Schonbein's wonderful aniline colours; Prussia, with enormous ingots of Krupp's steel; America, with some of her exquisite machines for economizing labour; Italy, with her reproductions in glass and gold of old Venetian and Etruscan fancies; France with stately steam-engines, in number this time sufficient to show that what had so lately been taken for her overstrained efforts had now become part of her regular routine work. All around were proofs that every nation had begun to rival us in some one of our great specialties, that ground was being gained upon us in every direction in which we were still ahead at a rate which we should be speedily distanced unless our own pace were soon and proportionably accelerated. Such was the writing on the walls of the "Brompton Boilers" for those amongst us who were skilled to decipher the monitory hieroglyphics. But the great majority even yet were warned in vain. The bulk of the nation after a fitful start or two, as in an uneasy dream, turned away to doze through another decade in the fancied security of their fools' paradise.

At last, at the Paris Exhibition of 1867, came a third warning, in tones to clear to be misinterpreted. English experts, of whatever class, were then unable to conceal from themselves that we were, not equalled, but beaten, and that not in some points only, but by some nation or other, in nearly all those points on which we had previously prided ourselves. Out of ninety classes of exhibited articles, there were barely a dozen in which pre-eminence was awarded to us. In ironwork, not only was Dupuy de Lôme's large marine engine more than a match for anything of the kind that we had to show, but from distant departments a multitude of French steam-engines and boilers had been collected, quite as well finished as any of ours, and so much more judiciously designed, as to be able, out of a given quantity of fuel, to obtain more power, in a proportion that more than made up for the difference in cost of fuel in England and in France. Of French forgings generally, it was observed that, if slightly dearer than the corresponding English, they had acquired a name for uniform excellence of material and for exactness of shape which more than compensated for their extra dearness. In steel-work, Prussia was perceived to be not less ahead of us than France in iron. In woollens, France, Belgium, and Austria were found to have made formidable advances on our position; and if in cotton goods we still retained the lead, it was chiefly in the coarser descriptions that our superiority was manifested, for, in the finer sorts, we had already become customers of other nations. Such was the appearance presented by the great British staples; nor did the generality of our minor manufactures cut a more creditable figure. Reversing the process of *ex pede herculem*, we might have guessed that as was the corporate mass, so would the separate members be; and so we are distinctly told both in general terms and in regard to numerous specified items. In almost everything either our inferiority was manifest, or our superiority was threatened. On this all witnesses agreed – Professors Tyndall and Frankland, Dr. Leon Playfair, Messrs. Mundella and Scott Russell, and all the other English jurors; Messrs. Lucraft and Conolly, and all the other English artisans who proceeded to Paris at the expense of the Society of Arts. Nor were the same authorities less unanimous as to the causes of the alarming phenomena they had witnessed, all explaining them thus: – The clear-sighted foreigners who in 1851 had been so much struck with what was then England's manufacturing supremacy, had satisfied themselves that it was due mainly to her possession of one natural and two acquired advantages – abundance, and consequent cheapness of coal and iron; vast accumulations of capital, and proportionate command over the mechanical auxiliaries of labour; abundance of labour and of supervising agency, both more efficient than any other country could at that time boast. They perceived that in the first of these respects England was unlikely ever to be equalled by any other European country, unless by reason of her own wilful waste of her mineral wealth; nor in the second, unless gradually; and that the best chance for her Continental rivals was in the third, in which England's superiority was the result of practice, with little aid from preparatory training or theoretical knowledge. They perceived how greatly, by adequate provision for the scientific instruction of Continental masters and men, both the quality of Continental labour and the mode of its application might be improved; and they hoped that increased manipulative skill, directed by increased intelligence, might do better and cheaper work than less skill and intelligence could do even with better tools and cheaper materials.

Now, had the industrial conditions of England and the Continental countries been reversed, and had the same educational ideas occurred twenty years ago to our leading statesmen instead of theirs, we have fair means of measuring the extent to which those ideas might by this time have become developed. We might probably be even now deeming it matter for congratulation that we had advanced beyond the stage at which, while all parties in the country were loudly proclaiming that something ought to be done, no two parties could agree what that something was, or would therefore permit anything to be done. At most we should have got the length of "optional compulsion," imposing, on whatever district volunteered to accept the same, the imperative obligation or not. "They order this matter better in France" as was presently discovered by the English artisans delegated thither in 1867. With envious eyes they noted that in every manufacturing town of any importance, a church or a baker's shop is not more a matter of course than an art-school, wherein whoever chooses may, on payment of little more than nominal fees, be initiated into all the mysteries of design. With jealous ears they heard of the facility with which the poorest French boy, of fair parts and application, may pass from communal school to communal college and thence to an university. Yet the impression made upon them by the contrast between French and English educational provision shows rather the scantiness of the latter than the abundance of the former; with which intelligent Frenchman themselves are far from being satisfied, holding, indeed, that if, among first-rate European powers, England be the worst educated, France is the next worst, as much below Germany as above England. Nor is there any overstrained modesty in this estimate; for not only in Prussia, but in each and every of those minor Teutonic States, too insignificant almost for separate English recognition, there is a complete network of institutions showering thickly over the narrow area of the land as much or more of technical instruction than is thinly sprinkled over the entire English superficies. In Würtemberg, for instance – a petty kingdom with a population barely two-thirds that of London – there are, and indeed already were in 1865–6, maintained chiefly at the expense of the State, – Firstly, at least as many elementary schools as there are communes or parishes, to which all children between the ages of six and twelve, for whose tuition their friends do not otherwise provide, are required to be sent in order to be taught to read and write fluently, and to get, in addition, a taste of and for the knowledge to which reading is the key: Secondly, as auxiliary to these, 450 industrial schools of a humble character, attended chiefly by girls: Thirdly, 523 farming schools and 108 trade schools, in which lads of twelve and upwards are fitted for husbandry or handicrafts by instruction given throughout the day to such as can spare the time, or for an hour or two in the morning and evening to those whom necessity compels too devote most of the intermediate hours to earning their bread: Fourthly, seventy six industrial academies in which more forward pupils are further advanced in science, pure, mixed, and applied: Fifthly, a great agricultural college at Hohenheim, and a great building-trades' college at Stutgardt; the one for giving thorough scientific training to farmers, gardeners, and foresters; the other, of which the most distinguished architect of Würtemberg is president, with twenty-eight professors and sub-professors under him, for fitting journeymen masons, bricklayers, carpenters, and the like, to become foremen in their respective crafts; foremen and moneyed apprentices to become masters; and small masters to become great contractors: Finally, a Polytechnic University at Stutgardt, amply equipped with lecture-rooms, modelling-rooms, chemical and physical laboratories, mineralogical museum, botanic garden, and astronomical observatory, where matriculated students may go through complete courses of mathematics, mechanics, natural philosophy, and natural history, engineering and architecture, with all their affiliated 'ologies, on payment of less than 5*l.* for the half-year, and where whoever chooses may attend the classes of any of the fifty-one professors, on payment of rather less than twopence the lesson.

From one, judge of all. From this brief outline of the educational condition of Würtemberg may be approximately inferred that of the generality of German States, among which Würtemberg stands educationally about midway, somewhat higher than most, somewhat below one or two. Not of Würtemberg only, therefore, but of Germany as a whole may France acknowledge the educational superiority. Yet, even as France looks up to Germany, may Germany in turn look up to Switzerland, which – having under the auspices of Pestalozzi anticipated both her neighbours in combining the teaching of thoughts and things with that of words – has, during the last seventeen years, gone beyond either in combining instruction in the real business of life with instruction in abstract science. In private and personal expenditure the Swiss are as frugal, not to say stingy, as we are profuse. Their wealth, national or individual, in comparison with ours, is poverty; but on many great public objects their lavishness stands out in humiliating contrast with our niggardliness. Their common national poly-technicon at Zurich – an edifice as grandiose as Buckingham Palace – is located the best model of a technical university which the world can show, the most perfect and symmetrical organization for training a rising generation in the practical duties of citizenship. In it everything that is most valuable in the arts or manufactures of other countries is taught by the most competent teachers anywhere procurable, in the best manner that experience can suggest, and with all the aid that the best material appliances can afford. There, as in the kindred establishment at Stutgardt, are an astronomical observatory, a chemico-mechanical laboratory, a laboratory of chemical research, a museum of engineering works and drawings, a museum of engines and machinery, a museum of architecture, collections – antiquarian, zoological, botanic, and geological. There a tutorial staff, sixty strong, deliver annually 145 courses of lectures, in groups adapted to the varying requirements of all who are either themselves ambitious of taking the lead in any technical career, or propose to make it their business to promote the technical progress of others – suited, that is, to agriculturists, manufacturers, mechanicians, engineers, and architects, to the general and political philosopher and the politician, and to all beside who either cultivate science or art or literature for its own sake, or take it up as a profession.

If now – recollecting that these several sets of educational apparatus were designed for the express purpose of enabling the countries to which they respectively belong to make up, by the more effective application of science to industry, for their inferiority to England in other conditions of industrial success – we proceed anxiously to inquire how far that purpose has been attained, we shall find all testimony continuing equally concurrent. Contrasting the textile products of France, Belgium, Prussia, and Austria, with those of Great Britain, "here," exclaims Mr. Huth, "is a machine working a machine; there, brains sit at the loom, and intelligence stands at the wheel." The previous training, whereby, "in the polytechnic schools of Germany and Switzerland, the future manufacturer or manager is made familiar with the laws of the great natural forces that must always form the bases of every intelligent industry," is pronounced by Professor Frankland to "more than overbalance the undoubted advantages which our own country possesses in raw material." "Englishmen," says Mr. Mundella, "possess more energy, enterprise, and inventiveness than any other European nation; but the best machines which Englishmen invent Germans and Frenchmen are enabled, by superior industrial education, to improve upon." While, "in Saxony, sons of the poorest workman receive a technical education such as the sons of our richest manufacturers cannot hope to obtain, how (asks the same keen observer) can it be otherwise than that the English workman should be gradually losing in the race?" Gradually losing, forsooth! Nay, rather does Mr. Lucraft feel bound to confess that "in the race we are nowhere; that our defeat is as ignominious and disastrous as it is possible to conceive; "that since 1862 we have "not only not made progress, but have retrograded," and that because "the mere mechanical workman has not the slightest chance with the workman of cultivated taste," It is "the Frenchman's familiarity with art," says Mr. Conolly, "and his early training in its principles, that enable him to outstrip us," insomuch that "we are becoming reduced to mere hewers of wood and drawers of water for other nations, manufacturing goods to be sold cheap, or producing raw material for them to work up;" but, as Mr. Randall adds, in the same strain, betraying our deficiencies "wherever intellectualism is concerned or an educated hand is required." Everywhere in the manufacturing establishments of the Continent, Mr. Samuelson found people of higher culture than our own, handworkers comparatively literate, foreman and managers with well-stored and well-exercised heads, masters often highly and variously accomplished.*

Such being the admitted difference in mental attainments between English and Continental directors and performers of labour, let us reflect on what that difference implies. That, whatever be the task, workmen in the habit of using their brains as well as their hands, will do it better than those who are not, will do it with less waste of time, exertion, and material, and will turn out work both fitter in itself and that will fit better into whatever other work it is to be combined with, is too clear to need pointing out: that managers whose only rule is that of thumb will, when, in cases of novelty, obliged to proceed by error also than if they had ascertained principles to guide them, is equally obvious; nor is if much less evident that a principal's or proprietor's competence to the supreme control of a great industrial business, will be proportionate to his comprehension of the processes which the business involves. What it may be somewhat less superfluous to note is, how greatly technical ignorance on the part of employers aggravates the evil of similar ignorance among the employed, and *vice versâ*, and how greatly the want of technical knowledge on one side tends to neutralize the efficacy of such knowledge on the other. Even bad workmen have a strong motive for doing as well as they can when working for a master who is a judge of work, while good workmen will be discouraged from putting forth their skill for the sake of a master who cannot tell good work from bad. Those who see that they will not get credit for doing their best will be apt to content themselves with doing the worst that will pass muster, and when the workmanship of all is brought to the same dead level of badness, the unionist demand that all shall be paid alike, no longer sounds unreasonable. Or if it be the master with whom is superiority of capacity, then, before venturing to introduce improved methods, he has to consider what his pig-headed foreman will have to say to such newfangled notions, and, before trusting his workmen with delicate mechanism, to reflect whether their clumsy hands will not be sure to put it out of order. Plainly the odds are too great against establishments conducted under such

* I must no longer delay mentioning that the principal authority for my statements and descriptions so far, is Mr. Scott Russell's very valuable work on *Systematic Technical Education* (Bradbury and Evans, 1869), some considerable portions of which I have endeavoured to epitomize in the text, although necessarily unable to present there more than the barest outlines of what in the original is set forth in rich and instructive detail.

disadvantages in rivalry with those in which authority graduates upwards *pari passu* with merit, where masters are managers and workmen looking upwards for instruction or direction accordingly – and where members of all grades, deserving and desiring each other's esteem, feel their common honour involved in the excellence of their joint productions.

As to the inevitable results of such overweighted rivalry, there is abundant evidence to be added to the warning notes already cited. Turning to recent parliamentary papers on the subject, we shall find foreigners; Dewsbury lamenting that, in the lighter and more woollens, Yorkshire is being superseded by the Continent; Hawick complaining that Verviers, by producing a superior article at the same price, has usurped a large portion of the Scottish woollen-trade; Birmingham, handing in a long list of wares, which used to be specialties of hers, and which are now partially or wholly displaced in common markets by corresponding articles from France, Prussia, and the United States; Nottingham, confessing that she is obliged to send large quantities of hosiery abroad to get it properly dyed; Macclesfield and Coventry, owning that it is no longer French, but also Swiss silks and ribbons they have to fear. Worst item of all in this sadly significant catalogue, Belgium boasting that in the fifteen years ending with 1867, the increase in her export of cotton goods was almost exactly twice that of England, or as 292 to 148 per cent. There is, in short, a dense cloud of witnesses reluctant or exultant, testifying to the manifold symptoms of England's industrial declension, declaring that both the manipulative dexterity and the mechanical contrivances, of which, in many departments of industry she had until lately almost exclusive possession, have now become common property; that improved means of transport equalizing the price of raw materials all over Europe, and that all competitors being thus much upon a level in these respects, the race will henceforth be to the swiftest to make scientific training. Nevertheless, we are as yet only thinking of girding up our loins, only thinking of putting ourselves in training for the novel contest: our scientific curriculum has still to be planned; the outlines of our scientific arena are still to be traced.

Yet that national unreadiness which has so often cost us dear, has at no juncture of our history been apparently fraught with more danger than now. Of our nation's many pressing wants, social or political, there is not one more urgent than that of technical education. Army reform, navy reform, readjustment of the relations between labour and capital, life and death matters as they all and each are, can yet comparatively afford to wait, for unless technical education precede them, they may soon be neither army nor navy to reform, nor much left of a class that, except metaphorically, will be entitled to be styled labouring. If a nation is to have soldiers or sailors or labourers, she must have adequate wealth to pay and employ them; and in England national wealth is little else than another name for commercial prosperity, one indispensable element of which is efficiency of labour, which again has now become a relative term, applicable or not, according as the industrial sections of a population excel or fall short of other countries in mental culture. And it is in this fundamental particular that we have allowed other countries to have twenty years' start of us. Even by so much were they earlier than we in discovering that not less in industrial than in other operations, knowledge is power, and science the surest basis of skill. If, at length, we too have recognized this truth, clearly we have not another moment to lose before striving in good earnest to make up for time already lost. Clearly, if we are really awake at last, we have no choice between remaining for ever fallen, and arising and bestirring ourselves at once.

If, however, resolved on immediate action, how are we to act? Whoever attempts to answer this question had need to be specially on his guard against exaggeration, which would here be more than ordinarily calculated to defeat its own object. Nothing is easier than, pointing to what other nations have done, to bid us go and do likewise; but if national exertions and sacrifices bearing the same proportion to ability as those of Würtemberg and Switzerland were really indispensable for our industrial reinstatement, our case would be nothing short of desperate, for such exertions and sacrifices would simply not be made. Würtemburg has, as we have seen, provided within the last twenty years for the technical instruction of a population of less than two millions, one university, two colleges of the first rank, and more than a hundred high-trade schools. To provide equally for its thirty millions of people, our triune kingdom would have to create fifteen universities, thirty colleges, and more than 1,500 high schools. Among Swiss cantons, that of Zurich alone, in addition to the Polytechnic University of which we have already spoken, maintains a veterinary school, a school of agriculture, two great *real*, as well as two great classical, schools , a normal school for teachers, fifty-seven secondary, and 364 primary schools. Few, if any, of the other cantons, it is true, do nearly as much as this. Still, in order that the proportion of the entire expenditure of the state devoted to education should be as high as the United Kingdom as in Switzerland, the House of Commons would have to pass annually an educational vote of at least five millions sterling. A vice-president of the Council daring enough to demand such a vote would be a sight fit for those gods whose delight it is said to have been to see a good man struggling with the storms of fate. Arguments for a good fight might, indeed, not be wanting. It might not be difficult for him to show that five, or twice five, millions of English money could scarcely be better spent annually than in first recovering and then maintaining England's manufacturing superiority. Merely as consumers, the tax-payers might not improbably receive for it full money's worth when all the home-made articles they had occasion to buy had become in consequence the best that skill could produce, instead of the worst dishonesty can palm off; while, in their quality of producers and purveyors, they would certainly get it all back many times over, if for every pound's worth of pig-iron or cotton-twist which the foreigner now takes from them, he were content to take as much hardware and cambrics as the iron and cotton could be converted into. Besides, it would surely be better, while we have the wherewithal, to consent to pay almost any amount of extra taxes rather than to lose the power of paying what we already pay, as we should do were there to be a great falling off in our export and import trade. Plainly, too, it would be better economy to spend, as the Swiss do, seven times as much on education as on pauperism and crime, than to go on spending, as we are actually doing, seven times as much on pauperism and crime as on education. All this would be same effect, would be without avail. The charmer, charmed he never so wisely, would have turned to him only the deafest of ears. The British public must be much less in need of education than it is before it will volunteer to be subjected to a special income-tax of fourpence in the pound for the sake of national education. Living, as we almost all of us who would not grudge for the common good, for the most vital of common objects, contributions that could come only out of a fund barely sufficing results of which the educational systems of other countries have been so fruitful, would not, seeing them to be beyond the reach of any exertions that we can prevail upon ourselves to make, be disposed to take what comfort he might from conjecturing that the grapes, after all, were very likely sour?

Such comfort I may myself seem to be offering in proceeding to suggest that the educational vines which have thrive so well abroad may not be precisely of the species best suited to our climate, or that, at any rate, an attempt to acclimatize them here would, for the present, be premature. One objection to them is, that they are prone to greater minuteness of ramification than there is here occasion for. At St. Etienne, there is a school for ribbon-making; at Mulhouse on for calico-printing. At the Ecole de la Marinière at Lyons, children are taught turnery, joinery, and iron-filing. At the Ecole St. Nicolas in Paris, trades are taught to 1,800 pupils. In West Flanders there are schools for weavers, in which near 1,900 apprentices are constantly practising at the loom. In Geneva are similar schools for watchmakers. In the laboratories attached to the *Polytechnica* at Berlin, Carlsruhe, Stutgardt, and Zurich, experiments go far beyond the utmost extent needed for illustration, and seem to aim at miniature mimicry of many of the grandest achievements of labour. But this sort of thing is, or, at any rate, would with us be, a decided mistake, involving needless expense on makeshift imitations of realities already existing close at hand, and needless protraction of lessons which might be got through much more satisfactorily and in much less time elsewhere. The proper function of technical seminaries of every degree is to teach the scientific principles which govern technical operations, not to teach the operations themselves. Pupils cannot, indeed, be taught too early the use of the tools and implements they will have to wield in after life, when this can be done without prejudice to matters of more moment; but still, for the manipulative part of any kind of work, there is no school like the workshop, or whatever else be the place in which the actual work is done. Mr. Squeers' notion that when a boy had learnt that b o t bot, t i n tin, bottin, n e y ney, bottiney, meant a knowledge of plants, he should be sent into the garden to know them, was sound in principle, however defective orthographically. More or less of didactic instruction should invariably precede, and, if possible, accompany, apprenticeship. The apprentice will learn much better and quicklier how to do things for knowing beforehand why he is bidden to do them a particular way; but knowing the why, he will learn the how quicklier and more effectually still in a real than in a sham workshop, in one in which work is done in earnest, and not merely played at, and where, besides, unless he or his friends can afford to pay for his being permitted idle, he may not only chance to be cuffed if he do not take pains, but may be paid if he do. Now, in these islands there is quite a sufficiency of genuine workshops and factories and foundries to do away with the necessity of attaching costly imitations of them as appendages to schools and colleges.

Then, that symmetric graduation, that taper rotundity of Continental systems, so often held up for admiration, may not, impossibly, be rather a defect than a merit. That regular arrangement of wheels within wheels – of double or treble rows of schools clustered round colleges, and of colleges circling round universities, necessarily implies a central authority prescribing and controlling all circumambient action; which might be all very well if central authorities were always as infallible as they commonly esteem themselves, but which, on any less flattering hypothesis, can scarcely fail to disseminate and perpetuate administrative errors. Enforcement of a national model on local imitation, must needs be, more or less, of a Procrustean process, lopping of here what can ill be spared, and jointing on there needless incumbrances; whereas, when local opinion is left free to mould local arrangements, and to adapt them to local peculiarities, a variety of examples will be produced to serve for each other's rectification. It were better, perhaps, that all schoolmasters should be trained at one and the same State school, than that no security whatever should be taken for their being properly trained. Still, considering how inclined they would be to communicate to their pupils whatever impulse they had themselves received, one could not without serious apprehension see them all started along one and the same hard and fast groove.

The paucity, moreover, and consequent high market value in an uneducated land like ours, of persons qualified to act as scientific teachers, would of itself prove a temporarily insuperable bar to the creation of an educational organization like that of any of the more highly educated countries of the Continent. Among English pedagogues, that would be a very middling one indeed who did not turn up his nose at the pittance of 300*l*. a year, which is all that the rector of the principal of the school in Prussia receives. If competent teachers in sufficient number were forthcoming, funds adequate to the rate at which they would appraise themselves would certainly not be; neither, if the money were, would the men be, for the latter do not yet exist, and would not for a long time to come be obtainable at any price. And even if this difficulty were got over, another not less serious would still remain. If, by the stroke of an enchanter's wand, England should become as thickly dotted as Prussia with technical seminaries of every degree, the majority would most likely be long left untenanted, except by the members of a sinecure staff. Out of a metropolitan population of some three millions, the world-wide fame of professors like Huxley, Frankland, and Percy, attracts barely a hundred students, regular and occasional, to the classes in the Jermyn Street School more than three or four times that number of class-men to Owens' College. Mechanics' Institutions were designed expressly for the scientific instruction of mechanics, but in only two English counties have they been of much avail for their main and original purpose. In general it has been observed of these establishments, that as soon as the lecturers begin upon science the lecture-rooms are deserted. There is but one agricultural college in England, viz. at Cirencester; and there are at least 300,000 farmers and other superintendents of agriculture labour whose patronage, however, has only of late years sufficed to keep the college tolerably full, and whose neglect, until of late, was always threatening to let it collapse from vacuity – even as our Civil Engineers actually suffered to collapse their solitary college at Putney. As long as existing institutions remain but half filled, the only certain effect of multiplying institutions of the same class would be that a greater number would be left half empty. It is not sufficient to place fountains of technic knowledge within people's reach in order to induce them to drink, – they must have, in addition, a taste for the beverage, and digestion vigorous enough for its assimilation; and these are qualities which neither come naturally, nor yet can be acquired artificially unless pains be taken to impart them. So Continental educationists failed not to perceive, and they made provision accordingly; and it is vain to think of copying the superstructure they have raised without taking pattern likewise from the substratum previously laid by them. The reason why the *Realschulen* and technic colleges of Germany are always crowded with scholars is, that primary schools are always sending forth scholars prepared for the *Realschulen,* which in turn are constantly doing the like for the colleges. Mechanics' institutes, although in respect to their scientific aim for the most part failures in England, have succeeded almost universally in Scotland. And why? Chiefly because Scotch mechanics generally have, while English mechanics in general have not, acquired at elementary schools enough of knowledge both to make them desire more and to qualify them for the following the more advanced teaching from which more may be obtained. This is the reason why, while the Birkbeck Institution casts by comparison only the shadow of a great name, the Watt Institution at Edinburgh and the Andersonian Institution at Glasgow are casting out light all round on continually increasing numbers of fitting recipients; and for a similar reason it is that the mechanics' institutes of Lancashire and Cheshire stand in such creditable contrast to those of the rest of England. In those two counties the quasi-compulsory educational clauses of the Factory and Colliery Acts are in active operation, with results which may be accepted as an earnest of the good that would arise if compulsion were universal. The enforced schooling of the factory children begets in the factory lads and lasses and in adult operatives a willingness to go on attending school-classes, insomuch that of the 123 mechanics' institutes constituting the Lancashire Union, seventy-five had, by the year 1868 become encouraged to open science classes, wherein, or in corresponding classes formed under the same auspices in the same part of the country, 2,250 students were under instruction, being more than one-quarter of the whole number in England and Wales availing themselves of similar means of instruction. All this shows that an indispensable preliminary to the furtherance of technical education, which from a level considerably below that of Scotland, must be raised to an equality at least with that of Germany. Unless this be done, everything beyond may as well be left unattempted; though, on the other hand, this having been done, much less than might be supposed will be left to do. This is the indispensable goose-step without which there can be no onward marching; but which, on the other hand, will of itself cover no small portion of the whole space to be traversed.

Regarded in a purely industrial light, the classes of persons amongst us in need of scientific instruction are four – subordinate labourers, skilled and unskilled; foreman and overlookers of labour; managers of superior grade; masters of principals on a largest scale. But for the first, and greatly more numerous of these classes, a very slight tincture of science will suffice for ordinary use. Not that its members can possibly have too much of it, or so much as to be thereby raised above their work, provided only they all share in it pretty equally. The lowliest workmen cannot, as a body, be too highly educated. It is only relative abundance of knowledge that puffeth up. Absolute abundance edifieth, increasing at once its owner's merit and his modesty. Whatever be the task, there is in its performance. Bees would have to use much more wax for cell-making were it not for their intuitive mathematics; and no doubt, if every carpenter and every tailor were an Archimedes, our tables and chairs and coats and trousers would be cut in all the more shapely wise, and with all the less waste of material. But although an artisan, in all probability, always does somewhat better for whatever science he possesses, he may yet do exceedingly well with very little. Provided science be at hand to guide, he need have very little science of his own to be able to follow. What is wanted for that is rather general intelligence, the development of which embraces a certain amount of special instruction. To inquire at all minutely to what extent the two might be combined, if social prejudice permitted poor and rich to be educated together as indiscriminately and universally in England as they actually are in Switzerland, where private schools, in our sense of the term, scarcely exist, and as they used to be in Scotland, might then become, primary education, infinitely better, in many respects, than anywhere within British territory is at present obtainable for love or money, might be imparted to children of rich and poor alike, at probably less expense, in the aggregate, than is no incurred by the rich for having their own children alone as indifferently taught as they for the most part are. Whatever there be which it is desirable that children of any degree should learn, children of every degree would then have equal facilities for learning, so long as they could be spared to remain at school. This, however, is not, as yet, to be hoped for. As long as purse-proud fastidiousness requires that the poor should be taught apart, the schools appropriated to them must continue to be more like what they are than what they might be, the improvements practicable in their organization being limited by the limited funds available for their maintenance. Fortunately, of the improvements most urgently needed, some would involve very little, and the rest no additional, expense. Only to get the three R's taught as they ought to be taught would be an immense advance. A child that, exchanging school for field or factory, cannot write and rithmetize fairly, and read without effort, might as well never have been at school at all, for it has learnt there nothing, that will not be presently forgotten. But the child must be a born idiot that cannot, within the half-dozen years commonly spent at a national school, learn this little, provided it care to learn an its master to teach, as both might easily be made to do by pressure which school-inspectors on the one hand, and employers of labour on the other, are in a position to bring to bear. Children who had learnt only as much as this would be in possession of at least the key of knowledge; but this, though a *sine quâ non*, without which nought else would much avail, would also itself avail little without some important accompaniments. The key would soon grow rusty from neglect unless curiosity about what it could unlock afforded adequate motive for frequently using it; and a schoolboy's curiosity on that point is usually more or less keen, according as his reading and other lessons have been more or less interesting. If the staple of these has been Canaanitish topography or Jewish pedigrees, the book-learning he has already taken in may well have been quite enough to surfeit him, and to leave him irreverently indifferent about the distance of Kadesh-barnea from Ezion-gebir, and whether it was Jochabed that begat Ahitub, or Ahitub that begat Jochabed. But he will probably be in a more receptive mood if the pages he has been accustomed to spell through have shown him the heroic three hundred standing up against the Persian myriads at Thermopylae, or the as heroic eight hundred dashing up Balaclava's valley of the shadow of death, or Etnal belching forth flames or St. Lawrence crashing down Niagra; or if he has had explained to him why Mars is red and the moon spotty, or why water rises in a syphon and does not go on rising in a diving-bell. These are things by feeding upon which, together with a judicious admixture of *Arabian Nights* and *Robinson Crusoe,*the childish appetite grows into an insatiable craving for more of the like nutriment; and of things of this sort, those which are specially suitable for serving as whetstones to childish faculties, are those which approach nearest to the domain of physical science. In the common occurrences of daily observation, a child whose eyes have been opened to some of their inner significance, will find inexhaustible matter to wonder and guess and question, and likewise to be eager to read about, and there are very simple ways in which early schooling may help to create an interest in such phenomena. To begin at the beginning is scarcely, perhaps, the best way. It has been settled in France – or, rather, had been, previously to the recent unsettlement of all things in that unfortunate land – that in the very humblest schools the elements of mathematics, mechanics, physics, and chemistry should be taught. But elementary abstractions are, for the most part, over-subtle for juvenile apprehension, and somewhat too dry for the juvenile palate; and instead of commencing with them, it would seem preferable to plunge at once *in medias res,* even as the late Dean of Hereford used to do at King's Sombourn school, when, with the aid of a squirt, a popgun, or a boiling kettle, he would explain the properties of air or water or steam; or as Professor Tyndall's plan was, when, by "illustrations drawn from the plough, the crowbar, or the see-saw in the playground," he used to make the lucky urchins of whom at one time he had tutorial charge "perfectly enthusiastic about their studies in practical mechanics." Every schoolmaster, it is true, is not a Tyrdall or a Dean Dawes, but neither need he be in order to adopt their method. He need but have that moderate amount of tact and patience without which he cannot be fit to teach anything, together with such an acquaintance with the special subject to be taught as, if he have it not already, he may readily acquire by merely reading a little ahead of his pupils, and as most national schoolmasters would speedily manage to acquire somehow, if forewarned that the pecuniary recommendations made regarding them in the periodical reports of the school-inspectors would depend on their doing or not doing so.

To the several recommendations implied in these remarks is to be added another, viz. this: that among absolutely obligatory subjects of national schooling should, as soon as may be, be included drawing, an accomplishment calculated to be quite as directly serviceable to the handicraftsman in his vocation as any even of the three R's, unless perhaps the first. This, however, is an innovation which must needs be delayed until time has been allowed for training up a body of sufficiently artistic masters; but with this exception, all the suggested changes in national school arrangements are readily practicable, demanding for their speedy adoption neither much additional expense, nor much of anything but will on the part of certain controlling authorities; while they would go far towards securing to the great bulk of the youth of the nation enough of preliminary instruction to fit them for engaging with adequate intelligence in whatever mechanical labour might subsequently fall to their lot. For patriotic prejudice apart, and owing possibly to their descent from long lines of operative ancestors, English work-people do really seem to inherit naturally unrivalled technical aptitudes. "It is remarkable," as Mr. Mundella says, "how well they do considering how little they know," that little according to the same well-informed witness, not, in the case of more than every other skilled labourer, going beyond ability to read a very simple paragraph, while, among the unskilled, not more than one in twenty can read at all. But with an amount of natural "go" about them, which even as it is makes such considerable amends for their inferior scholarship, no extraordinary quantity of scholastic lore need be combined to secure them against all possible danger of being outstripped by the most scholarly of their foreign rivals. For recruiting the rank and file of the army of industry, lads and lasses of the average English standard as to morale and physique, would with barely enough of culture to be able to read with some self-satisfaction, and to handle pen, and slate and lead-pencil with some little adroitness, be as good material as need be wished for, requiring only a moderate spell of active employment to convert them into first-rate privates, quite capable of following whatever lead their officers might give. It is only by the officers, and in order that they may better understand what lead to give, that more than a very slight tincture of science is needed, and to their requirements, therefore, in that respect, our attention may now be directed.

Here again we shall find that what is wanted is not so much the introduction of new as the more extended and more judicious application of old principles and systems. Regarding first the petty officers, – the foremen and overlookers, – we may observe that these rise almost invariably from the ranks, consisting of those more ambitious spirits who have laid themselves out beforehand for promotion by doing their best to fit themselves for it. Hitherto, such aspirants have sought to recommend themselves chiefly by general assiduity and manipulative dexterity; but, with the more enlarged views which better early schooling would give, they would not fail to see that the possession of some theoretical knowledge would sensibly help them to get on, and would look about for the means of acquiring such knowledge. And so looking they would not look in vain, but would presently learn that what they sought, if not already existing close at hand, was, as it were, only waiting to be called into existence. They would hear of a Government Department, located at Kensington, which by the way, would do well to take some pains to make itself and its beneficence more widely known, and which, whenever a number of manual workers choose to form themselves into shows, is sufficient to induce fairly competent teachers to officiate for an hour or two in the evening in national schools or mechanics' institutes. In Lancashire, where the comparative efficiency of primary education has rendered the working population comparatively appreciative of scientific instruction, classes thus aided have been formed to the number of more than sixty, and in order that they should go on multiplying in Lancashire, and that they should become proportionably numerous in other counties, it is only necessary that primary education should go on improving in Lancashire, and should rise in other counties to the Lancastrian level. The quality of the instruction given in these classes varies of course with the qualification of the teacher, which, however, cannot, consistently with the conditions of appointment, be less than respectable, and need not be more in order to allow of their owners training up scholars far fitter to become foremen than the generality of actual occupants of that grade. To speak of science in connection with the latter would, as yet, be cruel mockery, for in many districts inability to sign one's name is rather the rule than the exception amongst them. Mr. Mundella mentions one whom he saw making his mark by way of signature to a contract vesting him with the superintendence of a number of mines in Russia, and another whom he had himself deputed to his German establishment, but who presently came back because, while abroad, he could not correspond with his family, not being able to read their letters, much less to write them in return. On the other hand, in the science classes of the Kensington department, the instruction imparted is pronounced by Professors Huxley and Tyndall to be, "though elementary, sound;" neither is it so elementary but that classmen, whose sole preparation it has been, have, in several instances, competed successfully for the royal exhibitions and scholarships which have been recently created for the encouragement of poor scientific students.

But whether the scientific instruction which these easily-extemporised classes are capable of affording be or be not sufficient for ordinary foremen, in respect to whom a means of materially supplementing it will presently be indicated, it certainly is not all that is requisite for the superior officers – the managers or masters under whose direction foremen have to act. It is these – the captains and generals of our industrial forces – whose inferiority in theoretical attainments to their Continental correlatives affords most serious ground for apprehension. A certain proportion of them, no doubt, are average English gentlemen – fair specimens of their order in mental culture as in all else; but of the far more numerous remainder, those who have not, like foremen, risen from the ranks, have commonly belonged originally to that lower grade of middle society whose members are in the habit of sending their sons either to second-rate "grammar" schools or to so-called "classical and commercial" schools. Their pupils are not, indeed, liable, as soon as they have entered their teens, to be carried off to serve as scarecrows in a corn-field, or as "doffers" in a cotton-mill, but are usually suffered to remain until they are able to read, write, and perhaps cypher passably; but of any higher learning the quantity which more than one in ten of them carry away would be too highly honoured by being termed a smattering. To youths without more preparation than this it would not be of much use to offer facilities for indoctrination in mechanics or physics, after they have exchanged the school for the workshop. The scanty facilities of the kind which already exist will require no addition until middle-class schooling shall have been so improved as to talent may be latent in them. Fortunately, there are certain constituted authorities who may, if they please, be very instrumental in bringing about the improvement in question. Of the 3,000, or thereabouts, of endowed schools small and great, with which England and Wales are studded, nearly a third have been ascertained to be rich enough to admit of their being converted into efficient secondary schools; and until every one of these is converted accordingly, the Commissioners, to whom the superintendence of endowed schools has been committed by the legislature, will not have duly acquitted themselves of their trust. It will be their fault if almost every town or considerable village in the southern half of our Island be not before long in possession of a efficient public school, which all the private middle-class schools in the neighbourhood will have to take as their model, on peril of being abandoned by their best customers. The standard, too, by which middle-class schooling has of late years been regulated is that of the requirements of government and university examinations. The great ambition of its conductors is to enable their scholars to make creditable figures at those examinations. On which account it, in a great measure, rests with Government and the Universities to determine what place science shall occupy in English education. Let them but give it honour due, and none else will presume to slight it. Let it be ordained that – for appointments in the home service, civil or military, or in the Indian service, civil, medical, or miscellaneous, or for Oxford or Cambridge exhibitions or scholarships, or for admission into, and for success in, any university – proficiency in physical science shall stand competitors in as good stead as proficiency in any other branch of learning, and science will no longer want for votaries. One temporary consequence might, indeed, be sensibly to encourage cramming; but the main function of crammers is to do what has been left undone at school; and schoolmasters who had been apprised beforehand of what was necessary to prevent the bread from being taken out of their mouths, would so their best to avoid leaving any neglect of theirs for crammers to repair. At every upper as well as middle-class school at which there was efficient teaching of any sort, pains would be taken to teach science as efficiently as aught else, and of the scholars thence periodically issuing college-bound, a fair proportion would be both desirous and capable of commencing a college course of science. Whereupon, the extreme scarcity and almost entire absence of scientific or technical colleges would make itself felt as a national want, no longer appealing only to the sensitive imaginations of speculative educationists, but coming home to all men's business and bosoms; in view of which advent we may, without, it is to be hoped, extravagantly anticipating events, at once consider how the want may be best supplied. Not, in my own humble and heterodox, but not the less decided, opinion, at the expense of the public at large, or its representative, the State; which, though it might be clearly promoting the common interest were it even to force education on those who, for lack either of means or will, would otherwise go without it, has as clearly no occasion to cater in like fashion for those well-to-do people who are perfectly able, and will be perfectly willing, to supply their own educational requirements as soon as they rightly understand what those requirements are. Something, by way of example, the State may usefully do. It may present models of what technical colleges should be, by establishing for its own special purposes some two or three institutions like that which, in spite of the opposition of Parliamentary champions of free-trade in nescience, will presently be opened at Cooper's Hill, for training civil engineers for the services of the Government of India. But in order that the models should be suitable for their purpose, it is a *sine quâ non* that they be self-supporting. Whatever be the case in Germany or Switzerland, there is in England no sufficient reason why high scientific instruction should, except to a small minority of those by whom it is practically needed, be offered at a mere fraction of its cost price. At every English centre of industry there are hundreds of Mr. Tullivers, who, for such teaching as at the *Polytechnica* of Stutgardt and Zurich is to be has for 10*l.* a year, would gladly pay 100*l.* a year, were they but aware of its value. In Manchester, Birmingham, Leeds, there must be hundreds of such; and wherever there are but a single hundred, a revenue exceeding by two-fifths what Owens' College has to subsist upon would be available for the creation of a similar institution, which it would be available for the enterprise to suppose would not, in such circumstances, be forthwith created. Colleges entirely self-supporting would, indeed, be of little service for the most deserving, perhaps, and interesting of all students, those of great capacity but small means; but these might safely be left to the care of the private sympathy that would be enlisted in their behalf. The genus of public benefactors to which Mr. Owens of Manchester and Mr. Hartly of Southhampton belonged, is not one likely ever to die out amongst us. Whitworth is a name that will not pale beside that of either; and even as Mr. Whitworth is doing, there is in every manufacturing locality some Akroyd or Armstrong, or Crossley or Platt, prepared to do, only waiting till it be proclaimed by public opinion to be the right thing to be done. It needs only that the fashion be set, for the practice of founding scholarships and exhibitions and fellowships to assist working-class students in rising from the lowest elements to the highest eminences of science to become so general that, for a town to be without such an educational ladder, would appear as strange as for it not to have almshouses or an hospital.

In these remarks, I have been compelled to slur very hurriedly over several points which it might have been well to examine carefully had space permitted. Barely, however, is there room enough left to indicate the chief moral to be drawn from all that has gone before, which is briefly this – that in arrangements for placing technical education in England on a satisfactory footing, doing the like for general education will be more than half the battle. Were adequate provision made for the latter, a demand for the former would certainly arise quite "effectual" enough in an economic sense to be left to elicit its own supply. Wherefore, let Elementary School-Boards and Endowed School Commissioners understand that the great work which has been given to them to do, will not be done well unless withal it be done quickly, for, in proportion to their promptitude in the matter, will be England's chances of reinstatement in the industrial supremacy which, owing to her having allowed her industrial rivals twenty years' start of her in technical educational, she has of late by on imperceptible degrees been losing.

JOHN STUART MILL:
HIS CAREER IN THE INDIA HOUSE.

Thornton, William, "His Career in the India House",
John Stuart Mill: His Life and Works, Herbert Spencer et al.
(Boston: James Osgood, 1873) pp. 30–7.

This is one of the twelve character sketches in *John Stuart Mill: His Life and Works*, to which Herbert Spencer, John Elliott Cairnes, and Frederic Harrison also contributed. In this essay, Thornton depicted his personal relationship with John Stuart Mill as well as Mill's official career.

John Stuart Mill: His Career in the India House

I HAVE undertaken to prepare a sketch of Mr. Mill's official career, but find, on inquiry, scarcely any thing to add to the few particulars on the subject which have already found their way into print. Of his early official associates, all have, with scarcely and exception, already passed away; and there is no one within reach to whom I can apply for assistance in verifying or correcting my own impressions. These are in substance the following.

In the few last decades of its existence, the East-India Company's establishment, in Leadenhall Street, consisted of three divisions, – the secretary's, military secretary's, and examiners' offices, – in the last of which most of the despatches and letters were composed which were afterwards signed by the directors or secretary. Into this division, in the year 1821, the directors, perceiving an infusion of new blood to be very urgently required, introduced, as assistant examiners, four outsiders, – Mr. Strachey (father of the present Sir John and Major-Gen. Richard Strachey), Thomas Love Peacock (author of "Headlong Hall"), Mr. Harcourt, and Mr. James Mill; the selection of the last-named being all the more creditable to them, because, in his "History of British India," he had animadverted with much severity on some parts of the Company's administration. Two years afterwards, in 1823, the historian's son, the illustrious subject of these brief memoirs, then a lad of seventeen, obtained a clerkship under his father. According to the ordinary course of things in those days, the newly-appointed junior would have had nothing to do, except a little abstracting, indexing, and searching, or pretending to search, into records; but young Mill was almost immediately set to indite despatches to the governments of the three Indian Presidencies, on what, in India House phraseology, were distinguished as "political" subjects, – subjects, that is, for the most part growing out of the relations of the said governments with "native" states or foreign potentates. This continued to be his business almost to he last. In 1828 he was promoted to be assistant examiner, and in 1856 he succeeded to the post of chief examiner; after which his duty consisted rather in supervising what his assistants had written than in writing himself: but for the three and twenty years preceding he had had immediate charge of the political department, and had written almost every "political" despatch of any importance that conveyed the instructions of the merchant princes of Leadenhall Street to their pro-consuls in Asia. Of the quality of these documents, it is sufficient to say, that they were John Mill's; but, in respect to their quantity, it may be worth mentioning that a descriptive catalogue of them completely fills a small quarto volume of between three hundred and four hundred pages, in their author's handwriting, which now lies before me; also that the share of the Court of Directors in the correspondence between themselves and the Indian governments used to average annually about ten huge vellum-bound volumes, foolscap size, and five or six inches thick, and that of these volumes two a year, for more than twenty years running, were exclusively of Mill's compositions; this, too, at times, when he was engaged upon such voluntary work in addition as his "Logic" and "Political Economy."

In 1857 broke out the Sepoy war, and in the following year the East-India Company was extinguished in all but the name, its governmental functions being transferred to the Crown. That most illustrious of corporations died hard; and with what affectionate loyalty Mill struggled to avert its fate is evidenced by the famous Petition to Parliament which he drew up for his old masters, and which opens with the following effective antithesis: "Your petitioners, at their own expense, and by the agency of their own civil and military servants, originally acquired for this country its magnificent empire in the East. The foundations of this empire were laid by your petitioners, at that time neither aided nor controlled by Parliament, at the same period at which a succession of administrations under the control of Parliament were losing, by their incapacity and rashness, another great empire on the opposite side of the Atlantic."

I am fortunate enough to be the possessor of the original MS. of this admirable state paper, which I mention, because I once heard its real authorship denied in that quarter of all others in which it might have been supposed to be least likely to be questioned. On one of the last occasions of the gathering together of the Proprietors of East-India Stock, I could scarcely believe my ears, when one of the directors, alluding to the petition, spoke of it as having been written by a certain other official who was sitting by his side, adding, after a moment's pause, "with the assistance, as he understood, of Mr. Mill," likewise present. As soon as the Court broke up, I burst into Mill's room, boiling over with indignation, and exclaiming, "What an infamous shame!" and no doubt adding a good deal more that followed in natural sequence on such an exordium. "What's the matter?" replied Mill as soon as he could get a word in. "M—— [the director] was quite right. The petition was the joint work of—— and myself." – "How can you be so perverse?" I retorted. "You know that I know you wrote every word of it." – "No," rejoined Mill, "you are mistaken: one whole line on the second page was put in by ——."

In August, 1858, the East-India Company's doom was pronounced by Parliament. The East-India House was completely re-organized, its very name being changed into that of the India Office, and a Secretary of State in Council taking the place of the Court of Directors. But a change of scarcely secondary importance to many of those immediately concerned was Mill's retirement on a pension. A few months after he had left us an attempt was made to bring him back. At that time only one-half of the Council were nominated by the Crown, the other half having been elected, and the law prescribing that any vacancy among these latter should be filled by election on the part of the remaining elected members. On the first occasion of the kind that occurred, Mill was immediately proposed; and I had the honor of being commissioned to sound him on the subject of the intended offer, and to endeavor to overcome the objections to acceptance which it was feared he might entertain. I went accordingly to his house at Blackheath, but had no sooner broached the subject than I saw that my mission was hopeless. The anguish of his recent bereavement was as yet too fresh. He sought eagerly for some slight alleviation of despair in hard literary labor; but to face the outside world was for the present impossible.

Here my scanty record must end, unless I may be permitted to supplement its meagerness by one or two personal – not to say egotistical – reminiscences. The death of Mr. Mill senior, in 1836, had occasioned a vacancy at the bottom of the examiner's office, to which I was appointed through the kindness of Sir James Carnac, then chairman of the Company, in whose gift it was. Within a few months, however, I was transferred to a newly-created branch of the secretary's office; owing to which cause, and perhaps also to a little (or not a little) mutual shyness, I for some years came so seldom into contact with Mr. Mill, that, though he of course knew me by sight, we scarcely ever spoke, and generally passed each other without any mark of recognition when we happened to meet in or out of doors. Early in 1846, however, I sent him a copy of a book I had just brought out, on "Over-population." A day or two afterwards he came into my room to thank me for it; and during the half-hour's conversation that thereupon ensued, sprang up, full grown at its birth, an intimate friendship, of which I feel that I am not unduly boasting in declaring it to have been equally sincere and fervent on both sides. From that time for the next ten or twelve years, a day seldom passed without, if I did not go into his room, his coming into mine, often telling me as he entered, that he had nothing particular to say; but that, having a few minutes to spare, he thought we might as well have a little talk. And what talks we have had on such occasions, and on what various subjects! and not unfrequently, too, when the room was Mill's, Grote, the historian, would join us, first announcing his advent by a peculiar and ever-welcome rat-tat with his walking stick on the door. I must not dwell longer over these recollections; but there are two special obligations of my own to Mill which I cannot permit myself to pass over. When, in 1856, he became examiner, he had made it, as I have been since assured by the then chairman of the East-India Company, a condition of his acceptance of the post, that I, whose name very likely the Chairman had never before heard, should be associated with him as one of his assistant examiners; and I was placed, in consequence, in charge of the Public-Works Department. Not long afterwards, having lapsed into a state of nervous weakness, which for nearly a year absolutely incapacitated me for mental labor, I should, but for Mill, have been compelled to retire from the service. From this, however, he saved me by quietly taking upon himself, and for the space of twelve months discharging, the whole of my official duties, in addition to his own. Is it wonderful that such a man, supposed by those who did not know him to be cold, stern, and dry, should have been enthusiastically beloved by those who did?

It is little to say, that my own friendship with him was, from first to last, never once ruffled by difference or misunderstanding of any kind. Differences of opinion we had in abundance; but my open avowal of them was always recognized by him as one of the strongest proofs of respect, and served to cement instead of weakening our attachment.* The nearest approach made throughout our intercourse to anything of an unpleasant character was about the time of his retirement from the India House. Talking over that one day with two or three of my colleagues, I said it would not do to let Mill go without receiving some permanently-visible token of our regard. The motion was no sooner made than it was carried by acclamation. Every member of the examiners' office – for we jealously insisted on confining the affair to ourselves – came tendering his subscription, scarcely waiting to be asked; in half an hour's time some fifty or sixty pounds – I forget the exact sum – was collected, which in due course was invested in a superb silver inkstand, designed by our friend Digby Wyatt, and manufactured by Messrs. Elkington. Before it was ready, however, an unexpected trouble arose. In some way or other, Mill had got wind of our proceeding, and, coming to me in consequence, began almost to upbraid me as its originator. I had never before seen him so angry. He hated all such demonstrations, he said, and was quite resolved not to be made the subject of them. He was sure they were never altogether genuine or spontaneous; there were always several persons who took part in them merely because they did not like to refuse; and, in short, whatever we might do, he would have none of it. In vain I represented how eagerly everybody, without exception, had come forward; that we had now gone too far to recede; that, if he would not take the inkstand, we should be utterly at a loss what to do with it; and that I myself should be in a specially embarassing position. Mill was not to be moved. This was a question of principle; and on principle he could not give way. There was nothing left, therefore, but resort to a species of force. I arranged with Messrs. Elkington that out little testimonial should be taken down to Mr. Mill's house at Blackheath by one of their men, who, after leaving it with the servant, should hurry away without waiting for an answer. This plan succeeded; but I have always suspected, though she never told me so, that its success was mainly due to Miss Helen Taylor's good offices. But for her, the inkstand would almost certainly have been returned, instead of being promoted, as it eventually was, to a place of honor in her own and her father's drawing-room.

Mine is scarcely just now the mood in which I should have been naturally disposed to relate anecdotes like this; but, in the execution of my present task, I have felt bound chiefly to consider what would be likely to interest the reader.

* I may be permitted here, without Mr. Thornton's knowledge, to recall a remark made by Mr. Mill only a few weeks ago. We were speaking of Mr. Thornton's recently-published "Old-Fashioned Ethics and Common-Sense Metaphysics," when I remarked on Mr. Mill's wide divergence from most of the views contained in it. "Yes," he replied, "it is pleasant to find *something* on which to differ from Thornton's refutation of the wage-fund theory is only one out of numberless instances of his peculiar magnanimity. – B.

THE ECONOMIC DEFINITION OF WEALTH

Thornton, William, "The Economic Definition of Wealth", *Fortnightly Review*, April (23), 1875, pp. 566–74.

In this short essay, Thornton made an attempt to clarify one of the fundamental concepts in political economy, wealth, while stressing the three characteristics: utility, difficulty of acquisition, and exchangeability. In 1875, his opinion was put forward at the Political Economy Club.

The Economic Definition of Wealth

A Political economist, selecting this as a subject of discourse, may almost be suspected of wishing to bring contempt on his own special science, against which it truly is grave matter for reproach that, a full century after the earliest patriarch, the great Adam of Economics, put forth his "Inquiry into the Nature and Causes of the Wealth of Nations," his disciples should not have satisfied themselves what things are and what are not wealth. It is much as if geographers had not made up their minds whether by the earth, whose contour they undertake to delineate, is to be understood the globe which we inhabit only, or its atmospheric envelope also; or, as if astronomers had split into opposing sects upon the point whether the angelic, equally with the starry host, ought not be reckoned among heavenly bodies. At all events, the economic question before us, being notoriously still open, as widely open as ever, there can be no doubt of the paramount importance of closing it; for, lying, as it does, at the very basis of all economic speculation, it must, as long as it is left unsettled, continue to operate there as a perpetually disturbing force, and it is superfluous to insist on the inevitable shakiness of every superstructure raised upon perpetually reeling foundations.

What then is wealth? What are the peculiar qualities, the presence of which in some things causes those things to be classed as wealth, in opposition to others to which that appellation is denied? There are two such qualities. In the first place, it is plainly indispensable – etymologically indispensable, indeed – that wealth should possess utility, in the sense of conducing, or at least of being supposed to conduce, to human *weal* or well-being; in other words, that it should be capable of ministering to some human want or wish. No definition of wealth is admissible that does not exclude all things which, being utterly destitute of utility, real or supposed, no one can desire to possess. A thing must not, however, be useful only; it must, in addition, be somewhat difficult of acquisition. Nothing can be more useful than air; but, in ordinary situations, every one obtains without exertion as much as he wishes of such air as is then and there in anywise obtainable, and no one in such situations would be a whit the richer for having, in addition to the air supplied gratuitously to all present in unlimited abundance, air stored up in reservoirs for his own exclusive consumption. Even air, however, when unprocurable without effort may become wealth, and wealth of the most precious description. The captives in the Black Hole of Calcutta would very likely have surrendered all they had in the world for the sake of air enough to breathe; and an asthmatic old gentleman or lady, shut up in a stuffy railway carriage, would gladly give the guard a shilling to let a tight window down, and to let air in. Utility, then, and difficulty of acquisition are the characteristic constituents of wealth – of wealth in its widest and most comprehensive sense – in that loose and elastic sense in which it is sometimes colloquially treated; as, for instance, when we say that a man has a treasure in his wife or is rich in the possession of a contented disposition. Wherever both qualities exist in combination, there wealth is present: wherever either of the two is absent, wealth likewise is absent.

Political economists, however, have not been content with the definition here indicated. They have observed that, from combination of the two qualities just spoken of, commonly, though not invariably, results a third, viz. Exchangeability. If you have something, capable of being made over from yourself to another person, which another person desires to have but cannot independently acquire without trouble, he will, in order to be saved the trouble give you something else in exchange for it. If Brown and Robinson have between them the main materials of a dinner, Brown having a beefsteak, and Robinson a pot of porter, and if Brown long for some of Robinson's porter, and Robinson for some of Brown's steak, the idea of exchanging portions of their respective viands is pretty sure to occur to them, and equally sure to be acted upon. Wherefore it has by political economists been decided that upon the presence or absence of exchangeability shall depend the presence or absence of *economic* wealth. According to this view, everything whatsoever which is exchangeable is economic wealth: nothing whatever is economic wealth which is not exchangeable; and it may be noted in favour of this view that the maxims of political economy will be found to apply to exchangeable things only – that these alone are ever supposed to be subject to one of the so-called "laws" if the economic code.

In order, however, to be properly classifiable as economic wealth it is necessary that a thing should be *immediately* exchangeable. The exchangeability, which is the essence of economic wealth, need not be capable of being forthwith exercised, but may remain latent and dormant for an indefinite period. It will scarcely be asserted that Alexander Selkirk, all alone by himself on Juan Fernandez, was not, immediately after killing his first goat, and thus acquiring the prerequisites of his first meat dinner, a richer man than he had been just before. The goat's flesh was to him not the less intrinsically wealth because there was no one at hand with whom it might be exchanged for wealth of some other kind. Neither, of the goats subsequently killed or captured by him, will it be said that none of them became wealth until a vessel, chancing to touch at the island, brought thither customers with whom they might be bartered. Or, if this indeed be said, if the name "wealth" did not properly belong to the goats previously to the arrival of the customers, then equally ought it be withheld from all commodities whatever while on their way to market – from a cargo of corn, for instance, while passing from port to port. At this rate, the same corn which was indisputably wealth when shipped at Odessa, would cease to be wealth on reaching Liverpool or London. Such extreme analyzation may possibly be harmless, but it is certainly gratuitous, and no apology shall here be offered for disregarding it.

Wealth, then, of the economic sort, being perceived to be distinct from the miscellaneous compound colloquially so designated, and exchangeability being perceived to be its essence and recognised as its test, our chief perplexities might seem to be at an end. We have now got a perfect test, and have nothing to do but to apply it properly, in order to ascertain conclusively what things are and what are not economic wealth. In practice, however, this operation has not proved quite so easy as might have been expected. In respect to material, corporeal things, indeed, there is no difficulty. No one need remain for a moment dubious whether any one of these is or is not exchangeable. But with immaterial, incorporeal things, the case is somewhat otherwise, many of the most eminent economists, although agreed that exchangeability is the test of economic wealth, having classed under that head several things which are demonstrably incapable of being exchanged.

Thus, Adam Smith, Senior, Whately, and John Stuart Mill give, in their economic treatises, the name of wealth to all human qualities and aptitudes, bodily or mental, natural or acquired, which are capable of being employed in the production of material wealth they give it, that is, to the bodily strength and technical aptitudes of all productive labourers; plausibly arguing that, if two men, both equally penniless, but the one strong, intelligent, and expert, and the other weak, stupid, and clumsy, the first is intrinsically richer than the second. As, likewise, a country abounding with workmen able of body and mind is *pro tanto* richer than a country whose workpeople are, for the most part, feeble and shiftless. Other economists, and among them Mr. Dunning Macleod, go still farther, classifying as wealth all technical aptitudes whatever, even those incapable of being employed otherwise than unproductively; the skill, for instance, of a musician or an actor not less than that of a husbandman or an artificer; nor more, I presume, an actor or musician's talent than the symmetric plumpness of Mr. Jeames Yellowplush's calves, to which their owner is in great measure indebted for the high wages he receives. Others again (Mr. Macleod, if I mistake not, still included), would place in the same category not only the aptitudes themselves, but also every exertion of them by which their owner earns remuneration; they would place there a ploughman or mason's labour, the air played or the song sung by a musician, and the theatrical performance of a dramatist; they would place there, in short, not simply all aptitudes possessed, but all services rendered by virtue of those aptitudes; not simply the beauty of Mr. Yellowplush's calves, but also his display therof behind his mistress's carriage.

Now, with regard to all technical aptitudes, whether productive or unproductive, it cannot be denied that to them belong both of those primary essentials, power of gratifying human desire and difficulty of acquisition, and that they do consequently come well within the loose and expansible limits of the colloquial definition of wealth. Commonly, however, they lack the third essential unanimously insisted on by economists – they lack exchangeability. Except when embodied in the person of a slave, they cannot possibly become the subjects of exchange. The personal qualities of freemen may be wealth, but cannot possibly be economic wealth.

To be convinced of this it may suffice to bear in mind, that to every exchange there must be two parties, between whom a double transfer must take place, each of the two divesting himself of something which he previously possessed, making it over to the other, and receiving something in return – something which that other has parted with. Now, unless when a person either sells himself for a slave or, being already a slave, is sold by his master, it is impossible for any of his qualities, natural or acquired, to be transferred to a new owner. A freeman may lose his strength and skill by intemperance, or illness or lapse of time, but in no wise can he sell or transfer them; no one else can, by purchase or barter or any other means, become possesor of both of them. A clever man and a stupid man cannot, by any mercantile operation, exchange characters – the clever man becoming stupid and the stupid clever. Technical aptitudes, be it repeated unless embodied in a slave, cannot be exchanged, and cannot, therefore, except when so embodied, be economic wealth.

To this it is no reply to say, that the possessor of technical skill or knowledge may impart them to others by instruction. The very phrase, "imparting knowledge," is a misnomer. In the act of instruction, nothing is parted with by the instructor: instead of thereby lessening, he rather increases his own knowledge: he gives away nothing. What he does is to cause knowledge, similar to his own, to enter into or grow up in his pupil's mind, thereby doing to his pupil a service more or less important, and probably receiving from him a substantial recompense; but still neither effecting, nor participating in, any genuine exchange. That this is so, if not already sufficiently clear, may be rendered clearer by reference to services other than instruction. No service whatever can possibly exchanged. The performance of stipulated service is never the transfer to the employer of something previously possessed by the employee. When one person works for another, he is indeed colloquially described as giving that other his labour; but labour is not a thing, but an action. It is simply the exercise of certain powers or faculties, and to talk of giving away or selling it is tacitly to that in a mere metaphor, in a mere mental abstraction there is, or can be, property capable of being possessed and parted with. Truly, when such an expression is used, it is not labour itself, but the fruit or result of labour never belonged to the labourer. The result of a ploughman's toil is to cause land, previously hard and even-surfaced, to be broken up into ridges and furrows; the result of a weaver's operations is to cause threads to take a new special arrangement. Did, then, the ridges and furrows ever belong to the ploughman, or the special arrangement of threads to the weaver? And when we pay for hearing a musical performance, is there any intelligible sense in which the performance can be said to have become our property? Even if it were correct to say that the songs of airs we have been listening to were previously the musician's, is there any conceivable mode in which they can have ceased to be his and to have become ours? When we pay a guinea for a stall at the opera, or drop a shilling into the hat of a street bandmaster, is it for aught else than for the pleasure which we either expect to enjoy, or have been enjoying? But is the pleasure which we receive from hearing of the same kind as that which musicians derive from singing or playing? And even if it were of the same kind, would they be parting with a certain portion of their pleasure, and we be receiving the same identical portion? If not, if they do not part with pleasure, there can be no transfer of pleasure from them to us; and if no transfer, then, of course, no exchange of it with our money. Perhaps, in thus speaking, I may be considered to be over-refining – indulging in over-nice and fanciful distinctions. Perhaps, in spite of all I have said, it may still be contended that musical and theatrical performances are economic wealth, because payment may readily be obtained in return for them; if so, it may be proper to allude to certain other performances in return for which payment may similarly be obtained. People may be wheedled out of their money by flattery, or cheated out of it by false pretences are wealth? In scientific discussion no distinctions are too nice – none which we can disregard without imminent risk of becoming involved in very nasty perplexities.

Sufficient cause has now, perhaps been shown why certain descriptions of immaterial entities cannot be brought within the economic definition of wealth: faculties, bodily or mental, and mental acquirements, because they are incapable of being exchanged; and exertions or manifestations of faculties, because these, not simply cannot be exchanged, but cannot even be possessed. What then are the immaterial constituents, without, I believe, an exception, will be found, on examination, to resolve themselves into legal rights privileges. A privilege is never aught else than legal permission to its owner to do certain things which other people would like to do, but are legally debarred from doing. If, then, the privilege be practically and also legally transferable, there will generally be other persons willing to give something in order to get it transferred to them, and the privilege, being thus exchangeable, is by consequence, economically, wealth. Among privileges of this sort are copyright, or the exclusive right of printing and publishing certain books; patent right, or the exclusive privilege of the undertaking; the goodwill of a business, which is a little else than the right to occupy certain premises, which a certain set of customers, clients, or patients are in the habit of frequenting; and, notably, all kinds of credit; every species of lien on a debtor's assets, in whatsoever manner the lien be recorded, whether by bank notes of hand, bills of exchange, I.O.U.'s, debenture or other bonds, or simple registration. Whatever the right or privilege be, if it be one which other people covet, and the transfer of which is permitted by law, it is to all intents and purposes economic wealth in virtue of its exchangeability. Even empty titles or honour, even a baronet's right to place Sir before his name, and Bart. after it, nay even Lord Kingsales's right to wear his hat in a sovereign's presence, would be as distinctly wealth as the most substantial of goods and chattels, provided only the owners of the rights were at liberty to sell and could meet with customers silly enough to purchase them. But between the economic wealth thus immaterially constituted, between transferable privileges and material wealth, there is a most important distinction, a distinction deserving the most particular attention. Indeed, whatever practical value there may be in what has been already said, consists entirely in the lead thereby afforded up to what is about to be said at this point.

All material wealth, all tangible riches of whatever kind – lands, houses, merchandise, coin, bullion – are wealth, not simply to their individual owners, but also to the community at large, of which those individuals are members. Obviously, the greater the quantity of material property possessed by a particular individual, the greater likewise the aggregate quantity possessed by the whole community to which the individual belongs. Obviously, every fresh house built, every fresh piece of land reclaimed from the sea, every commodity newly produced, not only tends to enrich its possessor, but is also an addition to the total amount of national wealth; but with respect to transferable rights or privileges, which as we have seen, are the sole constituents of immaterial wealth, the case is widely different. To their immediate owners, indeed, the privileges are as completely wealth as any of the material things for which they are exchangeable. Their owners cannot, however, exercise them except at the expense of other people. What the owners gain by them, other people lose. In the same proportion in which those are enriched by them, these are impoverished. In precisely the same proportion, for instance, in which copyright enables certain persons to make profit by the exclusive sale of certain books, it prevents other persons from making similar profit, or prevents a portion of the profit from remaining untouched in the pockets of purchasers of books. So, likewise, of patent rights, and of the right involved in what is called the goodwill of a business; and so in especial of all kinds of credit. All credit implies the existence of an equal amount of debt; it signifies that certain things actually in the possession of certain debtors, belong not to those debtors but to their creditors. The whole value of credit consists in its empowering a creditor to recover from another's grasp what is his own – to take from another in order to take to himself. This power of recovery may be transferred to a third person by sale, and, being thus saleable or exchangeable, is, in the strictest economic sense, wealth; but to whatever extent it is wealth to the creditor, it is poverty to the debtor. By its exercise, not the smallest difference is made in the total of wealth previously belonging to both debtor and creditor; that total is not one jot either increased or diminished. Moreover, the power cannot be exercised, whether by the original creditor or by a creditor who has subsequently acquired it by purchase, without becoming extinguished. When completely exercised, it is completely extinguished; but by its extinction no wealth has been destroyed; the total of wealth belonging to both creditor and debtor still remains precisely the same as before. Liquidation, too, is not the sole means of virtually extinguishing debts; they may be repudiated, or all evidence of them may be lost. Suppose that in a fit of patriotic enthusiasm – like that with which the *noblesse* of France were seized on the memorable August night, when they laid the whole tree of feudalism in successive billets on Freedom's altar – English fundholders should unanimously resolve to commit to the flames all registers and records of the national debt; or suppose that, in some similarly semi-miraculous mode, all bank notes, bills of exchange, and other instruments of credit should suddenly be burnt or otherwise disappear; is it not clear that the community would be neither richer nor poorer in consequence? – that although multitudes would lose immensely, other multitudes would gain all that had been lost, the aggregate national wealth remaining just as before, without augmentation or diminution. Or suppose, conversely, that the legislature should authorise or require the Bank of England to double the nominal amount of money in circulation, by lavish issues of inconvertible paper; or that all the rich men in the country, after listening to such a sermon as Peter preached at Jerusalem on the day of Pentecost, should consent that henceforth all men should have all things in common, and should commence by a distribution of cheques among their poorer brethren, thereby conveying to the latter the whole of their bank balances; would the community, as a whole, be any richer than before? Would not the multiplication of bank notes, which conveyed to the recipients of the new notes a power of participation in the total stock of commodities on sale throughout the land, be productive of and accompanied by a depreciation of the currency, which would reduce, in precisely the same measure, the power of participation previously enjoyed by the holder of the old notes? Would not the supposed distribution of cheques simply transfer a similar power of participation from a number of rich to a number of poor? Is it not obvious that every multiplication or fresh creation of credits is tantamount to, nay, is identical with, the creation of an equal number and amount of new debts? And would it not be preposterous to suggest that individual members of a community can, by getting into debt, increase, nor a destruction of credits can diminish, national wealth, is it not self-evident that credit cannot possibly be one of the components of national wealth?

And as of credit – as of the creditor's rights and privileges in respect to his debtor – so likewise of all other exchangeable rights and privileges. Every privilege whatsoever implies the investiture of its owner with certain liberty of action abstracted from the liberty of action of some other person or person's. There are no privileges that can be exercised by their owners without preventing other people from becoming similarly enriched. The creation of new privileges or the abolition of old ones, how much soever it may add to or take from individual members of a community, can neither add to nor take from the aggregate wealth of the same community – cannot therefore augment or diminish national wealth by one iota. No privilege, therefore, can possibly enter into the composition of national wealth. Of *national* wealth, observe; for credit and all other exchangeable privileges are to their individual owners wealth, to all intents and purposes – wealth as distinctly and incontestably, notwithstanding their immateriality, as any of the material things for which they are capable of being exchanged. And not simply are they wealth, they are likewise economic wealth. This they are, in the strictest sense of the term, by virtue of their exchangeability; but it is not unimportant also, to point out that of one of the principal items of immaterial wealth – viz. Credit, in its various forms and guises – political economy takes scarcely less note than it does of the most solidly material wealth. To call, then, political economy, as is not unfrequently done, the science of national wealth, is very far from accurate; credit, albeit no element of national wealth, being a subject with which political economy is largely and closely concerned. And what is thus said of credit applies more or less to all other exchangeable rights. There is not one of these of which political economy does not or may not legitimately take cognizance; there is not one of them, therefore, which does not, not simply in virtue of its exchangeablity, but also for an additional reason, deserve to be classed under the head of economic wealth.

Nevertheless, although all immaterial wealth is undoubtedly entitled to be styled economic wealth, the expediency of its being so styled is a distinctly separate question, and there is good ground for urging that the word "wealth" when employed in economic discussions, should be rigidly restricted to material things, and should never be suffered to indicate immaterial entities. For material and immaterial wealth, although possessing in common the one single quality of exchangeability, differ so diametrically as to all other attributes, that to class them under the same name cannot but lead, as in fact it repeatedly has led, to disastrous confusion. It is this alone that can account for the amazing muddle with which the national debt and national riches are frequently found jumbled together, even in sensible people's minds; this which has given birth to all those paper-currency nostrums which from time to time have done such an immensity of mischief in our own and many other countries. It might greatly conduce to clearness of thought on mists were to agree either that by the word "wealth" they will understand material wealth only, or that they will never use the word without an adjective prefix, indicating whether material or immaterial wealth is the species referred to.

PROFESSOR CAIRNES ON VALUE

Thornton, William, "Professor Cairnes on Value",
Contemporary Review, October (28), 1876, pp. 813–15.

In this critical essay, Thornton discussed, with great precision, his own view on the laws of supply and demand, and also reviewed John Elliott Cairnes's *Some Leading Principles of Political Economy Newly Expounded.*

Professor Cairnes on Value

MOST members of the Political Economy Club must be familiar with an anecdote of Sydney Smith, who not many months after joining the club announced his intention to retire, and, on being asked the reason, replied that his chief motive for joining had been to discover what Value is, but that all he had discovered was that the rest of the club knew as little about the matter as he did. That this sarcasm, however, severe, was probably not unmerited, may be inferred from the haze with which the object of Sydney Smith's curiosity is still surrounded, and from the, at best, but very partial success of the recent attempt made by so powerful a thinker as my lamented friend, the late Professor Cairnes, to pierce the cloudy envelope.

In common parlance, the word Value has more than one signification, but, at the outset of his "Leading Principles,"* Cairnes represents all economists as agreed that in economic discussion, the term should be restricted to "expressing the ratio in which commodities are commercially exchangeable against each other" – against *each other,* be it observed, not against some selected commodity – and this ratio he proposes to call "exchange value." Evidently, according to this definition, "a general rise or a general fall of values is," as Cairnes says, "an impossibility, or rather a contradiction in terms," for, "if," as he continues, " a rise in relation to B, B must fall in relation to A: A and B cannot both rise or both fall in relation to each other: and what is true of two commodities is true of any number and of all commodities." Nevertheless, and although, according to his view, value "expresses simply a relation," Cairnes adds that "we may without impropriety use such expressions as 'a sum of values,' or 'an increase or diminution in the aggregate amount of values.' "

> "Where," he says, "the quantity of valuable things possessed by a community has been increased, the conditions of production remaining the same; or where, the quantity remaining the same, the conditions of producing commodities have been so altered as to cause a given quantity to exchange for a larger quantity than before of commodities of which the conditions of production have remained constant; in either of these cases we may not improperly say that the sum of the values or the aggregate amount of values has increased."

Here, however, it may naturally be asked, if there be such a thing as sum of such values as are here in question, how is that sum to be expressed? Suppose that,

* Some Leading Principles of Political Economy newly Expounded. By J. E. Cairnes, M. A. Macmillan & Co.

butter being commercially exchangeable for twice its weight of beef and six times its weight of bread, Thomson have one pound of each of those three articles of food, how can we, consistently with the definition, express their aggregate value otherwise than by saying that it consists of twice the beef's worth or six times the bread's worth of butter, half the butter's worth of beef, and one-sixth of the butter's worth of bread? But by such language not the faintest idea of totality is conveyed. For, if the quantity of Thomson's provisions should be doubled, if instead of one pound he became possessed of two pounds of each of the commodities named, the sum of their exchange values would remain unaltered, being still twice the beef's worth or six times the bread's worth of butter, and half the butter's worth and one-sixth of the butter's worth of beef and bread respectively? Again, if while as yet Thomson had consumed no part of his stock of food, butter's exchangeable value doubled, it would by no means follow that the sum of Thomson's values had increased, because his butter was now worth twice as much beef or bread as before, if on the other hand, his beef and bread had each become worth only half as much butter as before.

Cairnes imagines that use of the terms "sum of values," and "increase of diminution in the aggregate amount of values," may be illustrated and justified by analogous expressions employed with reference to power.

> "Power, like value," he says, "expresses a relation, and a general increase of the power of individuals or of nations in relation to each other is, of course, an impossibility. But this does not prevent our saying that the aggregate power of any given number of individuals or nations has increased, meaning thereby, not that their relative position has been altered, but that the elements which go to support power in them have been multiplied. We should thus say that the power of European nations has greatly increased within the last century. In a precisely similar sense we may speak, and it will often be convenient to speak, of an increase or diminution of aggregate values, value being only another name for purchasing power."

But here Mr. Cairnes overlooks an important distinction. Power in general, although like every other quality it may be relative, is not a mere relation, but an independent entity. The power of any given individual or nation would not the less be a reality even though there were no other individual or nation with would not the less be a reality even though there were no other individual or nation with whose power it could be compared, and would not the less be susceptible of augmentation or diminution. But exchange value, according to the definition, is a relation pure and simple, and nothing else; and, as Mr. Cairnes had just before conclusively shown, the relation of thing to other things cannot possibly increase without being accompanied by a corresponding decrease in the relation of those other things to it. If then it be true that political economy takes cognisance of no other value than "exchange value," and if the foregoing definition of exchange value be, as I believe it to be, strictly accurate, political economy plainly can no more recognize an increase or diminution in the aggregate amount of values than it can a general rise or a general fall of values.

Cairnes seems to me to have complicated the question and to have deceived himself by pronouncing "exchange value" to be but another name for "purchasing power." For he had already accepted "exchange value" as but another name for "ratio of exchange," and purchasing power is obviously not simply ratio of exchange, but also, or rather, to use Cairnes' own words, "the sum of the conditions which determine that ratio." Understood in this enlarged sense, the purchasing power of the whole world not only may, but must, increase or decrease simultaneously with any increase or decrease in the total quantity of purchaseable commodities existing in the world, inasmuch as it must necessarily coincide with that total quantity. But, as we have seen, the quantity of each of the commodities might be doubled, and their aggregate exchange value of that other decreasing in precisely the same proportion in respect of it. Wherefore, "exchange value" and "purchasing power" are clearly not synonymous terms. Nay, if they were, it would on that very account be absolutely impossible to sum up the total purchasing power of the world in any such language as would convey the smallest notion of its amount. Nothing, for example, would be gained by simply saying that it was equal to so much more of butter than of beef or bread, or to so much less silver or gold than of butter.

Yet there can be no doubt that economists, when speaking of value, are often, and indeed generally, thinking of a quality the aggregate amount of which may increase or diminish, and may also be expressed in words or figures. Undoubtedly they do generally use the term in a sense according to which, if one man possess twice as much of precisely the same articles as another man, the value of the first man's possessions is double that of the second's. Moreover, if it be desired to state the total value of the property of either of the two, that may readily be done, all that is requisite for the purpose being to specify for how much of butter, or of gold, or of silver, or of any other selected commodity, the whole of the property might be exchanged. But evidently the sense in which the term value is used on such an occasion is very different from that to which Cairnes' definition would restrict it. The fact is that not in common parlance only, but also in economic discussion, value signifies not one thing but two things, indicating sometimes what Cairnes calls "exchange value," sometimes what he calls "price," but for which I would suggest in preference the name of "pecuniary value," as denoting not merely the exchangeable relation between any given commodities and metallic or paper money, but also the same relation between them and whatever commodities were selected as the instrument of exchange – as, for instance, *pecudes*, heads of cattle or sheep, from whose employment in primeval Italy for the purpose of commercial valuation the word "pecuniary" is derived. Of this second species of value Cairnes speaks as follows: –

> "Though commodities in general cannot rise or fall simultaneously in relation to each other, they may rise or fall in relation to any selected one amongst the number, and if gold or silver be the one selected, commodities in general may rise or fall in

relation to a commodity thus selected is called price. It is plain, then, that while a general rise or a general fall of prices is a perfectly possible, as indeed it is a not uncommon event."

When Cairnes has taken such pains to distinguish between exchange value and price, we ought not hastily to suspect him of afterwards inadvertently confounding them; yet it is certain that he has confounded them so far as to attribute to one a faculty which, according to his own showing, belongs exclusively to the other. He has unconsciously attempted the impossible feat of including two distinct things within one and the same definition. His definition of exchange value is unimpeachable while confined to its proper subject, but it cannot be stretched beyond its legitimate domain without involving palpable inconsistencies. Obviously enough, prices or pecuniary values may be summed up into a total, and that total may subsequently increase or diminish; but sums total of and augmentations or diminutions of general exchange values are, quite as obviously, impossible conceptions.

Yet, distinct as exchange value and pecuniary value are in one essential particular, there are three conditions common to both – three conditions indispensable to the existence of either in any commodity. There must be – first, utility, in the sense of ability real or imaginary of conducing to the gratification of some human desire; secondly, difficulty of acquisition, since no one will give that which cannot be obtained without trouble for a thing which he can obtain by simply wishing for it; thirdly, transferability, since it is impossible to exchange a thing of which the owner cannot divest himself, and which he cannot make over to another person. These propositions are palpable truisms, affording no ground for intelligent controversy; but as to what constitutes utility, there has been and still is sufficient doubt among economists to require that a word or two should be said on the subject, though for the sake of brevity, I shall, without referring to the opinions of others, restrict myself to indicating my own.

By utility, whether the term be used colloquially or in economic discussion, is invariable to be understood the quality of conducing to the gratification of some human desire. Such utility is commonly independent of the ease or difficulty of acquiring a commodity. Water, for instance, would equally quench thirst, and perform most of its other offices, whether obtainable for nothing or obtainable only a great expenditure of labour. Sometimes, however, the utility of an article is partly due to the difficulty of acquisition, its utility in that case consisting partly in gratification of its owner's vanity. If diamonds were to become as common as pebbles, they would still be equally pleasing to the eye; but, the possession of them having ceased to be a distinction, there would no longer be the same desire to possess them, the ability to gratify which desire constitutes great part of their present utility. Difficulty of acquisition therefore, besides being always an indispensable condition of exchangeability, is sometimes a principal element in utility likewise.

Thus much being premised, let us now attempt a somewhat higher strain *paulo majora canamus:* warning being at the same time given that we are about to enter the high latitudes of the science, where closer attention than the reader may perhaps be much disposed to bestow will be requisite in order to steer clear of rocks and breakers. He should remember, however, that it is the track taken by Professor Cairnes through these ill-explored regions which I propose to examine, and that the navigation must needs be more than ordinarily intricate where so skilful a pilot has, as I expect to be able to show, fatally mistaken his course.

In a digression which he finds it necessary to make into the region of supply and demand, Cairnes begins by pointing out, more clearly than had ever been done before, what only needs to be pointed out in order to be forthwith perceived to be true in one special set of circumstances, that

> "conceived as aggregates, supply and demand are not independent phenomena of which either may indefinitely increase or diminish irrespective of the other, but phenomena strictly connected and mutually dependent; so strictly connected and interdependent that (excluding temporary effects, and contemplating them as permanent and normal facts) neither can increase or diminish without necessitating and implying a corresponding increase or diminution of the other."

As long as commercial transactions are confined to barter – as long, that is, as no selected commodity is employed as a medium of exchange, supply is the quantity of commodities offered for sale, demand the quantity of commodities which customers offer or are about to offer to purchase. But to offer either to sell or to buy is to propose that certain kinds of goods shall be exchanged for other kinds. Every offer to sell is therefore equally an offer to buy, and every offer to buy is equally an offer to sell. The sum total of goods which customers offer to purchase is consequently identical with the sum total offered for sale. Of any particular commodity, indeed, either the supply may increase without any increase in demand, or the demand may increase without any increase in the supply. But "aggregate demand cannot increase or diminish without entailing a corresponding increase or diminution of aggregate supply; nor can aggregate supply undergo a change without involving a corresponding change in aggregate demand."

All this is self-evident as soon as stated,* but the truth which it embodies is rather curious than important, and, moreover, ceases to be truth when extended, as it is by Professor Cairnes, beyond the domain of barter. Cairnes has most

* It may be objected that among the articles offered for sale, may be some for which, on account of their having become obsolete, or for any other cause, there may be no demand, in which case aggregate supply will be in excess of aggregate demand. But to such hypercriticism Mr. Cairnes might fairly have replied that articles which have ceased to be objects of human desire have likewise ceased to be, in an economic sense, goods or commodities, and cannot therefore really form a portion of supply.

seriously misapprehended and underrated the changes consequent on the adoption of a medium of exchange, or, in other words, of money in any of its various forms. He does indeed observe, and in this instance also he was, I believe, the first to make the observation, that under a monetary *régime* supply and demand become distinguishable, which they previously were not. He very justly points out that, after money has come into general use, money without much inaccuracy be regarded as *representing* "general purchasing power," inasmuch as every proposal to sell is now an offer of money, while doubt, therefore, it now becomes possible to distinguish between aggregate supply and aggregate demand, the former consisting of all goods offered for money, the latter of all money offered for goods. But Cairnes is surely mistaken in regarding money as not merely the representative, but also the *measure*, of purchasing power, and therefore the measure likewise of demand, for the supply of money in circulation, or even in existence at any given time and place, is almost always worth many times less than the whole quantity of goods on sale, and requires to be used over and over again in order to effect the purchase of that whole quantity; and large purchases, too, are continually made upon credit by persons who have no money in hand. A yet more serious mistake on his part is that of supposing that the entire *supply* of goods still continues to represent an equal *demand* for goods. No doubt equally under a *régime* of barter and under a monetary *régime* every offer to sell is at the same time an offer to buy, the only difference being that under the one *régime* it is an offer to buy one or more of all the various commodities in the market, and in the other to buy only the particular commodity or commodities which have been selected to serve the purpose of money. No doubt, therefore, under a monetary *régime* the aggregate supply of goods constitutes a precisely equivalent demand for money in exchange for goods; but it by no means follows that there is a corresponding demand for goods in exchange for money. Purchasing power is not, as Mr. Cairnes supposes, identical with demand. The possessor of purchasing power is not, as he tacitly assumes, bound forthwith to exercise the power. Neither the actual holders of money, nor those persons who may if they please successively obtain money on credit, necessarily require immediately as much of the whole stock of goods in the market as they have the means of immediately purchasing; and, if not, they will probably content themselves with purchasing as much as will suffice for their immediate requirements, and will reserve part of their money or credit for the subsequent requirements. Perhaps it may be objected that, according to this view, the employment of money may diminish the demand for goods, and it may be asked, How can this be, seeing that money is merely the instrument of exchange, and that goods and services alone are ultimate objects of exchange? Of course money can have no such effect. Of course the same total of goods will be bought and sold, whether money be or be not used in aid of the operation. Yet there is a real and material difference between the two cases, for in the one the aggregate of goods brought to market would greater than in the other. While trade was carried on by barter no dealer would offer goods for sale unless he desired certain specific goods in return; neither would he offer more than he supposed sufficient to procure for him the quantity which he needed of those specific goods, whereas under a monetary *régime* a dealer would offer for sale whatever quantity of goods he expected to be able to sell at a remunerative price for money, whether he were or were not prepared immediately to lay out the whole of the expected sale proceeds in the purchase of other goods. I submit, then, in direct opposition to Mr. Cairnes, that the relation of general supply and general demand to each other is very materially affected by the employment of a circulating medium, and becomes essentially different under a monetary from what it was under a barter *régime.* I submit that, under the former, supply and demand *are* "facts of a different order," not indeed "incapable of comparison and measurement," but still "independent facts which may increase or diminish irrespectively of each other." Cairnes stigmatizes all assumptions to this effect as "baseless and absurd." Cairnes did not often permit himself to indulge in such hard words, and it would have been as well if on this occasion also he had adhered to his habitual sobriety of language.

On the strength of the reasoning cited above, Cairnes proceeds to object to the definitions of supply and demand given by Mr. Mill, viz., *the** quantity supplied and *the* quantity demanded, and proposes to substitute the following:–

> "Demand: the desire for commodities or services, seeking its end by an offer of general purchasing power, seeking its end by an offer of general purchasing power. Supply: the desire for general purchasing power, seeking its end by an offer of specific commodities or services."

Among other arguments urged by Cairnes in support of this view is this: that the element of desire involved in both supply and demand is "in each case indefinite and practically unlimited." Now doubtless there is no bound to the quantity of "general purchasing power" (money) which any one offering commodities for sale would be glad to receive in exchange. If he have ten sheep to sell, and expects to get £30 for them, he will not, because he finds he can sell them for £4 instead of £3 apiece, content himself with selling five and withdraw the other five from the market. But on the other hand, if any one who requires ten sheep, and is prepared to pay £40 for them, finds he can get them for £30, he will not necessarily buy thirteen instead of ten, but will more probably prefer to spend only £30 on sheep, and retain the other £10 for subsequent expenditure. Although, therefore, in supply the element of desire be unlimited, in demand it is not so. Among other reasons why Mill's disciples may hesitate to accept Mr. Cairnes' definitions in lieu of those of their master is this, that with Cairnes general purchasing power and money are synonymous terms, and that consequently the form of words

* The definite article is here italicized, because Cairnes inadvertently represents Mill as pronouncing supply and demand to be each simply *a* quantity.

suggested by him could apply only to a monetary *régime*, leaving the *régime* of barter unprovided for.

On a basis thus shown to be unsound, Cairnes proceeds to build up a superstructure which, in spite of the excellence of portions of the workmanship, necessarily partakes largely of the character of the foundation. The fabric consists of somewhat novel theories of cost and production and normal value; but to point out in regular order the several errors which these conceal, might be too severe a tax on the patience of the reader, whose convenience will perhaps be better consulted by my confining myself for the most part to an exposition of what I myself conceive to be the truth of the matter under discussion. I may, however, observe at the outset that, even if Cairnes' novelties were perfectly correct, they would be rather illustrative and amplificatory of, than antagonistic to, the teaching of Mill. It is indeed simply astounding that Cairnes should have so completely misapprehended the meaning of his great predecessor as to suppose the later to have confounded the *cost* with the *results* of production – the *sacrifices* which productive labour exacts with the *reward* which the same labour confers. It is really almost incredible that whereas Mill merely says that, *to the capitalist,* the cost of production consists of the wages and profits which he, the capitalist, *pays and advances,* he should be represented as declaring it to consist of the amount which the capitalist ultimately *receives* for the finished product.

Of all commodities whatsoever, the actual exchange or market values are liable to indefinable fluctuations. In regard, however, to such commodities as are capable or indefinite multiplication, and which moreover are not subject of monopoly, these fluctuations, to whatever distance they may extend in opposite directions, always tend after a while to return to an intermediate level, called by Adam Smith *natural* price, by Mill *necessary* price, and by Cherbuliez and Cairnes *normal* price. This level can, I think, be shown to be determined exclusively and invariably by cost of production, because no one will voluntarily persevere in an occupation the products of which do not usually yield him at least the full equivalent of what they have cost him, so that if they do not yield this equivalent, they will cease to be produced; and, further, because no one will persist in an occupation a given quantity of the products of which commonly exchange for a smaller quantity of the products of some other occupation, in which he is at liberty to engage, than he could procure for himself if he did engage in that other occupation. Whenever, therefore, the vicissitudes of supply and demand cause earnings to differ very sensibly in different employments, capital and labour will be attracted from the worse to the better paid occupations, until, by reason of diminished supply of the products of the former, and augmented supply of those of the latter, both sets of products come to be exchanged in proportion to their respective costs of production.

The essence of the question, however, is barely touched by these remarks. The main point at issue is, whether demand is "measured by the quantity of purchasing offered in support of the desire for commodities," or by the quantity of "particular commodities for which such purchasing power is offered," and the importance of the point cannot easily be overrated, for on it depends the truth or falsity of the wages fund dogma. Now there are "three capital theories in economic science" – those of "wages, money, and foreign trade, in each of which supply and demand form pivots of the doctrine, the two poles on which the exposition turns." Let us then inquire whether it be true, as Cairnes maintains, that in those theories "demand is in every instance regarded as represented and measured, not by the purchasing power offered."

At the threshold of the inquiry it may be observed parenthetically, in regard to commodities proper – in regard, that is, to commodities as distinguished from services – that except when they are put up for sale by auction, an offer of anything in exchange for them is rarely made, it being usually the owner of the commodities who offers to sell them at a certain price, which may be and often is less than the customer would, if necessary, have consented to pay. In respect of commodities proper, then, the price which the customer agrees to pay is no measure of the intensity of his demand, no indication of the maximum amount which he would have been prepared to pay for the gratification of his desire. It is otherwise, indeed, with regard to services. It is usually the employer in quest of labour who offers in the first instance a certain wage; but besides that his first offer is determined with reference to the rate which he supposes the labourers would have demanded if they had taken the initiative, he is often compelled to raise the rate originally proposed by him, yet still may not have to raise it so high as he would have been prepared to do rather than not secured the services he required. As then of commodities proper, so likewise of services, the price finally agreed upon does not measure or constitute demand.

For money, indeed, the demand is undoubtedly identical with the quantity of goods offered for sale. It is so for a reason assigned by Mr. Mill. Every dealer in goods is at the same time a customer for money – not, however, for any definite sum, for he desires to obtain as much as he possible can; and though he commonly names a price at which he is prepared to sell, that price is always the highest at which he expects to be able to sell. Neither is there any price so low that he will not consent to sell at it if he is convinced that by holding out he will not obtain a higher. Clearly, then, demand for money cannot be the quantity demanded, for there is no such quantity, and it must consequently be admitted to be the fact that the sole measure of the demand for money, if it have any measure, is the supply of goods; but this is likewise a fact to which we cannot attribute much importance without great risk of deceiving ourselves. We were but just now priding ourselves on the discovery that the introduction of money enables us to discriminate between aggregate supply and demand, by regarding the former as an operation of dealers in goods, and the latter as an operation of customers for goods. But if, after drawing this distinction, we proceed to treat supply of goods as demand for money, we shall be not discriminating but confounding. We shall be using the same term in senses directly opposed to those just before assigned to them. If, to use Cairnes' own words, demand be simply "desire for commodities or services seeking its end by an offer of general purchasing power," "desire for general purchasing power seeking its end by an offer of specific commodities or services" cannot be demand. Besides, we must never forget that commodities and services alone are ultimate objects of exchange, and that money is merely the medium of exchange. If we choose to consider money as a final object of demand, and if we also treat the entire supply of goods as the measure of demand for money, then the quantity of money in circulation must be equal in value to the entire quantity of goods on sale, whereas it is almost always of far less value. Although, then, the entire supply of goods is in one sense the measure of demand for money, it is so only in a sense in which the terms cannot be employed without manifest inconsistency.

We come now to foreign trade, in regard to which the question that here concerns us is whether a country's "exports represent the force of its demand for foreign products." Now if the country's foreign trade were carried on exclusively by barter, they might at first sight appear to do so. The immediate object of the exporter from any country – say, from England – would then be to exchange the whole of the exports for foreign products, and, however much smaller than he had expected might prove to be the quantity of the latter obtainable in exchange for the former, he might probably accept that smaller quantity rather than be at the trouble and expense of sending home again any part of the English exports. It must be admitted that here demand could not be the quantity demanded, for no definite quantity was demanded. The exporter's desire was to obtain at least the quantity he expected; but, also, if possible, a larger quantity, and the largest quantity possible. It may thus be that even "as the imports of each country represent in relation to it the measure of foreign supply, so its exports represent the force of its demand for foreign products." But it is on the other hand to be noted that although the desire involved in demand for foreign products is not desire for a definite quantity, inasmuch as what the exporters wish for is the very largest quantity obtainable in exchange for their exports, it is yet a quantity not less than would have sufficed to render the exporting operation remunerative. The exporter may indeed be compelled to accept a quantity smaller than this, but if so, the cause is simply that he has miscalculated. If he had foreseen that the quantity obtainable would not be large enough to yield him a profit on resale, he would certainly not have exported so largely, while, contrariwise, he would have exported still more largely if he had hoped thereby to obtain a proportionably larger quantity of foreign products and to be able to resell that larger quantity advantageously. The actual quantity of exports was offered in support of a desire, not for the particular quantity of foreign products actually received in exchange, but for some larger quantity, so that even if it showed – which it does not – what was the maximum of English goods which the exporters were willing to give in exchange for foreign goods, it would still only show that they were willing to exchange this maximum for a quantity large enough to compensate them for the trouble and expense they were incurring – not for any quantity, however small. The total of exports cannot, therefore, with any accuracy be said to represent the force of demand. Rather, and much more appropriately, even, if without perfect propriety, may demand, in accordance with Mill's view, be described as the quantity, albeit not a definable quantity, is at any rate not less than some certain definite quantity.

And if Cairnes' definition of demand does not hold good in connection with foreign trade under a *régime* of barter, still more obviously is it inapplicable under a monetary *régime*. What is then the immediate object of exporters is to sell their exports for money; but whether they subsequently expend the whole of the sale proceeds on the purchase of foreign goods for importation into the originally exporting country depends upon whether or not they believe that they will be able advantageously to resell in that country the entire stock of goods so purchased. If they do not believe this, such of them as are resident in the originally exporting country will cause part of the sale proceeds to be remitted thither, where the consequent influx of money will tend to raise the prices of home produce at least as much as the efflux of money from abroad will tend to lower in foreign countries the prices of foreign products, and where, therefore, the demand for foreign products will be at least as likely to be checked as to be stimulated. Clearly, in such circumstances, the total quantity of exports from any country will not necessarily represent that country's demand for foreign products.

Thus, of the three cases cited, one, that of money, is not a case in point, while in neither of the two – labour and foreign trade – does Cairnes' definition hold good. I have elsewhere* stated reasons for considering that even Mill's definitions require some addition in order to render them strictly correct, and that supply or demand is not simply the quantity supplied or demanded, but the quantity supplied or demanded at some specified price. With these emendations, to which I have reason to believe that Mr. Mill did not object, his definitions would apply universally – would apply perfectly in regard to labour, and sufficiently in regard to foreign trade. Cairnes himself admits that it is "frequently highly convenient and, perhaps, even necessary" to use the terms in question in Mill's sense, Most unfortunate would it be if there were any real need to use terms of such prime importance in opposite senses. True, it might, as Mr. Cairnes says, be "only requisite to distinguish them in thought," but this simple necessity would infallibly prove to be in practice a simple impossibility. No extremest care could prevent the two senses from being continually confounded even by the same thinker, and still less by different thinkers, to an extent which would furnish abundant justification to the numerous scoffers with whom economical discussion is already but another name for endless and barren logomachy.

Here it may not be superfluous to observe – palpable truism as the observation is – that cost of production "means sacrifice, and cannot, without risk of

* On Labour, Book ii. chap 1, 2nd edition.

hopelessly confusing ideas, be identified with anything that is not sacrifices;" that "it represents what man parts with in the barter between him and nature, which must be kept eternally distinct from the return made by nature upon that payment." Neither is it simply not superfluous, it is highly desirable, to point out that in the earliest of industrial stages the sacrifice in question consists exclusively of the toil and fatigue, the privations and sufferings of whatever sort, involved in the act of labour. Such is its composition when a savage, nourished and invigorated solely by berries or cockles of his own collecting, and aided solely by implements of his own manufacturing, runs down and kills a stag. The stag's cost of production consists entirely of labour – partly of the huntsman's previous labour that had provided him with hunting tackle and with food for sustenance during the chase, partly of that which he had undergone in the chase itself, but still solely and exclusively of labour. Now, if this huntsman, returning to his wigwam laden with the day's spoils, should meet a tribesman similarly wending homewards with the products of a day's fishing, and if the two should desire to barter part of their respective acquisitions, the principle on which the exchange would take place would be that of the labour ordinarily required for similar acquisitions. The huntsman would expect in return for his venison as much fish as, with the same labour as the venison had cost him, he might probably himself have caught if he had gone fishing instead of hunting; the fisherman in exchange for his fish would expect as much venison as, with the same labour as his fish has cost him, he might probably have captured if he had gone hunting instead of fishing. For even though the huntsman had persuaded some companion, whom he had noticed to be cleverer than himself at making darts or bows and arrows, to undertake that operation for him on condition of being subsequently paid with venison for his pains, the venison's cost of production would still consist entirely of labour – partly of the actual huntsman's labour, partly of that of the acquaintance who had equipped him for the field. Before this second case could occur, however, industry must have made an important step in advance of its primitive stage. The entire savage community could no longer be living from hand to mouth. One savage at least must have become capable of abstinence enough to lay by for future use part of the produce of his labour instead of consuming the whole of it upon his immediate lusts, and so to be able to engage in a lengthened sedentary occupation. By so storing up food and materials for the sustenance and exercise of future labour, this provident savage had already created capital, had already become an embryo capitalist: nay, more, had already discovered a mode of profitably investing his capital. For he would scarcely have consented to stay at home making implements for another, unless by so doing he had expected to save himself some trouble. Rather than do that he would have preferred basking in the sun until his provisions were consumed, and then have gone out hunting again on his own account. As he insists upon being paid for his bows and arrows with somewhat more venison than he could himself have obtained with the same inconvenience as it costs him to make the bows and arrows, the difference between the quantity which he receives from his customer and that which he might probably have procured for himself constitutes profit on his capital. As society advances, and individuals engage largely in agriculture and manufactures, the number of capitalists goes on increasing, until at length the industrial portion of the community becomes divided into two great classes – to wit, of capitalists who, whether working for themselves or not, employ others to work for them, advancing to these all the prerequisites of labour, on condition of being repaid with the entire produce of the labour of the employed; and of labourers working for employers, without prospect of further benefit to themselves than that of the remuneration which the employers have advanced or promised to them. When this state of things is reached, the conditions of production have lost their original simplicity, and have become exceedingly complex. No act of production is now the act solely of the labourer immediately engaged in it, for its performance involves the use of tools, materials, and perhaps of buildings which previous producers had provided. Thus the cloth-weaver would be helpless without the loom, for which he is indebted to the miner, the ironfounder, and the machine-maker, or without the yarn, for which he has to thank the shepherd, the wool-comber, and the spinner, not to speak of the carriers who have conveyed the raw materials and manufactured articles from place to place.

Moreover, the miner, ironfounder, and the rest were probably all in the employment of capitalists, who advanced to them the prerequisites and also the remuneration of labour, and who did this only for the sake of profit, which profit must have been included in the total expenditure incurred by the final employer before he could set the weaver to work. In these circumstances the cost of production must be regarded from new point of view, from which it assumes a very different aspect from that which it previously presented. In one sense, indeed, it still, as much as ever, consists exclusively of the amount of labour of different kinds which has taken part in production; but, understood in the sense, it no longer has any direct bearing upon normal value. To raise twenty tons of coal from the mine requires far more and far severer toil than to make a gold watch; any one competent to perform both operations would find himself much more exhausted in body and mind after the former than after the latter; yet the market value of coal at the pit's mouth would probably be less than half of that of a fairly good watch in the shop of a wholesale dealer, and the market values of the two exhibit no tendency towards a level at which they will correspond with the quantities of labour required respectively for the production of coal and of watches. The reason is that the capitalists, to whom the coal and the watch in the first instance belong, have had to pay at very different rates for the labour employed upon them, and cannot, therefore, afford to offer them for sale at the same price. All labourers, as Cairnes has well shown, are divided into unskilled and skilled groups, the skilled, again, being subdivided into groups requiring for their several avocations very different degrees and very different kinds of skill, the acquisition of which, demanding as it does opportunity, leisure, and ability to pay for special education, is practically open to comparatively few. With in each group, individuals can compete freely with each other for employment, thereby keeping wages at about the same level throughout the group, but competition between members of different groups, the rate of wages may vary indefinitely. If, indeed, these variations become exceedingly large, more labour will be attracted to the better paid employments, in which the rate wages will consequently be somewhat reduced, whereas, in the worse paid employments, owing to the diminished influx of labour, the rate will somewhat rise; for, even though none of the labourers actually engaged in the worse paid employments should feel themselves fitted to compete for superior work, there are always plenty of young labourers growing up and as yet undisposed of, whereof a larger proportion than before will endeavour to qualify themselves for whatever kind of work has of late become unusually well paid. As already explained, however, only comparatively few will have the means of thus qualifying, and the rate of wages, therefore, in different employments, although prevented from varying to an unlimited extent, may continue to vary as much as it previously did. Such variation obviously implies that the irksomeness of labour has ceased to be the measure of labour's remuneration; that the sacrifice made by the labourers who have produced a commodity no longer represents that commodity's normal value. The whole pecuniary cost of production is now defrayed by capital, which will not continue such expenditure except in the belief that the finished product will exchange for the equivalent of the cost, together with profit at the current rate thereon. If, in any employment, this profit cease to be obtainable on the average of transactions, capital will eschew that employment, and will betake itself in preference to some other. True, of the capital already invested, so much as is locked up in buildings, machinery, or the like, may be incapable of transference; but, as of labour, so also of capital, there is always a considerable quantity as yet undisposed of, and the whole of this, unlike labour, is able to enter with equal ease into any and every employment from which it is not shut out by legal barriers. Whenever, therefore, owing to fluctuations in market value, the rate of profit, or of the net return obtained by the capitalist for his sacrifices of every sort, varies materially in different employments, capital will be attracted to the more profitable employments and repelled from the less profitable, and production will increase in the former and decrease in the latter, and prices of commodities of all kinds will tend to become such as to equalize profits in all employments. For this reason, Mill and indeed all economists, with no other exception, I believe, than Cairnes, ordinarily treat cost of production as meaning nothing but the sacrifices made by the capitalist; and, understood in this sense, it obviously is, within one and the same country, the sole arbiter of normal value, with which the sacrifices of the labourer have nothing whatever to do, or at least have no direct connection. The truth of this conclusion is in no degree invalidated by the fact which Mr. Cairnes was the first to bring to notice, and on which he has thrown a great deal of very valuable light, of the distribution of labourers into numerous non-competing groups. This fact does indeed most seriously affect the wages of labour, which is determined not by what the labourer has suffered, but by what the capitalists pays. The capitalist advances all the pecuniary expenses of production, and the mutual competition of capitalists necessarily gives to the market values of commodities a tendency to correspond with the pecuniary expense of producing them. Within one and the same country, then, every portion of whose capital can freely compete with every other portion, the "law" of normal value, if the word law were here permissible, would be that normal value depends absolutely and exclusively on cost of production. Operation of reciprocal demand, which Cairnes calls in as an auxiliary, is here altogether out of place. What the *law* would be in respect to commodities interchanged between different countries, whose respective capitals are not in competition with each other, is a different question, and one of great interest and intricacy, which I hope to find some future occasion for discussing, but which we need not at present enter.

Of the three epithets, "natural," "necessary," and "normal," employed to denote a particular species of value, the first and earliest, the one adopted by Adam Smith, is perhaps the least objectionable. The exchange value which a commodity could not fail to possess if supply and demand did not interpose their disturbing influence may, without much impropriety, be termed its "natural" value; whereas that surely is not *necessary* value with which, actual value *need* never coincide, nor is that *normal* value which, as a rule, always differs more or less from actual value. Nevertheless, normal value being the term selected by Mr. Cairnes, it may as well be adhered to in an examination of that economist's teaching.

As to actual or market value – the value for which, at any given time and place, a commodity is actually sold or offered for sale, all economists until lately – indeed, if I may presume without undue egotism to say so, until the publication of my own book "On Labour" – were agreed that it depends on the proportion between supply and demand, falling when supply exceeds demand, and rising when demand exceeds supply, and subsiding at last to a point at which supply and demand are equalized. This opinion I undertook to refute, admitting indeed that, provided goods be offered unreservedly for sale, price must fall if supply exceeds demand, but showing that even then it need not rise because demand exceeds supply; that it may either rise or fall, although supply and demand remain unaltered; and that, whether it rise or fall, the price finally resulting need not be one at which supply and demand will be equalized. Mr. Cairnes accepts my refutation as complete, but declares himself dissatisfied with the theory proposed by me in substitution of the one which he acknowledges me to have displaced. Now what I contend for may be briefly summarized as follows. It is competition alone, and primarily and mainly the competition of dealers upon and varying with – not the actual relations of supply and demand – but the varying estimates formed of those relations by competitors of very various degrees of sagacity, and the more or less powerful influence exercised by those estimates on competitors subject to very different degrees of necessity. The object of every dealer is to get in exchange for his whole stock the largest aggregate price which he can get within the period during which it will suit him to keep part of his stock unsold. If there were but one single dealer, he would probably ask the highest price at which he thought all his goods would be purchased within the period; but if there be several dealers, each must guard against the danger of being undersold. All dealers, therefore, while considering at what price they shall offer their goods, consider, each for himself, the actual state and future prospects of the whole market. Each takes stock, as well as he can, of the quantities already in hand of the commodity he deals in; estimates, as well as he can, the additional quantities likely to be brought in within the period during which he can manage to wait, and also the quantities which, within the same period, customers will be likely to take off at different prices; and conjectures, as well as he can, to how low a price rival dealers will be obliged to descend in order to get rid, within that period, of the portions of their respective stocks which they will respectively be impatient to sell. He then considers whether at that price he will be able, within the time, to get rid of the whole of his own present stock. If so he adopts that price. If not he adopts one still lower. In this manner each frames his own calculation, and judges for himself what will be the best price to ask; but different dealers in the same market, of every gradation of experience, shrewdness, and neediness, may calculate differently, or may draw different inferences from the same calculations. Some may estimate lower than others both the quantities that will be brought into the market and the quantities that will be demanded at different prices; or may think that the same estimate requires a lower price; or some may not be able to wait so long as others, and may be compelled to adopt a price which will enable them to dispose of their goods more rapidly than others would care to do. But whatever be, for whatever reason, the lowest price at which any resolve to sell, that price becomes, for the time being, the current price, and what causes it to be so is competition. What caused certain dealers to adopt that price in the first instance was the fear that otherwise competition would prevent their selling as fast as they desired. What prevents other dealers from asking higher prices is the knowledge that they will be undersold by their competitors if they do. Plainly, then, it is competition, and competition alone, that regulates price; and equally plain is it that competition is not regulated by supply and demand, for, in precisely the same relations of supply and demand competition may vary indefinitely. What then does regulate competition? My answer is simply, Nothing. There is no regularity about competition – competition is not regulated at all. If it can properly be said to depend upon anything, it depends partly upon individual necessity, partly on individual discretion; and, as for the first of these there is proverbially, and for the second manifestly, no law, so likewise is there no law of competition. Neither, if there be no law of competition, and if competition be, as it has been shown to be, the determining cause of price, can there be any law of price.

This being my view, Cairnes declares himself altogether dissentient. He will not admit that there is no law for individual necessity, possibly supposing that such a law might be adequately expressed by the words "What must be will be." Neither will he admit that there is no law for individual discretion, and he is satisfied that, "whether we are able to discover it or not, there is a law of market price, just as there is a law of normal price, as there is a law of wages, of profits, of rent, as there are laws of the winds and tides and seasons, and of the pheonomena of external nature." His conviction of the existence of this law is in no wise shaken by perception of the non-existence of any "constancy of relation between the proportion of supply and demand and market price, such that, knowing the relation in any given case, we should be able to predict what the price would be in the event of a change in the conditions of the market." He acknowledges that the "idea of proportion between demand and supply as furnishing a clue to the connection of demand and supply with market price must be abandoned," yet while acknowledging this he proceeds to lay down "the nearest approximation he can make to the law of market price," and in so doing simply expresses sentiments which in substance are always either absolutely coincident, or at least perfectly consistent with mine, the sole point of difference between us being one of nomenclature.

He begins by pointing out that there is in every market a price, designated by him *proper* price, "a price at which it is desirable," in the interest of dealers as well as consumers, "that the commodity, whatever it may be, should sell at that time and place." Price is "too low" when, by excessively stimulating consumption, it threatens to cause the existing stocks to be taken off before fresh supplies, adequate to what will then be the demand, can come in. It is "too high" when, by needlessly checking consumption, it threatens to cause part of the existing stock to remain on hand on the arrival of those fresh supplies. In either case "the error is in time discovered." In the former case, competition among dealers slackens, and prices are augmented; in the latter, competition quickens and prices are reduced; augmentations and reductions alike converging towards the *proper* price – the "price just sufficient, and no more than sufficient, to carry the existing supply over to meet the new supplies forthcoming."

"Dealers, while thus simply pursuing their own interests, are unconsciously performing for the community a service of first-rate importance – a service which has been will compared by Archbishop Whately to that rendered by the captain of a ship, who, taking account of the stock of provisions at his disposal and the length of his intended voyage, adjusts to these conditions the rations of his crew. Such is the *tendency* of the speculation of the market, and the *end* is *attained in proportion to the intelligence* and the *knowledge* of those who engage in the pursuit. Of course mistakes are often made, sometimes very serious mistakes; and then we have reaction, oscillation, and perhaps commercial crisis. But under all circumstances the *price in the market is determined by the opinions of dealers,* founded upon their knowledge of demand and supply – of dealers pursuing their interests under circumstances which, in proportion to the intelligence and knowledge at their command, *favour* the establishment of the proper market price."

Such is Cairnes' exposition, which he prefaces with an intimation that he is utterly unable to agree with me, but with which, nevertheless, I find myself almost unreservedly agreeing. How can I help agreeing in the main with what is little else than a repetition or expansion of what I myself had previously said? Cairnes does not describe *proper* market price as one with which *actual* market price need ever necessarily coincide, but only as one towards which it always tends, and towards which it will "approximate in proportion to the intelligence and knowledge of the dealers." But while as yet only in course of approximation to proper price, actual price must needs be *improper* price, and, whether proper or improper, Mr. Cairnes pronounces the price in the market to be under all circumstances determined by the opinions for the dealers in the market founded upon their knowledge of supply and demand. It is these opinions which quicken competition when price is "too high," and slacken it when price is "too low," thereby causing prices to fall in the one case and permitting them to rise in the other. Is there, then, some pregnant distinction between opinions of individuals founded on knowledge and varying with intelligence, and the "individual discretion" of which I have myself spoken, and which I have coupled with "individual necessity" because it would be anything but discretion if it did not take account of such necessity? If not, Cairnes and I are so far at one, and only using different words to express the same idea. We both agree that competition is the immediate arbiter of market price, and that competition depends upon what I call individual discretion, the sole difference between us being that, whereas he styles our common conclusion an economic *law*, I refuse to accord to it so dignified an appellation. To the question of nomenclature thus arising, the answer obviously depends upon what economic or other scientific law really is. According to Cairnes, it consists in the "constancy of relation" between facts and the condition that produce them." Now, of course, all conditions being precisely the same, precisely the same consequences must ensue, and if this "constancy of the relation" be a law, it is a law of universal application, holding good in every department of science, and therefore in the region of economics among the rest. But I submit that this is not so much a scientific law as the principle to constitute a scientific law it is indispensable to specify the conditions from which certain specified facts will infallibly result, and Cairnes, as we have seen, admits that exactest knowledge of the proportion between supply and demand would not enable us to predict what would be the actual market price at any given time an place. *That,* he says, would depend on the opinions of the dealers, and these again upon their intelligence? No doubt two persons, the conditions been precisely the same, would, if placed in precisely the same circumstances, from precisely the same opinions and adopt precisely the same line of action. But it is equally indubitable, not merely that there cannot possibly be two such persons, but also that one and the same person cannot possess precisely the same intelligence at two different periods, for this, if for no other reason, that some addition must have been made to his experience during the interval between the two periods. Cairnes and I agree that although actual market prices are almost always what he would call *improper* prices, their tendency is always towards proper price. This tendency of theirs is by Cairnes affirmed, and by me denied, to be the *law* of market price, and I feel that I am risking little in asking the impartial reader to decide which of us is in the right.

Cairnes ends his investigation of value with a chapter on some if its derivative laws; but without dwelling upon this further than to observe that it will be found to be exceedingly profitable reading, I will now bring the present paper to a close by briefly recapitulating its principal conclusions.

Value, in economic language is of two distinct kinds, and cannot therefore be brought within the limits of a single definition. Sometimes it signifies *exchange* value, or the ratio in which, in open market, any commodities, or all commodities whatsoever, are exchanged against each other; sometimes it signifies *pecuniary* value, or the ratio in which any commodities, other than some one selected commodity, are exchanged against the one selected. Sum of pecuniary values – increase or decrease of the aggregate amount of pecuniary values – are perfectly intelligible and highly useful, indeed indispensable, expressions, signifying the total quantity of, and any augmentation or diminution of the total quantity of, some selected commodity which may be had in exchange for the total of all other commodities. But sum of exchange values, and increase and decrease of the aggregate amount of exchange values, are unmeaning phrases and impossible conceptions; for every rise in the ratio of any one commodity to any other, or to all other commodities, is necessarily counterbalanced by a precisely proportionate fall in the ratio of that other or those others to it.

Supply is the total quantity of commodities offered for sale at a given time and place, at specified prices. Demand is the total quantity of the same commodities which customers are prepared to purchase at the prices specified.

Value of either species, exchange or pecuniary, is subdivisible into market value and *natural, necessary,* or *normal* value. Market values are the prices at which commodities are anywhere actually offered for sale. Normal values are values towards which market values, whatever be their intermediate fluctuations, always tend eventually to return; and these normal values, within one and the same country, are determined invariably and exclusively by cost of production.

Cost of production consists solely of the sacrifices which production exacts; and these, in the earliest of industrial stages, consist exclusively of the labour engaged in production. In all subsequent stages, however, they generally consist less of labour itself than of payments made by employers, and always consist in part of payments on account of labour other than that engaged in the final act of production. In short, except in the every earliest industrial stage, the sacrifices that constitute the cost of production which determines natural or normal value are made in far larger measure by employers of labour than by actual labourers, and are generally made entirely by employers. The sacrifices of labourers may be as great or greater than ever, but they have ceased to enter into cost of production in the economic sense of that expression.

Market price is determined by the competition of dealers, the keenness of which competition depends upon the estimates made by different dealers of the actual and prospective condition of supply and demand. But as these estimates and the lines of action suggested by them are made by dealers of very various characters and tempers and also very differently circumstanced, they cannot be depended upon as being the same on any two separate occasions. There cannot, therefore, be any law of competition, nor, consequently, any law of market price.

The foregoing conclusions differ essentially from those of Professor Cairnes; neither are they strictly coincident with those of Mr. Mill. They are, however, in complete accordance with these latter, from which they differ chiefly in being somewhat amplified and expanded.

THE WAGES FUND

Thornton, William, "The Wages Fund",
Nineteenth Century, August (6), 1879, pp. 293–307.

This is another review essay on John Elliott Cairnes's *Some Leading Principles of Political Economy Newly Expounded.* The review features three different figures (Thornton, Cairnes, and John Stuart Mill), with three different views on wages, and was written after Cairnes's death.

The Wages Fund

WHEN Professor Cairnes – between whom and myself, during the latter years of his life, a close intimacy subsisted – was engaged upon his new exposition of "Some Leading Principles of Political Economy," he one day told me that he was sorry to have been compelled to take up a position of direct antagonism to Mr. Mill and me in respect to the Wages Fund. I replied that when his new book appeared I would not fail to read it carefully, and that I would then either publicly answer the portions directed against us, or publicly acknowledge my inability to answer them. I regret exceedingly that circumstances prevented me from redeeming this pledge while my friend was still living, and I regret it the more because I am thereby deprived of the satisfaction which I might otherwise have had of convincing him that, on the point specially referred to, there was little or no real difference between us. On some other points, indeed, scarcely less vital, connected with the remuneration of labour, our views, as will presently appear, do differ very materially; but upon these it is rather I who dissent from him, than he who dissented from me, for to the best of my recollection I have never hitherto had occasion to express in print any opinion regarding them, either on one side or the other.

I begin by offering an epitome of that portion of Mr. Cairnes's general theory which exhibits his conception of the wages fund, and I pledge myself to furnish no pretext for suspicion that I am doing this the less faithfully because, for the sake of brevity, I substitute words of my own for his. His expressions shall be rigidly adhered to wherever deviation from them might involve the possibility of his meaning being mistaken.

The object of his inquiry is to discover "the causes determining the general or average rate of wages." As to the strongly marked differences in relative rated – as to the distribution among various classes of labourers of the total amount applied to their remuneration in proportions bearing no relation to the numbers of persons belonging to each class, and to the consequent differences of rate observable in different employments, Cairnes had already shown that these are due to the division of the whole body of labourers into numerous non-competing groups, but he was fully aware that he had thereby thrown no light upon the causes which decide what the total remuneration of labour shall be. Neither to the inquiry what these causes are, would there, as he intimates, be any approach to an answer in saying that the total depends upon the supply and demand for labour. In the case of commodities, indeed, the total amount applied to their purchase may, allowably if not with strict accuracy, be said to depend upon supply and demand. Whatever be the demand for any commodity at a price not below the normal value thereof, that is to say, not below the cost of production *plus* profit at the current rate on the cost, supply invariably tends to accommodate itself to demand, because, if supply be unequal to demand, the price will rise and the rate of profit, rising simultaneously, will attract more capital to production, while, if supply exceed demand, the price will fall, and profits, likewise falling below the current rate, will cause capital to be transferred from production of the commodity in question to other employments in which the current rate of profit has been retained. Whatever, therefore, during any somewhat lengthened period, be the demand for a commodity at a price corresponding with its normal value, the total amount represented by that demand will be the total applied to the purchase of the commodity. But, in respect to the point under consideration, there is no analogy between commodities and labour. Production of commodities, being an onerous operation, is undertaken only with the prospect of remuneration sufficient to compensate the trouble it involves, and will cease if that prospect be withdrawn. But production of labour, or rather of those embodiments of labour termed labourers, instead of an onerous operation, is compliance with one of the strongest instincts of our nature, the indulgence of which is its own more than sufficient reward, insomuch that the raw material of labour is often born into the world in quantities greatly in excess of what there is demand for: the education and training necessary to convert the raw material into effective labourers being moreover bestowed by parents from motives of natural affection, from a sense of duty or from habit, with comparatively little reference to the extent of employment likely to be opened to the finished labourers. Thus there cannot be said to be any cost of production of labour in the sense in which we are accustomed to speak of the cost of production of commodities, and if no cost of production then no normal value, nor consequently any demand for labour at a price corresponding with normal value, whereunto the supply of labour can conform. The actual price of labour at any given time does indeed depend upon the keenness, with which employers, actuated by their several estimates of supply, may compete for labour; yet still, even as the supply of labour is governed by circumstances very different from those which govern the supply of commodities, so also is the demand. In the case of commodities, according to Cairnes, demand depends partly on the desire for their possession, partly on the purchasing power at the command of customers; wheras, in the case of labour, demand in any given state of the national wealth depends, in his opinion, partly on the proportion of that wealth which its possessors are disposed to convert into capital by investing it for the sake of profit in productive industry, and partly on the character of the various national industries. After showing with his usual clearness that the proportion of wealth employed as capital depends upon the degree in which its owners are influenced by the love of profit and of accumulation rather that by the temptations of immediate enjoyment, and partly by the opportunities of profitable investment open to them, he proceeds to show that, of any given amount of invested capital, the proportion expended upon labour must always vary greatly in different employments, and may vary sensibly from time to time in one and the same employment. In almost all employments the capital invested undergoes a threefold distirbution, part being expended on buildings, fixed machinery, or other implements and material varies according to the nature of the work to be done, being much greater, for instance, in agriculture than in a textile manufacture. And, even though the quantity of labour required were always the same, the amount of money required to procure it would vary with every variation in the supply, and every consequent variation in the price of labour, and these variations would affect the distribution of the entire capital. Suppose, for example, that the amount invested in a certain employment is 10,000*l.*, whereof 5,000*l.* is required to procure implements and material, and that, to utilise these, 100 labourers are needed whose services cannot be procured for less than 50*l.* a head – the amount expended on labour will then likewise be 5,000*l.* But now suppose the current rate of wages to be 40*l.* instead of 50*l.* a head – the same number of labourers will then be procurable for 4,000*l.*, and there will remain 1,000*l.* available for the purchase of more implements and material, and for the hire of more labour in the same proportions as before. In the second of these cases, although the whole number of labourers will be 111 instead of 100, the total of their hire will be only 4,400*l.* instead of 5,000*l.* It thus appears that, the total of the capital invested being given, the quantity expended on labour will depend partly on the nature of the employment, partly on the current rate of wages; and, as what is thus seen to be true of each employment separately must be equally true of all, it follows that, in any given condition of the national wealth, the factors which determine how much of that wealth shall be expended on labour are, first, the readiness of its possessors to invest it as capital; secondly, the extent of the field available for investment; thirdly, the nature of the national industries; and fourthly, the rate or rates of wages current. To the amount resulting from the combined action of these factors Cairnes gives the designation of "wages fund;" and the quotient resulting from division of that fund by the whole number of labourers among whom it is divided is styled by him the general or average rate of wages – the words *general* and *average* being here treated by him as synonymous.

In the reasoning thus summarised there is much in which I cordially agree, but there is also a good deal from which I am compelled to dissent. Among minor objections to it may be mentioned this – that in order to discover the average rate of wages it will not suffice to divide the aggregate wages by the number of their recipients. The many various rates of wages, and the number of labourers in receipt of each rate, must also be taken into account. It may be pointed out, too, that of a given amount of invested capital, the proportion expended on labour will be affected not only by the actually current price of labour itself, but also by that of the accessories of labour – implements and materials. If the total of capital be taken at 10,000*l.*, whereof 5,000*l.* is required for the hire of 100 labourers, and if implements and materials sufficient to keep those labourers fully employed can be procured for 4,000*l*., there will remain available for further investment 1,000*l*., whereof more than half will fall to the share of labour. A fifth factor, therefore, viz., that of the market price of implements and materials, must be added to the four enumerated by Cairnes. Nor is it unworthy of notice that, other things remaining the same, wages cannot fall in one employment without causing profits therein to rise, thereby attracting capital from other employments; whereupon, although wages will again rise somewhat in that one employment, they will fall somewhat in the rest, settling down finally in all at a somewhat lower level than before.

These, however, are trifles. A more serious defect on Cairnes's part is the omission to explain how the extent of the field of investment is determined. No doubt, the extent of the field being given, the aggregate of wages will be determined by the action of the other factors specified above; but what is it that determines the extent of the field? To this question Cairnes attempts no sort of reply, although rather contemptuously rejecting the answer suggested, if not formally tendered, by Mr. Longe, viz. demand for commodities. This nevertheless will, I think, prove on examination to be the correct solution of the problem. National wealth consisting as it does of the entire quantity of things at once useful and exchangeable in a nations possession, is distributed amongst two classes of persons – those who have, and those who have not, more than enough for the bare subsistence of themselves and their dependents. The former class may, for our present purpose, be distinguished as rich, the latter as poor, and it is members of the former class only who are in a condition to lay aside any portion of their wealth with a view to its investment as capital by being employed in productive industry. With every individual capitalist the sole motive for so investing part of his substance, instead of consuming the whole of it on his lusts, is the expectation that its products will exchange for at least so much more than their cost of production as will yield a profit sufficient to compensate him for his abstinence and trouble. But upon what does every such expectation rest? Surely on the probable degree of eagerness with which the products will be sought for by customers – in other words, on the capitalist's estimate of the demand for his commodities. Be the commodities what they may – houses, shoes, or what not – no builder will build more houses, no shoemaker will make more shoes, than he hopes to be able to sell within a reasonable period at prices that will fully compensate him for his pains. If he is disappointed in this hope, he will withdraw part of his capital from its previous employment, and either let it remain idle for a season or transfer it to some other employment whose products are at the time in greater request. The proportion of any individual's capital invested in any employment whatever depends upon the estimated demand for the products of that employment: it is that demand which in any on particular industry defines the limits of the field of investment. But what does this in each particular industry must needs do it in all industries; in all, as in each, the proportion actually invested of the total available for investment will depend on the demand for commodities of all descriptions. As of each section of the field of investment, so of the entire field, the limits will be set by the demand for commodities.

This being the position which Mr. Cairnes undertakes to controvert, what has he to urge against it? He very justly observes that the demand for products of any particular kind, although determining the relative proportion of the aggregate capital that will be applied to a particular kind of production, does not determine the absolute quantity of capital so applied. Demand in various degrees of intensity for houses, shoes and commodities of all other sorts "determines," he says, "the proportion in which the total of available capital shall be distributed over the whole field of production, those proportions adapting themselves to the proportions of the various demands;" but to argue that demand for commodities will necessarily cause capital to be applied to production in quantities sufficient to satisfy the demand is, as he justly considers, equivalent to arguing that "because a man distributes his income in the proportion of his needs, therefore the greater his needs, the larger must be his income." In opposition to such an imaginary argument he quite conclusively demonstrates that neither an individual nor a nation can possibly invest a greater amount of capital than that of which he or it has the disposal. Incontestable, however, as are Mr. Cairnes's observations on these points, they are also widely beside the question, which is not what decides how much of a given aggregate is invested in the whole field. The total so invested cannot of course be greater than the total national capital, but neither Mr. Longe nor any one else ever pretended that it could, and I, for my own part, submit that it need not be nearly so great. The whole capital may, and generally does, exceed the quantity for which profitable employment can immediately be found, and a portion is then held in reserve, and remains for a while inactive. As to the capital, be it the whole, or only a part, which is at any time in a state of activity, what calls it into that state is the prospect of profitable employment, or the probability that its products will be sold at a profit. And this probability is but another name for the estimated demand for the products, which, again is but another name for the field of investment. It is then the demand for commodities of all sorts that defines the extent of the whole field – that defines how much of the entire national capital shall be immediately employed, and how much reserved for future use.

So far Mr. Longe, if I correctly interpret his language, seems to me to be in the right, but I am unable to agree with him that the demand for commodities determines not only how much of the existing national capital shall within any given time be applied to production, but also how much of the capital so applied shall be expended upon labour. Mr. Cairnes seems to me to have finally disposed of this latter notion by pointing out, as we have already seen, that, whatever the amount of capital in active employment, the proportion thereof devoted to the payment of labour will vary with the nature of the employment, and with the supply and actual market price of labour, the expenditure on labour will be greater when the total of capital invested is large, and less when the same total is small. It follows, therefore, that although the demand for commodities is very far from precisely determining, it does very materially affect, the expenditure on labour; and Mr. Longe, perhaps, did not mean to affirm more than this.

Even as thus restricted, however, the proposition would not have found favour with Mr. Cairnes, but would have been objected to by him on the same moral grounds on which he assails it when brought forward without qualification. With neither more nor less of warrant in one case than in the other, he might have denounced it as being "among the most popular fallacies," and as being likewise "the root of a whole cluster" of demoralising maxims, such as that "the extravagance of the rich is the gain of the poor, and that profusion and waste are for the good of trade." But a maxim may quite possibly be demoralising without being false. That certain actions are pleasant though wrong is not a fact tending greatly to edification, yet it is a fact all the same; and a not unplausible plea may be urged on behalf even of the very maxims which Mr. Cairnes singles out for reprobation. Probably enough, a selfish spendthrift may be well content to salve his conscience by fancying that his prodigality affords additional occupation to the poor, but to suppose that this reflection will render him more extravagant and wasteful, to suppose that he will be induced to squander more upon himself for the sake not of pleasing himself, but of benefiting others, is surely to credit him with a degree of philanthropy which he is exceedingly unlikely to possess. And unless it can be proved that the wealth which he has wasted, by expending it upon idle vanities would, if not so wasted, have been applied to the maintenance not simply of productive industry, but of productive industry of one peculiar kind, it cannot be denied that the extravagance and profusion of the rich may quite possibly be for the benefit of the poor – quite possibly for the good of trade. If so, there may even be moral satisfaction in regarding the result as another example of good coming out of evil – a satisfaction undisturbed by the reflection that more evil will be likely to be done in order that good may come of it. Now the outlay on the illuminations which take place on the Prince of Wales's birthday does undoubtedly transfer from the pockets of his Royal highness's tradesmen to those of gas companies to manufacture gas for the replenishment of their diminished stocks. Undoubtedly *some* good is thereby done to trade; *some* gain is in consequence made by the poor. If the money had not been spent on illuminations, what would have become of it? Would the use made of it have done more good to trade, have enabled the poor to make more gain? Possibly, though not at all probably, the original owners might have found immediate employment for it in their own businesses; but, even so, only part of the money would have been paid away as wages, and not necessarily a larger part than the gas companies would similarly have paid away. Most likely, however, it would consist of spare cash which the Prince's tradespeople could afford to spend upon articles for domestic or personal consumption. Suppose it to be so spent: the simple difference would then be that the money, instead of passing into possession of gas producers, would be transferred to producers of other articles, who would presumably employ most of it in replenishing their diminished stocks; and, here again, it would by no means follow that more of the money would be applied to the direct hire of labour. Or perhaps the Prince's tradespeople, preferring to lay the money by, would deposit it with their bankers, in whose custody it might, in a season of pecuniary plethora, lie idle for a considerable time, its power of employing labour remaining meanwhile dormant, and labourers remaining without the wages they would have earned if the money had been employed in producing gas to replace what had been wasted. And even though the money in deposit were forthwith issued in loans to persons engaged in productive industry, still, just as in all the previous cases, whether more or less would be expended upon labour would depend upon the nature of the industry engaged in. There is, indeed, one group of industries, the selection of which by capitalists may be especially advantageous to labourers. If capital be employed in the reclamation of land, in improved agricultural processes, in mining, whale fishing, or in any other mode by which the national stock of materials is augmented, labour may obtain a twofold benefit, by reason firstly of demand for it in order to manufacture those materials. But in all industries other than those of this description, the amount paid as wages depends upon the proportions in which the particular work to be done requires that the invested capital shall be distributed between materials, implements, and labour, and the proportion assigned to labour will not necessarily be less because the commodities produced are available for mere luxury and ostentation instead of being suitable for some more rational purpose. On the contrary, labour's share will be much larger if a given quantity of flax be metamorphosed onto Brussels lace, than if it be converted into coarse linen. In the interest of labourers the essential point is that there be a demand for the products of labour itself, and the former demand will not be a whit the less effective because it arises out of extravagance or waste rather than out of rational consumption.

The conclusions which Mr. Cairnes deduces from the reasoning which I began by epitomising are three: – 1. That the wages which within any given period come into possession of the whole labouring population constitute a definite aggregate whose amount is of course identical with that of the total sum applied to the direct purchase of labour. 2. That on the proportion of this aggregate to the whole number of labourers depends the general average rate of wages. 3. That the same aggregate stands in a definite relation to the whole national capital, that relation being determined by the nature of the various industries among which the capital is distributed, and by the rate of wages actually current. The first of these propositions is self-evident, needing no demonstration, and obnoxious to no cavil, unless indeed to this, that if of the tripartite capital devoted to productive industry, the portion which is expended upon labour can properly be styled a Wages Fund, the two other portions may with equal propriety be termed Implement and Material funds. If by "wages fund" be signified no more than this, Mr. Cairnes may be said to have rather created than to have rehabilitated it; for while no one ever dreamt of denying, so probably it may never previously have occurred to any one to affirm, the existence of so obvious a reality.

The second proposition seems, as I have pointed out, to require to be somewhat differently worded, but in its essence it likewise is self-evident. No one who perceives its intention can possible deny it, and Mr. Longe, who appears to deny it, and who is in consequence treated by Mr. Cairnes with wholly unmerited scorn, does so only in appearance. That, intermediate between the highest and lowest rate of wages, there must be somewhere an average rate, just between the Koh-I-Nohr and a glass bead or a farthing rushlight there must be an average price of raw material, and between an armourplate rolling mill and a gimlet and average price of implements, Mr. Longe would of course at once allow, though he probably thinks, as I do, that it would be idle to seek for such averages, seeing that there is no one of them which would not be utterly valueless when discovered. The fact is that he and Mr. Cairnes are here at cross purposes. Although both treat general and average rates as synonymous expressions, he uses them in one sense and Mr. Cairnes in another. All that he maintains is that, inasmuch as each particular employment has its own particular rate of wages, there cannot be one rate general to all; and his assertion of the non-existence of such a *general* rate, if equally superfluous, is also quite as incontestable as Mr. Cairnes's affirmation of the existence of the *average* rate.

I may here explain that my observation thus far, although strictly relevant to the subject under consideration, are in no degree required for my own personal vindication. Mr. Cairnes does indeed, in an early part of his exposition, "presume that Mr. Thornton would say something," neither which nor the like of which I ever dreamt of saying, and then, adding that "substantially the same language is held by Mr. Longe," winds up by remarking that "the theory put forward by Mr. Longe apparently finds favour with Mr. Thornton also." But I earnestly protest against being held responsible for the presumptions or suppositions of any one but myself, for any language which I have not myself employed, or for any theory with which I have not directly or indirectly signified my concurrence, and I have never until now had an occasion to say one word either for or against the first two of Mr. Cairnes's propositions. It is not until he reaches the third, according to which "the amount of a nation's wealth expended on wages at any given time stands in a definite relation to its general capital," that he has any even apparent pretext for joining issue with me.

In order to show the nature of the difference, real or supposed, between us, Mr. Cairnes extracts a passage from my book *On Labour*, which I also may be permitted to transcribe:–

> If there really were a national fund, the whole of which must necessarily be applied to the payment of wages, that fund could be no other than the aggregate of smaller similar funds possessed by the several individuals who composed the employing portion to the nation. Does then any individual employer possess any such fund? Is there any specific portion of any individual's capital which the owner must necessarily expend upon labour? Of course, every employer possesses a certain amount of money, whether his own or borrowed, out of which all his expenses must be met, if met at all. With so much of this amount as remains after deduction of

> what he takes for family and personal expenses, he carries on his business – with one portion of that balance providing or keeping in repair buildings and machinery, with a second procuring materials, with a third, hiring labour. But is there any law fixing the amount of his domestic expenditure and thereby fixing likewise the balance available for his industrial operations? May he not spend more or less on his family and himself according to his fancy, in the one case having more, in the other less, left for the conduct of his business? And of what is left, does he or can he determine beforehand how much shall be laid out on buildings, how much on materials, how much on labour? May not his outlay on repairs be unexpectedly increased by fire or other accident? Will not his outlay on materials vary with their dearness or cheapness, or with the varying demand for the finished article? And must not the amount available for wages vary accordingly? And even though the latter amount were exactly ascertained beforehand, even though he did not know to a farthing how much he would be able to spend on labour, would he be bound so to spend the utmost he could afford to spend? If he could get as much labour as he wanted at a cheap rate, would he voluntarily pay as much for it as would be compelled to pay if it were dearer? It sounds like mockery or childishness to ask these questions, so obvious are the only answers that can possibly be given to them; yet it is only the assumption that directly opposite answers must be given that the wages fund can for one moment stand. For if in the case of individual employers there be no wages fund – no definite or definable portions of their capitals, which, and neither more nor less than which, they must severally apply to the hiring of labour – clearly there can be no national wages fund. And be it observed, fixity or definiteness is the very essence of the period be disbursed in the form of wages. The only question is whether the amount be *definite* or *indefinite*. If *indefinite*, it cannot of course be divided, and might as well not exist for any power it possesses of performing the sole function of a wages fund – that, namely, of yielding a quotient that would indicate *what* is *about to be* the average rate of wages.

From this extract it may be at once perceived that the wages fund theory which Mr. Cairnes defends differs essentially from that which I impugn, affirming as the latter does, not simply that within any given period a definite amount is actually applied to the payment of labour, but also that there is, previously to such actual application, a definite amount which, and neither more nor less than which, must, owing to the influence exerted by predetermining causes on the wills and actions of men, be necessarily so applied. The first of these doctrines is in substance manifestly true, and, even if false, it would be at worst but at harmless fallacy, whereas the second would, if true, be fraught with very malignant consequences, opposing an insuperable barrier to social progress in one of the most important directions. Now, as will presently be seen, one principal question between Mr. Cairnes and myself is whether this second doctrine was or was not, at the time at which I wrote, generally entertained by economists, and regarded as the essence of the wages fund theory.

By Mr. Mill, whom Mr. Cairnes pronounces to be, "if not the originator of the wages fund, certainly its most able and effective expositor," its principles are thus set forth:–

> Supply and demand entirely govern the price obtained for labour. The demand of labour consists of the whole circulating capital of the country, including what is paid in wages for unproductive labour. The supply is the whole labouring population. If the supply is in excess of what the capital can at present employ, wages must fall. If the labourers are all employed, and there is a surplus of capital still unused, wages will rise. . . . There is at any given instant a sum of wealth which is unconditionally devoted to the payment of wages. This sum is unalterable, for it is augmented by saving and increases with the progress of wealth, but it is reasoned upon at any given moment a predetermined amount. More than that amount it is assumed that the wage-receiving class cannot possible divide among them. That amount and no less they cannot but obtain. So that, the sum divided being fixed, the wages of each depend solely on the divisor, the number of participants. In this doctrine, it is by implication affirmed that the demand for labour not only increases with the cheapness, but increases in exact proportion to it, the same aggregate sum being paid for labour whatever its price may be.

"This series of deductions." Mr. Mill remarks "is generally received as incontrovertible. they are found, I presume, in every systematic treatise on political economy, my own certainly included."

It is this doctrine, believed by Mr. Mill to have been entertained by all economists in common with himself, that I ventured to challenge, and Mr. Mill, after carefully scrutinising the arguments advanced by me against it, avowed himself convinced by them, "pleading guilty to having, along with the world in general, accepted the theory without the qualifications and limitations necessary to make it admissible." Moreover, although it is also one in regard to which Mr. Cairnes proclaims antagonism to Mr. Mill and myself, he commences his attack upon us with words which would seem to imply that we are all three of one mind

> It must (he says) at once be conceded that in the sense in which Mr. Thornton understands the predetermination and limitation of the wages fund, his position is unassailable. Undoubtedly there is no specific portion of any individual's capital which the owner must necessarily expend upon wages. There in no law fixing the amount of any man's domestic expenditure, and thereby fixing likewise the balance available for industrial operation; nor is any man bound to spend in the payment of labour the utmost he can afford to spend.

And he goes on to strengthen, although fancying that he is weakening, this concession by adding that "if economic doctrines in general are to be understood in the sense assigned" (by me) "to the wages fund, there is not one within the whole range of economic science that could endure ten minutes' "criticism." Proceeding, however, to illustrate this last remark by examples, Mr. Cairnes, to my utter amazement, treats me as the author of the very absurdity which I was foremost to expose. He assumes that it was not my opponents, but myself, who had contended for the existence of "principles which compel human beings to the adoption of certain courses in despite of their own inclination and will;" that it was I, and not they, who had formed so "radically erroneous a conception of economic law" as to imagine that the "determination" thereby "expressed means the necessary realisation of certain results independently of the human will." "He would," he says, "have confidently asserted," not simply "that no economist, but that no reasonable being, had ever advanced the theory of a wages fund in the sense" supposed by me, "were it not that Mr. Mill has accepted the reasoning quoted" from my book "as a refutation of that theory." The amazement which this last sentence excited in me must, I think, be shared by every reader whose memory reaches ten years back. The theory which Mr. Cairnes could scarcely conceive to have been advanced by any other reasonable being than Mr. Mill is not obscurely implied in the teaching of Ricardo, is distinctly enunciated by M'Culloch, is by Professor Fawcett ranked among "the elementary principles of political economy," and among "fixed and well-ascertained laws as certain in their operation as those which control physical nature," It is, moreover, the stock argument with which the *Edinburgh* and *Quarterly Reviews*, the "leading journal" and its whole host of followers, politicians in Parliament, and economic professors in the lecture-room, were, within a yet unexpired decade, accustomed to demonstrate, to their own triumphant satisfaction, the utter futility of trades-unionism was continually achieving. But why multiply testimony? With the evidence of Mr. Mill before us, what need of further witness? That "most able and effective expositor of the wages-fund theory" surely must have known, if any one did, what was meant by "wages-fund," and he declared in unequivocal terms that I had accurately interpreted its meaning. Yet there is one other witness too important to be overlooked, inasmuch as he is no other than Mr. Cairnes himself, who, after vehemently denouncing the theory as absurdity almost too wild for any sane person to entertain, nevertheless proceeds to reaffirm it.

He begins by recapitulating a portion of his previous reasoning with which, at least in the shape in which I am about to restate it, I cordially agree, to the effect that "in the existing state of the national wealth, the character of Englishmen being what it is," a satisfactory prospect of profit will determine "some part of that wealth to productive investment," the quantity invested being distributed among the various national industries in such proportions as the several investors may deem to be best for their interests. But then, forgetting another portion of his previous argument, to which, with some slight reservations indicated above, I likewise assent, he goes on to say that "the form of the investment" – in other words, the characters of the various national industries – "will again *determine* the proportion of the whole capital which shall be paid as wages to labourers" – that proportion

> *not being* a *matter within the discretion of capitalists,* supposing they desire to obtain the largest practical return upon their outlay. To accomplish this (he continues), the instruments of production, labour, fixed capital, and raw material, must be brought together in certain proportions – a condition which requires, the supply of labour being given, a distribution of the aggregate capital in certain proportions among those instruments. Supposing now capitalists to succeed in forcing down the rate of

> wages below the point at which, having regard to the number of the labouring population, the amount which the fulfilment of this condition would assign to the payment of wages was absorbed. Either the capital thus withdrawn from the wages fund must remain uninvested, and therefore unproductive, or if invested, and not invested in wages, it would take the form of fixed capital or raw material. But by hypothesis the fixed capital and raw material were already in due proportion to the labour force, and they would consequently ensue, *and what could this end in but* a *restoration to the wages fund of the amount withdrawn from it?...* In a word, my argument brings me back to the position from which I started, that, the aggregate investment being determined by certain mental and physical conditions, and the national industries being such as they are, there is but one distribution of the capital invested which is consistent with the greatest advantage to the possessors. But distribution involves a certain proportion spent in the payment of wages, and it is to this result that capitalists, if true to their own interest, *must* conform their conduct.

Here, while reiterating what no one ever denied – that, given the amount of national wealth, the character of its owners, the extent of the field of investment, and the nature and profitableness of the various industries among which that field is divided, a *definite* portion of wealth will be applied to production – Mr. Cairnes is by implication agreeing with Mr. Mill and myself that, even though all other conditions remain the same, the portion so applied must vary with every variation in the character of the owners of wealth, becoming such circumstances *indefinite.* It is when proceeding to intimate that, given the aggregate capital invested in productive industry, and provided that the capitalists are intent on obtaining the largest return upon their outlay, the same proportion must necessarily in all circumstances be expended upon labour, that Mr. Cairnes really opposes us. This, however, he does in unmistakeable terms when declaring that the proportion in question, styled by him "wages fund" is so far from a matter within discretion of the capitalists that if, by reason of a reduction in the price of labour, some portion of the wages fund be temporarily withdrawn, the portion withdrawn must eventually be restored to the fund. Here is a distinct restatement of the doctrine against which I protested, and against which Mr. Mill, on reflection, joined with me in protesting. It would not be easy to affirm more explicitly that "there is at any given instant a certain proportion of the national wealth which constitutes a wages fund, whereof the whole, and neither more nor less than the whole, must be expended upon labour."

Assuredly, then, Mr. Mill and I were not fighting with our own shadows. Assuredly the creed which we undertook to controvert was at the time universally in vogue, and it would indeed be hard if, simply because we had succeeded so completely in exploding it that no trace of it remained, we were to be taunted with having assailed an absurdity which none but ourselves had ever held. In truth, however, even if, in consequence mainly of Mr. Mill's repudiation, it seemed for a while extinct, it has since revived, and is apparently little less rife than ever, now that its professors have, in virtue of the passages just quoted, some pretext for claiming Mr. Cairnes as one of their number. Luckily, there is no difficulty in showing that, when writing those passages, Mr. Cairnes had forgotten what he had little before written, and was not less at variance with his own previous self than with those against whom he was for the moment arguing. On turning a few pages back, the reader of this paper will find Mr. Cairnes supposing the case of a capitalist starting with 10,000*l.*, whereof one half enables him to procure implements and raw materials enough to give full employment to 100 workmen whose wages at the rate of 50*l.* a head would absorb the other half of his capital. Here, according to Mr. Cairnes, is a wages fund of 5,000*l.* of capital still disposable, which he proceeds to invest in the same business. To this end it is necessary to distribute it among the instruments of production in the same proportions as before, that is to say, to lay out 550*l.* on additional implements and material, and with the balance of 450*l.* to hire eleven more labourers, whereupon the distribution of the entire capital stands thus:–

Implements and material..............	5,550*l.*
Labour..................................	4,450*l.*
	10,000*l.*

In this case, of the 1,000*l.* temporarily withdrawn from the original so-styled "fund" not the whole, but less than one half, is eventually restored to the fund. And it might similarly be shown that if, in consequence of a fall in the price of implements and of material, instead of in that of labour, 1,000*l.* had been temporarily withdrawn from the implement and material funds, only 450*l.* would have been restored to these latter funds, the balance being added to the original wages fund and raising its amount from 5,000*l.* to 5,550*l.*.

Mr. Cairnes had thus conclusively shown that, even with a given amount of capital invested in a given industry, the proportion of capital expended upon labour is *not* a predetermined and unalterable sum, but a sum which may vary materially with circumstances; and it is impossible to affirm more explicitly than he repeatedly does that the circumstances which influence the investment of capital are continually varying. That these were his deliberate opinions is clear from the general tenor of his discourse, and it can have been only in a moment of forgetfulness that he was able to express himself in an opposite sense. But, holding these sentiments, it is impossible that he should not really have agreed with me, first, that in the case of individual employers there are no definte or definable portions of capital which, and neither more nor less than which, they must necessarily apply to the hiring of labour; and, secondly, that if there are no such portions of capital in the case of individuals, neither can there be an aggregate of such portions constituting a national wages fund, the whole of which, and neither more nor less than which, must necessarily be divided among the entire body of labourers. Yet these two propositions compose the whole sum and substance of my thesis; and nothing, I submit, need be added to show how little ground

Cairnes had for imagining there to be any discordance between that thesis and the matured results of his own reflections.

Here then I stop, gladly closing a discussion on which I very reluctantly entered. Nothing indeed has been said which Cairnes, were he still living, would not have received with the welcome with which every genuine seeker after truth greets objections to his own prepossessions; but still it has been painful to me to be obliged to make to him a reply to which a rejoinder is no longer possible. In such circumstances my own credit, were that alone at stake, should cheerfully be sacrificed to the claims of friendship like ours. But a far more serious interest is involved, and Cairnes would have been among the last to desire that any considerations should deter me from combating what I deem to be one of the most pernicious of economic fallacies. It is, too, the reverse of a disservice which I have rendered to his memory, if I have succeeded in showing that the adherents of that mischievous doctrine have no sufficient warrant for appealing to his high authority in its behalf.

PARLIAMENT WITHOUT PARTIES

Thornton, William, "Parliament without Parties",
MacMillans Magazine, January (41), 1880, pp. 259–66.

Thornton wrote this essay with the explicit intention of criticising the current English prejudice and perception of the alternative political system. The essay was published when he was 66 years old, just five months before his death.

Parliament without Parties

In a recent number of contemporary journal, M. de Laveleye has drawn a striking picture of the anarchy which has hitherto seemed to be the normal condition of the Italian Parliament. The Chamber presents indeed the usual Continental features of Right, Left, and Centre, and there are also a Left Centre and an Extreme Left; but not only is each of these primary divisions without any character or policy common to all its members, and without any recognised leaders – the minor groups into which it is broken are equally undistinguishable by any peculiar tenets. There may be a Carioli, a Crispi, a Nicotera, a Depretis group, named after some prominent politician near whom they usually sit, but it is only by vague ties of alliance and comradeship that the individual associates are connected with him or with each other. They have not agreed upon any comprehensive plan of common action. Although now and then found voting all together on some particular question, they may presently afterwards be seen splitting their votes in all directions: they have no settled programme, no watchword, no emblem or bond of internal union. An assembly composed of such heterogeneous and mutable materials cannot possibly furnish a homogeneous majority on which a united ministry may rely for the furtherance of any systematic policy. Of the followers of to-day many may to-morrow be deserters to the opposite camp, and it is only by a series of negotiations, compromises, and bargains that the cabinet can hope to carry any of its points. Besides, an Italian ministry is never really in union with itself. Inasmuch as, while it was in process of formation, there was no large parliamentary party prepared to sink minor differences for the attainment of great ends, it was necessary to endeavour to propitiate as many groups as possible by selecting from them different ministers, each of whom carried with him into office some favourite crotchet which he could not waive, even if he would, without risking the defection of the group whom his selection had been designed to propitiate. It is obviously impossible that in such circumstances a government should be either collectively strong, or should in its corporate capacity enjoy a prolonged existence. The slightest accident may suffice to bring to light personal differences signalised by individual resignations: these provoke interpellations, followed by a crisis, and terminating in an arrangement which may possibly expected to be permanent, but which always turns out to be temporary, for it never fails to exhibit a fresh series of intestine disputes, internal changes and interpellations, resulting first in another crisis, and then in another arrangement as temporary as that which it superseded. In the eighteen years of Italy's constitutional life there have been twenty-five ministerial crises, and at this moment some seventy or eighty ex-ministers have seats in the Italian chamber. The only thing certain about any new ministry is that it will be of short duration. Actual occupants of office are never allowed time to familiarise themselves with the details of their respective departments, or to impress a definite line of conduct on their subordinates, and administrative impotence and disorder are the inevitable result.

For these evils, the gravity of which cannot easily be overrated, M. de Laveleye sees no remedy save in the gradual growth, in the country and in the chamber, of two or more parties sufficiently numerous to be able, with adventitious aid occasionally derived from one or other of the minor groups, to constitute, each in its turn, a compact majority competent to place and maintain in office selected exponents of its distinctive views. "Government by parties and by the majority is," he says, "the only one which can give strength and efficiency to parliamentary institutions." Without a majority so completely dominated by certain primary ideas as to be content to sacrifice for their furtherance all secondary objects, administrative stability and vigour are, he thinks, impossible. These conclusions are so specious, have so much to recommend them, are so generally entertained, and are moreover so consonant with ordinary English prejudice, that it may be not unprofitable for an Englishman who believes them to be equally erroneous and mischievous to state in some little detail the grounds of his dissent.

In doing so it may be convenient to begin with an impartial examination of the system which is desired to be substituted for that which actually prevails. "In England, where parliamentary government works in a typical manner, the result of the elections determines the majority, and the majority places in office the men who best represent the ideas of the triumphant majority." Most members of the latter have virtually pledged themselves to their constituents to march under their party's banner, which they cannot desert without being branded as traitors and treated accordingly. Whatever, therefore, their individual opinions on minor matters, on all matters, great or small, they as a rule vote straight at the word of command; and, as long as their numbers continue undiminshed, the chiefs whom they support can govern with as much thoroughness as though their power were absolute. The general accuracy of this description will be recognised by all who recollect how despotically one English premier was accustomed to impose silence on his supporters, even to the extent of preventing them from answering the objections urged by the Opposition to his proposals, and how another found it unnecessary to let his well-trained bands know beforehand what it was that he proposed, secure of their readiness to register the accomplished acts, whatever they might be, wherewith it amused him to startle the world. But is it possible that such exceeding loyalty can be really conducive to the public weal? Is it not, on the contrary, utterly inconsistent with the spirit and intent of representative government, which surely means, if it means any thing, that the feelings of the country shall be reflected in parliament, and that the government shall in all things be carried in accordance with the predominating national will? But although there always is, and necessarily always must be, such a will in regard to everything in particular, there neither is nor possibly an be with respect to things in general. Among men who think for themselves there can scarcely be – not any considerable parties – but any two individuals, who think alike on all political subjects. Make any question whatever the subject of a *plébiscite*, and it will no doubt be carried one way or the other by a majority of votes. But though all questions so treated might be so carried, scarcely any two questions would be carried by majorities composed of precisely the same persons. Of the many who were in favour of Catholic emancipation a very large proportion were violently opposed to emancipation of the Jews. From the myriads who fifty years ago had shown themselves so eager for Parliamentary reform, thousands broke away when their suffrages were appealed to in behalf of poor-law reform. It is thus impossible for the mass of electors to be divided into parties ready for a stand-up fight with each other whenever their leaders give the signal, whatever that signal be; and if nevertheless there be such parties in Parliament it follows that the national spirit is not adequately represented there. That it should be perfectly represented is indeed morally impossible. In every separate constituency there must needs be infinite diversity of political opinion, and since it is hopeless for electors who do not agree amongst themselves to seek for any one agreeing with them all, their best alternative is to select as their deputy that candidate on whose judgment they severally most rely, and to leave him at liberty, with certain specified reservations, to act according to his own discretion. But the deputies cannot fully discharge their legitimate duty unless on all questions, great or small, as to which they have been left unpledged, they speak and vote strictly according to their conscience.

True, without more constant support than could be expected from men like these, no ministry could attempt to carry out any comprehensive programme of their own devising without incurring defeats which, according to the law of honour at present in vogue, would necessitate their resignation, and their replacement by successors who would presently have in their turn to resign. True, likewise, that the prevalence of this law may furnish a plausible excuse for the present practice, on either side of the House of Commons, of voting for or against measures, not according to their merits, but according as they are proposed or opposed by the cabinet. In every political assembly, however conscientiously independent its individual members may be, there cannot but always be two main streams of thought, one in favour of and the other averse from progress, and either Liberals or Conservatives may honestly deem it more for the general good to make occasional sacrifices of principle than, by steadfast adherence to the principle, to risk the displacement of a ministry whose general procedure they approve by one bent on pursuing a policy which they esteem mischievous. But the notion that ministers are in honour bound to resign after unequivocal defeat is based on utter misconception of the true character of ministerial functions. So much mere etymology may of itself suffice to prove. In every country deserving to by styled constitutional, though king or queen may reign, the governing power must reside mainly with Parliament, which, inasmuch as it has a veto on the appointment of ministers, but its servants – should minister, not be ministered unto – should do as Parliament may bid, not attempt to impose their bidding upon Parliament. That, this being their vocation, they should nevertheless give themselves the airs of dictators, would, had not long habit familiarised us with the practice, appear even more preposterous than if a coachman should insist on taking one road while his master wanted to go another. For the individual coachman may at least be firmly convinced in his own mind that his choice is the best, whereas a cabinet, being a noun of multitude signifying many individuals necessarily differing each from the other more or less in temper, humour, and judgment, can seldom, if ever, have an equally firm common conviction. Any conclusion to which they may have come must be the result of mutual compromises, and represents consequently rather everybody's objections; yet a policy of which no one of its authors thoroughly approves is to be forced upon Parliament without other choice than between it and a wholesale ministerial strike. Mere vulgar trades-unionism, in its most imperious mood, never goes such lengths as this. The nearest parallel to it is perhaps that of Lord Sefton's French cook, who resigned the premiership of the kitchen on being told that his lordship had been observed at table to put salt into the soup; though it is not recorded that even then all the under-cooks and scullions followed the example of their chief and threw up their appointments in a body. And what heightens the absurdity of the ministerial usage is the singular sense of honour which underlies it. If a coachman has reason to fear that by taking the dangerous road enjoined upon him he might upset the carriage and break his own neck and his master's, he may be fully warranted in giving warning rather than obey; but, even so, prudence, not honour, is his justification, for honour would rather prompt him to share his master's peril in order that he might do his best to abate it. And similarly, it would seem, should a right-minded ministry, perceiving Parliament to be bent on what to them seemed a mistaken course, nevertheless refrain from deserting their posts as long as they were permitted to retain them, in order that so they might save the vessel of the state from some of the disasters on which, under worse guidance, it might rush. They would be very obtuse if they failed to perceive that to be allowed in such circumstances to continue at the helm was about the highest compliment that could be paid them.

All this is so obvious that the prevalence of diametrically opposite sentiments, not in England only, but in all other constitutional countries, might seem unaccountable, were it not that those latter countries, taking English constitutionalism as their type, have too servilely copied its more prominent features. They might have reflected that the English constitution was not made suddenly, but grew gradually, and adapted itself in growing to the varying circumstances of successive generations. For a lengthened period, and until a date will within living memory, party government was with us a necessity, due principally to the gross imperfection of our representative system. During the

Tudor, Stuart, and Georgian eras, most members of Parliament were mere nominees of territorial magnates, with whom, as with the generality of mankind, personal interest was the first consideration, and patriotism at best the second, and with whom personal and political objects of supreme moment were so inseperably blended that political success and political failure were to them matters of life and death. Political passion ran proportionately high, descending also very low, and thoroughly permeating every stratum of society. While the question at issue lay, or seemed to lie, between Clericalism and Puritanism, a monarchy and a republic, a Jacobite and a Hanoverian dynasty, revolutionary anarchy and preservation of Church and State, all who took any heed of political matters spontaneously and half unconsciously coalesced into separate leagues, each with its distinctive cry too loudly and constantly vociferated to allow of any other being much attended to, and each instinctively aware of the need of internal discipline and of subordination to those prominent exponents of its dominant sentiment whom it had accepted as its chiefs. The party zeal thus generated throughout the country was faithfully represented in Parliament. The lords and gentlemen by whom so much of the elective function was practically monopolised were careful to impress upon all whom they suffered to be elected the paramount obligation of collective action, of presenting a compact front, and of voting black white rather than permit individual scruples to endanger the realisation of the common object. When quieter times succeeded, weaker motives sufficed to produce a similar result. The primary aim, both of the grand electors and of their nominees, continued to be, as it had always been, the constitution of a majority for the purpose of placing and maintaining their leaders in power, not simply for the furtherance of some special public policy, but also in order that they might themselves participate in the sweets of office, which the leaders on their side were careful to distribute in such mode as seemed best calculated to conciliate the possessors of parliamentary patronage, and thereby to preserve and augment the number of their adherents. The conditions out of which this state of things arose have now in great measure passed away. Members of the House of Commons are now, for the most part, returned by independent constituencies, and might, if they and their constituents chose, act on all occasions independently and conscientiously. But the traditions of former days have hitherto been too strong for any for any approach to so salutary a change. Party spirit is still supreme, and still exercises a universal fascination. Who is insensible to the manifold charms of that "Strife of Freedom, wherein," as Carlyle says, "everyone may get a share of what is going," to the strong personal attachments and bitter hatreds it begets, the excitement of conflict, the joy of triumph, the exultation over the spoils of victory? Who doubts that a Whig opposition would again be as unanimous as before in its tacit encouragement of Hyde Park rioters for the sake of embarrassing a Tory administration, or that "no leap in the dark" would be too appalling for gleeful Tories hopeful of thereby finally "dishing the Whigs"?

What though, meanwhile, howsoever parties rave, the public rues? The English public loves too well the pleasure it has so long enjoyed to care much about its punishment. The best chance for us is that other nations, taking warning from our example, may strike out a better line for themselves and set us a better example. The circumstances of Italy are particularly favourable for such an experiment. The parliamentary anarchy which M. de Laveleye, in common with some eminent Italian statesmen, so much deplores, implying, as it does, no more at worst than absence of rival parliamentary archons with quasidespotic, albeit temporary authority, only requires to be rightly understood in order to be quite otherwise appreciated. What it really does is to leave the ground clear for the erection of improved institutions. If it continues long enough, ministers, finding themselves incapacitated from posing as dictators, must sooner or later accept their legitimate *rôle*, and acquiesce with becoming docility in parliamentary dictation. Whoever thence forward may bring on a motion, will have to take the sense of the whole chamber upon it, not in form and appearance only, but in all sincerity. Having no trained bands on whose allegiance he can in any case rely, he will be unable to carry his proposal except by convincing a majority of its general expediency, accepting too any amendments on which any majority whatever of the deputies may agree, and thereby bringing it into accord with the dominant feelings of the chamber, and presumably also of the country. The superiority of a system so genuinely representative over that which it would supersede speaks in great measure for itself, and will be more manifest the more minutely we consider how the plan would be likely to work. There would still be a cabinet with an at least nominal premier, an inner council of ministers with a titular president, and although without solidarity or mutual responsibility, only the more thoroughly imbued with omnifarious aptitude by reason of its exemption from those shackles. Each separate minister would probably be well enough disposed, and might moreover be formally required, to consult his assembled colleagues on all matters of moment, yet without being bound to follow their advice. Each might be accountable solely and exclusively for the transactions of his own department or of any business outside it of which he might voluntarily assume the conduct; and no defeat which he might sustain would, unless implying direct censure and want of confidence, necessitate his resignation. Neither, even when it did, would it necessitate that of his colleagues likewise, who would have learnt to repudiate the monstrous notion that official fellowship could impose on them the obligation of publicly defending official misconduct which they had not shared, and against which they might have privately remonstrated, or of insisting in participating in the retribution which such misconduct incurred. Partial ministerial changes would take place whenever required, but sudden subversion of an entire ministry would be no longer possible. Worthy and unworthy would no longer all go out together in order to make way for others, some of whom would inevitably be less worthy than those whom they had supplanted. An Italian ministry, of which, as has been said, the one thing that can at present be predicted is that it will be short-lived, might in its corporate capacity live for ever under the new *régime,* amputation effete members, judicious grafting and infusion of new blood sufficing to maintain it in perpetual health. Every individual minister, perceiving that he held office during pleasure – pleasure contingent on his own individual good behaviour – would perceive likewise that the surest mode of prolonging his tenure was by assiduous attention to the duties of his department, to which he could give his whole time when freed from the incessant interpellations with which he, in common with his colleagues, is now pestered, and from the incessant and incumbent upon them in order to preserve or recruit a majority ever on the point of melting away. In the conduct of his own departmental business indeed he might still be subject to abundant criticism, but that criticism would be no longer factious, for the Chamber would no longer be divided into factions: when there was no organised body of ministerial partisans to overthrow, and organised opposition would be without a *raison d'être.* There would continue to be – it would be a great pity if there did not – abundance of personal ambition outside the cabinet, abundance of individual aspirants to office; but each of these would best consult his own interests by singling out some particular post as the object of his aspirations, and by making himself master of its details so as to justify his own candidature for its reversion. But the intelligent criticism to be expected from such quarters would, if accepted in a proper spirit be, however hostile, the reverse of harmful to those against whom it was directed, inasmuch as, causing them to take more heed to their ways and aiding them to direct their steps, it would strengthen instead of weakening their hold on office. On such conditions an Italian Palmerston, when once appointed, might remain foreign minister, or an Italian Gladstone or Northcote or Forster or Cross, Finance or Home Minister, during the rest of his public life, or until his proved and ever-increasing efficiency in one position was rewarded by translation to another more arduous or dignified. Disappointed aspirants might chafe impatiently, but even they would scarcely pretend that the reins of government could continue too long in hands ostensibly the very fittest to hold them. And let it not be apprehended that the ministers would be less strong collectively than individually. The habit of asking and taking each other's advice would naturally engender a disposition to act together, all the more because whatever agreement or union subsisted among them would be based upon genuine conviction. On all great occasions, indeed, some considerable degree of concord would be indispensable. No foreign secretary would venture to propose the alternative of war without the concurrence of the heads of the finance and military and naval departments; nor would the most headstrong of premiers attempt to initiate a serious organic change in domestic arrangements to which the bulk of his colleagues had declared themselves adverse; while, on the hand, any measure on which the parliament's own *élite,* their very flower and cream, were agreed, would commend itself with hitherto unprecedented force to general acceptance. Thus the general course of national policy would be steadily continuous, deviating from inherited traditions in so far as varying circumstances and calm deliberation suggested, but no longer oscillating violently from extreme to extreme with every capricious change in the national humour.

It need not be asserted that these immense gains would be without their drawbacks. In foreign affairs, more especially, a parliamentary government which may be required to submit every premeditated movement to public discussion must often be very inferior to an autocracy in promptitude of decision and execution; yet it may fairly be doubted whether this serious defect would not be moderated rather than aggravated under the supposed new *régime*. Ministers, every one of whom parliament had itself selected, and whose increasing efficiency had, as already hinted, been ever since justifying the original choice, would presumably not be denied the confidence which experience had shown them to deserve, and would, if they were worth their salt, on any adequate emergency not scruple to take full liberty of secret action, on the necessarily implied condition of being held responsible for the consequences of the discretionary powers they had assumed. Quite possibly they might, on sufficient cause subsequently shown, obtain an applausive bill of indemnity for interrupting fruitless negotiations with Austria by seizing on the mountain passes into the Tyrol, or for guaranteeing Greece against Turkish invasion on condition of the cession of Corfu.

The experiment thus imagined to be tried in the first instance by Italy would presumably, if successful there, be imitated in other countries, and eventually, though not until very late, by such slaves of habit as ourselves. Yet for England the plan suggested would possess some signal recommendations over and above those already indicated, and, among others, this – that it would, in anticipation of Mr. Hare's admirably contrived scheme for extent for the representation of minorities. The object of such representation is not to enable a minority to rule, but simply to enable it to obtain a hearing. It is not more inevitable than, in the long run, desirable that a majority should have its own way in all things; and at any rate a minority must needs submit as long as it remains a minority. But provided only it can insist on being listened to, whatever truth there may be in its utterances is sure in the end to prevail to the benefit of all concerned, that majority of course included by whom it had previously been opposed, and whom it has at length converted. Now there is probably scarcely a shade of popular opinion which, even as the House of Commons is at present constituted, is not entertained by one or more of its members, who, when partisanship had ceased to enjoin silence, would not fail, as often as fitting opportunity offered, to express openly their previously hidden sentiments. Thus without any change in the present mode of election, the sense of the entire nation might be in so far represented in the House as that the thoughts upon any given subject of every minority of thinkers could compel attention to them, and gradually obtain whatever influence comparison between them and those of superior numbers might show them to merit. One consequence, be it observed parenthetically, would pretty certainly be general recognition of the want of a much completer and more direct representation of minorities, as perhaps the most crying political want of out time, while concomitant advantages of the new *régime* would be that caucuses and similar devices for Americanising our institutions would be perceived to be unnecessary, even if it not necessarily baneful, and that political differences would cease to be regarded as disqualifications for local appointments. Whigs and Tories equally in Tory boroughs, and Tories and Whigs equally in Whig boroughs, would be deemed eligible for town councils, vestries, and school boards; the most specially serviceable men, whatever their political creed, would everywhere be in request for every special local service.

Enough, however, of this for the present, though a good deal more of the same kind must be said in order to make much impression on the deeply-ingrained prejudices against which it is directed, and although it might have been well, if space had permitted, to point out how sensibly the difficulties with which the French Republic is just now beset would be lightened by adoption of the principles advocated above. But the few foregoing pages will not have been written altogether in vain if they induce any one to reflect how incompatible is party spirit with patriotism, and how very imperfect a specimen of representative government must be the best imaginable form of government by party.

A NEW VIEW OF THE INDIAN EXCHANGE DIFFICULTY

Thornton, William, "A New View of the Indian Exchange Difficulty", *Westminster Review*, July (114), 1880, pp. 173–92.

This essay was published after Thornton's death. In it, contrary to his contemporaries' view points, Thornton attributed the falling exchange value of the rupee between 1861 and 1872 to an increase in Council Bills rather than to a depreciation in the price of silver.

A New View of the Indian Exchange Difficulty

No one is at all likely to bestow a glance on the following pages who is not already aware that, during the sixteen years ending with 1878, the Indian Government has annually sustained a loss, always considerable and latterly enormous, by reason of its having to meet bills, equivalent in amount to many millions sterling, drawn annually by the Secretary of State for India in Council. These bills – Council Bills as they are called – which are necessary to provide the Council with the means of making corresponding sterling payments in England, are drawn in rupees, and as the exchange value* of the rupee has during the same sixteen years fallen to various rates very much below the normal rate of 2s., the Council have been compelled to accept proportionately smaller sums in sterling for drafts upon the Government for any given sums in rupees, and consequently to draw for a proportionally larger total of rupees for the satisfaction of all their English requirements.

The following Table [see p. 92] shows the amount of Council Bills, the average rate of exchange, and Government loss by exchange in each of the said sixteen years, and also the first two particulars for three earlier years:–

It will be observed how immensely the loss by exchange has increased since 1872, and when it is considered that the price of silver began to fall in 1873 from its immediately previous and normal rate of 60*d.* per oz., and that in 1878 it averaged only 52$\frac{9}{16}$*d.*, the inference may at first seem irresistible that the intermediate increase of loss was mainly due to the depreciation of silver. Such, indeed, is the general and almost universal opinion, that of the late Mr. Bagehot and other equally eminent authorities included; and one novelty in the view about to be placed before the reader will consist in its treating this opinion as altogether erroneous, and in representing the depreciation of silver as not having as yet affected the Indian exchange in any appreciable degree.

So startling a paradox may not improbably be summarily dismissed as unworthy of serious examination, but to any one who will vouchsafe me a hearing I hope to be able to prove, and to prove, not by complex argumentation, but by simple logic of undisputed and indisputable facts, that, however apparently absurd, it is really almost literal truth.

The first fact to which I would invite attention is that, although the

* "Exchange value" is, perhaps, a somewhat ambiguous expression, but wherever used in this paper the reader is requested to understand by it simply and solely the value of the rupee, as measured by the price payable for bills of exchange drawn either by foreign countries on India or by India on foreign countries.

Year	Amount of Council Bills	Average Rate of Exchange	Loss by Exchange
	£	R	£
1860–1	797	2	—
1861–2	1,193,729 (Besides £120,000 on London, purchased in India on Government Account.)	1-11⅞	—
1862–3	6,641,576	1-11⅞	—
1863–4	8,979,521	1-11⅞	11,640
1864–5	6,789,473	1-11⅞	42,700
1865–6	6,998,899	1-11¾	84,662
1866–7	5,613,746	1-11	165,223
1867–8	4,137,285	1-11⅛	63,758
1868–9	3,705,741	1-11⅛	132,139
1869–70	6,980,122	1-11¼	142,555
1870-1	8,443,509	1-10½	554,623
1871-2	10,310,339	1-11⅜	382,288
1872-3	13,939,095 (Besides £403,040 on London, purchased in India.)	1-10¾	750,318
1873–4	13,285,678	1-10⅜	924,851
1874–5	10,841,615	1-10⅛	863,995
1875–6	12,389,613	1-9⅝	1,391,454
1876–7	12,695,800	1-8½	2,129,962
1877–8	10,134,455	1-8¾	1,606,582
1878–9	13,948,565 (Besides £516,193 on London, purchased in India.)	1-7¾	2,963,796

depreciation of silver did not commence until 1873, the exchange value of the rupee had, during the twelve years immediately preceding, fallen from 2*s.* at which it had stood in 1860, to 1*s.* 10¾*d.* in 1872. So far, at all events, unless an antecedent can result from a subsequent, the fall in the value of silver cannot possibly have had anything to do with the fall in the exchange, which must plainly have been wholly due to other causes, whereof it may suffice to specify one, quite adequate of itself to account for the phenomenon. The amount of Council Bills (and of bills on London purchased in India) which had been only £797 in 1860, became more than two millions sterling in 1861, and reached to between fourteen and fifteen millions in 1872, the total during the twelve years ending with that one being more than eighty-four millions, and the annual average about seven millions. How so great and rapid a multiplication would operate is readily perceived. All English sellers of bills on India, finding themselves with an article on their hands which had become a comparative drug in the market, would be far more eager to sell than customers to buy, and would have and would have to accept much less sterling money than before for paper representing any given sum in rupees; while Indian customers for bills on England, becoming conversely more anxious to buy than sellers to sell, would have to give many more rupees than before for paper representing any given amount of sterling. Now that this twofold operation was by far the principal, if not the exclusive, cause of the fall of the exchange during the twelve years ending with 1872, is admitted on all hands; but if that first fall from 2*s.* to 1*s.* 10¾*d.* may so be sufficiently explained, a similar explanation might equally suffice for the further fall which took place during the six years immediately succeeding. In that second period, during which the exchange fell from 1*s.* 10¾*d.*, to 1*s.* 7¾*d.*, the total amount of Council Bills and of Bills on London purchased in India on Government account, was little short of seventy-five millions sterling, and the annual average twelve and a half millions, and whoever is aware in how very much more than mere rule-of-three proportion the price of any article is lowered by a considerably additional supply while demand remains the same, need have no difficulty in believing that if an average annual issue of seven millions of Council Bills had reduced the value of paper rupee money by five farthings in every two shillings, an annual issue of twelve and a half millions might well suffice to occasion a second reduction of twelve farthings. One thing at least is demonstrably certain. Wheather this second reduction was or was not exclusively due to the superabundance of Council Bills, and whatever other causes, if any, may have contributed, the depreciation of silver was not among the number – not at least as a direct material agency. What moral influence it may possibly have exerted indirectly will be adverted to hereafter, but of its absolute nullity in any more distinct sense, there is the following positive proof.

In order that the increased abundance and consequent cheapness of silver bullion on this side the globe should have affected the exchange value of the rupee, two things were indispensable; firstly, more silver than usual must have been followed by an increased coinage of rupees. Otherwise, the comparative abundance of silver in Europe and America, and its comparative scarcity in India, could not lower its price in India any more than superabundant wheat harvests in India could lower the price of wheat in England as long as the whole of the superabundance was retained in the land of its growth. In either case, no doubt, apprehension of importation, on the part of dealers in the commodity concerned, might produce some effect of the kind, but as soon as it was discovered that the apprehended importation neither did nor was likely to take place, both the apprehension and its effect would vanish, and the price, whether of silver or of wheat, would revert to the point from which it had fallen. Again, even though silver had been imported into India in infinitely larger quantities than before, still the consequently increased cheapness of the raw material of rupee could, unless accompanied by increased coinage, have no more lowered the value of the rupee than a fall in the price of silver-paper – the raw material of bank notes – could of itself lower the value of bank notes. For the purchasing power of rupees does not, any more than that of bank notes, depend upon intrinsic value of the material of which it is composed: it depends upon the utility of the rupee as an instrument of exchange and upon the demand for it in that capacity. A rupee cannot, indeed, possibly become worth less than a piece of silver of the same weight and fineness, nor a bank note worth less than a scrap of paper of like size and quality; but either rupees or notes may, and inevitably will, become worth more, if their issue do not keep pace with the demand for them. Clearly then, however large might have been the importation of silver into India subsequently to 1872, the exchange value of the rupee could not have been affected in consequence, unless a greater coinage than usual of rupees had taken place simultaneously. Now in the three years next after 1872, both the imports of silver into India and the coinage of rupees there, instead of increasing, sensibly decreased. During the four years ending with 1872, the imports had averaged £3,877,448, and the silver coinage £3,715,766, but during the next three years (1873-1875) the yearly average of silver imports was £2,897,794: that of silver coinage £3,272,369. It is thus clear that during at least three out of the six years under review, that is to say during 1873, 1874 and 1875, the Indian exchange was not affected by the depreciation of silver.

One thing indeed which these figures seem to indicate is that the depreciation had not in 1875 as yet extended to India at all, notwithstanding that it already represented in Europe and America a fall of price of from 60*d.* to 56⅞ *d.* per oz., or not quite 5¼ per cent. For, inasmuch as in India the coinage is perfectly unrestricted, any one who pleases being entitled to take silver to the Mint and have it coined there, it is certain that, if silver had in any appreciable degree been worth less there in an uncoined than in a coined condition, it would at once have been coined in quantities sufficient to restore equilibrium between the two conditions. Unluckily as to this particular point only hearsay evidence is immediately accessible: still, in so far as such imperfect testimony can be relied upon, it is distinctly corroborative of the above stated inference; every one, with any pretension to acquaintance with the subject to whom I have referred, assuring me that to the best of his knowledge, the price per oz. of bar silver in India has not sensibly varied for several years.

The facts already adduced might perhaps suffice to prove my case, in so far as it applied to the period ending with 1875, but others may be cited in their support. In whatever degree, if any, the fall in the exchange value of the rupee may have been due to depreciation of the metal of which it is composed, general prices must necessarily have risen in India in the same proportion – not indeed as much as the price of bills on England has risen, for no one doubts that this latter rise is in part due to increased demand for bills on England - but as much as the price of such bills has been raised by depreciation of the silver composing the rupee. For a fall in the value of the rupee occasioned by depreciation of silver, and a rise of all prices expressed in rupees, are convertible terms. The one means the other and means nothing else: it means simply that a rupee will no longer exchange for the same quantity of commodities as before, because a quantity of silver equal to that contained in the rupee will no longer exchange for the same quantity. Did the Indian prices in general rise when silver became depreciated? Of some few articles, wheat for example, the price did for a while rise slightly; but, in every such instance the rise can be traced to variations of supply or demand or other circumstance affecting exclusively the particular article concerned; while, with regard to the great majority of commodities, either prices have remained stationary, or if there has been any change, the movement has taken a downward more frequently than an upward direction. The one striking exception is that of bills on England, but if, while these have risen enormously in price, the price of almost everything else has remained comparatively unchanged, the inevitable inference is that the relation between them and rupees has been disturbed by some special cause or causes affecting themselves exclusively, not by any cause affecting rupees exclusively.

Unless the accuracy of our statistics be open to doubt, the inference drawn from them would seem to be as irresistible as it is obvious, but it must be admitted that one portion of the evidence is almost as startling as the opinion in behalf of which it is cited. How, it will naturally be asked, is it possible that if - provided it were sent to India – it would there become worth more by being coined, it was not forthwith coined? To say in reply to the first of these questions that time was required for silver to find its level in all parts of the commercial world is merely to restate the difficulty, not solve it. Why in this instance was so much time required? If at Bombay or Calcutta there were heaps of jute or hides, or seeds or sugar in store, the transfer of which to England would ensure a profit of five per cent. over and above the ordinary rate, the transfer would, instead of occupying three years, probably by completed in as many months. Why, then, should three years have been necessary for an article so much more easily portable as silver? With some hesitation I venture to suggest as a possible explanation that, profitable as it might have been to remit silver from England, it was still more profitable to remit bills. Merchants who, while silver was at 60*d.* per oz., might have had to give £100 for the quantity coinable into 1000 rupees, would, with the price at 56⅞*d.* per oz., have to give only £94 15*s.* 10*d.* for the like quantity; but on the other hand, with the exchange at 1*s.* 10*d.* the rupee, the average rate of the three years ending with 1875, he could buy a 1000 rupee bill on India with only £91 13*s.* 4*d.*, a difference in favour of remittance by bill amply sufficient to cause that mode to be universally preferred. Besides, be this as it may, if there had been any extraordinary importation of silver into India, part of the extraordinary supply must inevitably have gone to the Mint to be coined, and against that supposition at least the negative testimony of the Mint records is absolutely decisive.

Let us here pause for a moment to report progress, briefly restating the point already arrived at, and the path by which it has been reached. In the twelve years beginning with 1861 and ending with 1872, the exchange value of the rupee fell from 2*s.* to 1*s.* 10¾*d.*, but as the depreciation of silver did not commence until 1873, it can have had nothing to do with this first fall, which must therefore have resulted from quite different causes, whereof an increase of Council Bills was certainly the chief, if not the only one. During the three years immediately succeeding and ending with 1875, the exchange underwent a further fall to 1*s.* 9⅝*d.*, for which the simultaneous increase of Council Bills form an annual average of seven, to one of twelve and a half millions, would perfectly account, and would no doubt have been universally supposed to account perfectly, if it had not been overlooked in the consternation produced by a fall in the value of silver from 60*d.* to 56⅞ *d.*, which also took place simultaneously, and to which the entire discredit of having lowered the exchange was immediately and generally transferred. But in order that the depreciation of silver should even co-operate in thus affecting the exchange, it was indispensable both that more silver should be imported into India than in previous years, and that more of the silver should by coined, whereas, in point of fact, between 1872 and the end of that depreciation of silver had no more to do with the fall of exchange during 1873–5, than it had with the previous fall during 1861 and 1872.

Unless some flaw, which altogether eludes my own jealous scrutiny, can be detected in the reasoning thus summarized, my case thus far ought, I think, to be admitted, but I am far from flattering myself with the hope of readily obtaining such an admission. That silver should fall in value by 5¼ per cent. in three years throughout the greater part of the commercial world, without sensibly lowering the exchange in every country in which silver money is the sole legal tender, and where coinage is absolutely unrestricted, is so contrary both to all experience and to that indolent opinionativeness which is apt to be complacently confounded with common sense, that the reader may probably be tempted to exclaim "the thing's impossible and cannot be," and to add that only by some juggle of words and figures can it have been made to appear to be. Neither can it be denied that except in very peculiar and extraordinary circumstances the thing would be as impossible as it seems: but then, in the particular case with which were at present dealing, the circumstances are most peculiar, if not unexampled; their peculiarity consisting in the fatal obligation under which India groans of having to make annually to England remittances – economically of the nature of tribute – of many millions sterling, for which she gets no return. How disastrously this obligation affects India's commercial position will be seen if we consider what that position would be without it. India's imports from and her exports to England would presumably then about balance each other, as would likewise the bills annually drawn by one country on the other; and as long as the relative intrinsic values of the metals respectively composing the sovereign and the rupee remained without alteration, the exchange between the two countries would be pretty constant at par. If, however, the relative values of the precious metals became seriously deranged, or to put the case as it has actually occurred, if silver became greatly depreciated, its price in the first instance becoming much lower in Europe and America than elsewhere, then, indeed, other circumstances remaining as above supposed, silver would assuredly pour into India: large coinage of rupees would immediately ensue; and all prices whatsoever would rise in consequence, the price of bills on England of course rising among the rest, though neither more nor less than prices in general. The fall in the exchange value of the rupee which the rise in the price of Bills of Exchange would constitute, would then be permanent – would last as long as the depreciation of silver lasted – inasmuch as, so long as the rupee remained shorn of part of its previous purchasing power, while the sovereign retained all of its previous purchasing power, more rupees would obviously be needed to purchase a bill representing a given number of sovereigns, while fewer sovereigns would suffice to purchase a bill representing a given number of rupees. But, although so long as the rate of exchange continued to fall, dealers might be much inconvenienced by the increased difficulty of estimating the eventual sale proceeds of their wares, and might be entrapped into unexpected losses – compensated, however, quite possibly, by equally unexpected gains – the inconvenience would be only temporary, and would cease whenever the rate of exchange reached the lowest point marked out for it by the depreciation of silver. At that point, whatever it might be, the exchange would remain constant, unless or until silver recovered part of its former intrinsic value, and merchants would base their calculations upon it, and arrange their prices accordingly, making neither more nor less profit than before by reason of the lowness of the rate. For it is, I submit, a complete mistake to suppose that reduction of the exchange value of the rupee, *when caused by depreciation of silver,* can either stimulate India's export or check her import trade.

In saying this I am, I am aware, advancing a second novelty, and am moreover directly at variance with economists of no less mark than the late Mr. Bagehot and Mr. Goschen; but, with all respect, I submit that the reasoning of those eminent authorities on this point is fatally vitiated by a very singular exchange value of the rupee considerably below par, a merchant sending foreign goods to India and selling them there at the same prices as prevailed before the exchange fell, and consequently obtaining for them only the same number of rupees for a £1,000 bill upon England, and would therefore find his eventual profit on the transaction proportionately reduced; while on the other hand, a merchant sending Indian goods to England would, with the sovereigns obtained by him as their sale proceeds, be able to buy a bill on India for many more rupees than formerly, so that his total profit would be proportionately augmented. In thus speaking, however, they assume that Indian prices remain stationary, unaccountably overlooking the utter impossibility of their so remaining while the exchange was falling *by reason of depreciation of the rupee due to the depreciation of the metal composing it.* Mr. Bagehot did, indeed, perceive clearly that, in such circumstances, Indian prices must sooner or later rise, but, throughout his book, he assumes that – at the time he wrote, they had not as yet fallen; and Mr. Goschen's language distinctly treats "depreciation of silver in India," and a consequent "depreciation of the Indian exchange," unaccompanied by a rise of Indian prices, not "simply as a possible contingency, but as an actually existing fact."* But surely the co-existence of a depreciated currency and of stationary prices is a flat contradiction in terms. Depreciation of silver currency, in a country in which silver is the sole legal tender, signifies a rise of prices and signifies nothing else. It is a rise of prices alone which indicates it; nay rather, which constitutes its essence. The quantity of silver contained in a given number of rupees has ceased to be worth the same quantity of miscellaneous commodities as before; so, more rupees than before are needed to purchase the same quantities of commodities; in other words, general prices have risen, In whatever measure, great or small, depreciation of silver has contributed, or may hereafter contribute, to lower the exchange value of the rupee, in precisely that same measure must Indian prices in general have simultaneously risen already, or hereafter rise simultaneously. The necessity of the case forbids one moment's interval between the two events. It does not suffice to sat that prices must sooner or later rise in virtue of the depreciation; if they have not risen already the depreciation has not yet commenced. Although, therefore, the importer into India of English goods, if buying bills of exchange on England with depreciated rupees, would have to pay more rupees for them, he would, in the increased number of those rupees obtained by him in payment for his goods, have acquired the means of doing so without incurring any diminution of his previous rate of profit; while, on the other hand, the exporter to England of Indian goods, although able with the sale proceeds of those goods to buy bills on India representing more rupees than before, would find those rupees worth no more in India than the smaller quantity were formerly, and would not therefore find his trade more profitable than of yore. There would thus be no increase of profit to stimulate India's export trade; the amounts of the two would retain their old proportions, and so too would the amount of bills drawn by one country on the other, on purely commercial account. If all this be true, and it is not so much demonstrable truth as a string of palpable truisms, it follows that Mr. Bagehot was mistaken in supposing that a fall proceeding from depreciation of silver could ever "cure itself," or that "the ordinary laws which govern foreign exchanges" could correct a fall proceeding from that cause. Both import and export trade and everything connected with them, would follow the same routine as before without other change than this, that inasmuch as the Indian currency had become depreciated, all Indian prices would rise, and notably the

* See Evidence before the Silver Committee, Question 1371. From Question 1377, it would seem that the fallacy here alluded did not escape the sharp eyes of Professor Fawcett.

price of foreign bills of exchange payable in gold. The natural tendency for the so-called "laws which govern foreign exchanges" is to place exchange at par; par of exchange signifying that rate at which the bullion contained in any given number of the coins of one country will exchange for a quantity of foreign coin containing an equivalent quantity of bullion. But between two countries like England and India, one using silver and the other gold money, the rate representing par must needs change if silver becomes depreciated, so that if, after the Indian rate of exchange had fallen in consequence, the laws which govern foreign exchange should restore it to its previous height, the results would be not parity, but imparity, of exchange.

Returning from this short and indispensable digression, in which we have examined the purely hypothetical case of an India exempt from tribute, but with a silver currency depreciated by reason of a decrease in the intrinsic value of the metal composing it, lit us now turn to the actually existing case of an India saddles with enormous tribute obligations. Between 1861 and 1873, previously to which latter year silver had undergone no depreciation, the progressive increase of Council Bills had reduced the exchange value of the rupee by five farthings. During the next three years, 1873–5, the annual average amount of Council Bills was further increased, and was not, indeed, very much less than doubled, and the exchange value of the rupee underwent simultaneously a further fall of three farthing or of twopence in all. Is it possible that this second fall can have been exclusively due to the same cause as the first, and that the reduction by one-twentieth of the value of silver bullion had nothing to do with it? Assuredly, if India had been exempt from tribute, it would have been impossible for silver to be worth more by 5¼ per cent. in Europe and America than in India, without pouring into India in quantities sufficient to produce equilibrium between its price there and elsewhere; and it would have been similarly impossible that the influx should not have been accompanied by an increased coinage of rupees sufficient to establish equality in India between the value of uncoined and coined silver. How then can it be that the existence of the tribute has prevented all this from actually happening? In reply I can only repeat my former conjecture that the progressive increase of the tribute, represented as it was by a corresponding multiplication of Council Bills, lowered the exchange to a point at which it was still more profitable to remit bills than to remit silver to India; but this answer ought, I submit, to suffice, confirmed as it is by the fact that the imports of silver and likewise the coinage of rupees, instead of increasing, decreased between 1872 and the end of 1875, and that, as a further consequence, notwithstanding the depreciation of bar silver in Europe, the silver currency of India underwent no depreciation during the period mentioned.

Now at length, perhaps, I may fairly claim to have proved that down to the end of 1875 at all events, the depreciation of silver had not appreciably contributed to reduce the exchange value of the rupee, the low rate of which was mainly, if not exclusively, due to the excessive issue of Council Bills. But though this be true down to the date mentioned, what about the future? In respect to the immediate past, we have some new and curiously instructive particulars. Whatever may have been the causes which, in spite of the extreme cheapness of silver in Europe, checked for a while its importation into India, those causes ceased to operate immediately after 1875. The net imports, which, having been £6,552,375 in 1871, fell to £715,144 in 1872, and after rising to £2,495,824 in 1873, and to £4,642,203 in 1874, fell again to £1,555,355 in 1875, sprang suddenly to £7,198,870 in 1876, and by another and still more surprising bound to £14,676,334 in 1877; while the coinage of rupees, which in the four years ending with 1872 had averaged annually £3,715,706, but only £3,272,369 in the next three years, became £6,271,122 in 1866, and in 1877 reached the unprecedented height of £16,180,326. In 1878 it was £8,176,373. A comparison of these figures with some of those in the tabular statement entered on the first page of this article [see p. 92, above] will afford a striking confirmation of the soundness of the views here set forth. In 1877, when the importation of silver was by far the greatest that had taken place for more than twenty years, and the silver coinage by far the greatest ever known, the rate of exchange, instead of falling rose by one farthing above that of the previous year, for the amount of Council Bills was less by two millions and a half than that of 1876. In 1878 the imports fell from about 14½ to about 5½ millions and the coinage from about 16 to about 8 millions, yet the rate of exchange fell four farthings, for the amount of Council Bills rose by nearly 2½ millions above that of 1877. Now, seeing that the enormous additions made to both imports and coinage in 1877 did not affect the price of bills of exchange, we may rest satisfied that they did not affect the prices of things in general; we may fairly conclude that India's appetite for silver – her *argenti sacra fames* – whetted by the short diet of the four preceding years, was keen enough to allow of her absorbing even those enormous additions without showing any symptoms of surfeit, and we may still more be strengthened in this conclusion on observing that when, in 1878, the amount of Council Bills became half as much again as in the preceding year, a decrease of about one-half in both silver imports and silver coinage did not prevent the exchange from suffering almost the severest fall it had ever experienced within an equal space of time. Can more decisive proof be desired that the cause of the fall in 1878 was the same as in all pervious years – a great increase, namely, in the issue of Council Bills, unaccompanied by an increase in the demand for them; and that consequently, down to this moment, the depreciation of silver has not sensibly contributed towards the fall?

Next as to the future. Undoubtedly if silver continue to be as is present very much cheaper in England than in India, silver must sooner or later flow from hence into India, perhaps in a continuous stream, perhaps only by fits and starts, but in one way or the other, sufficiently to bring its prices in India and England to virtual equilibrium, and in whatever degree silver may in consequence become depreciated in India, the Indian currency must needs be depreciated likewise, and the Indian exchange be affected accordingly. The degree, however, in which these effects will exhibit themselves will obviously depend on the price of silver in England and Europe generally, and there are strong grounds for believing that that price will speedily recover from its present depression, inasmuch as all the causes which have hitherto contributed to depress it may be confidently expected to become shortly inoperative.

Some readers may perhaps be surprised to be told that among those causes, the discovery of new and extraordinarily productive mines in the United States of America occupies only a very subordinate place. It may be true, though there is much reason for believing the figures to be greatly exaggerated, that whereas the North American out-turn of silver had ten tears before been scarcely worth mentioning, it was nearly six millions sterling in 1872, more than seven million in both 1873 and 1874, and nine millions in 1875, and has since shown but slight symptoms of dimunition, being stated at £3,400,000 for the first six months of the present year. But however abundant the new supply from this source, one thing certain is that none of it has found its way to Europe, for the total exports from the United States, instead of annually during the four years ending with July of that year, then that the supply from the United States, instead of increasing, fell off after 1872, having averaged £3,414,440 and only £3,346,198 in the next six and a half years. It is plain as a material factor in the fall of the gold price of silver, "except in so far as the apprehension excited by the discovery of the new mines may have affected a market already in an exceedingly perturbed and sensitive condition."

A factor of real efficacy was Germany's demonetization of silver and monetization of gold, which has acted in three-fold wise – to wit, by throwing on the market fifteen millions sterling worth of silver coin withdrawn from circulation, by stopping the demand for that silver which had previously been required to maintain the German silver currency at a proper complement and by creating a larger new demand for gold, and thereby enhancing the absolute value of that metal at the same time that its value relatively to silver was being increased by reason of the independent depreciation of the latter. The combined effect of this simple action might nevertheless have been almost unfelt but for the suicidal perversity of France and the other members of the Latin Monetary (and Bi-metallic) Union, which taking alarm at Germany's procedure, resolved, and publicly announced their resolution, to restrict within the narrowest possible bounds their own silver coinage, and thereby did their best to increase the very depreciation at which they had taken fright. By this step the Union were abandoning the fundamental principles of their association, and the step was not more dastardly than disastrous. If they had remained true to their bi-metallic faith, and, continuing to manifest by their conduct the courage of their opinions, had trusted bi-metallism to take care of itself, bi-metallism would have shown itself equal to the occasion, and able to bear with perfect ease the new strain to which it was being subjected. Of course silver would then have been taken in larger quantities to the various Mints of the Union, and the consequent issues of silver coin would gave proportionately displaced gold money, and possibly, though most improbably, might gave caused the latter to disappear entirely from circulation. But even in this extreme case, what then? The public inconvenience that might otherwise have resulted from the substitution of less portable for more portable metallic money, could easily have been obviated by a more general adoption of bank notes or other paper for large or distant payments; and although the Union Mints might have been somewhat severely tasked in order to meet the extraordinary demand for silver coin, with the prospect, too, of having to perform a converse task whenever the tide should turn, and gold be demanded at the Mint in substitution for silver, they might have abundantly compensated themselves for the extra trouble by the pecuniary gain they would have made, if, in anticipation of the action of individuals, they had themselves bought up depreciated silver with the gold they had in stock, and then reissued it with the additional value it would have derived from being coined. If this course had been pursued, the depreciation of silver would have been arrested almost as soon as it commenced; the extraordinary supply, such as it was, by which the metal was temporarily cheapened, would have been met by a corresponding demand which would presently have restored the price to nearly, if not quite, its previous height, and things would have gone on much as before. For the one solitary physical factor then remaining would have been Germany's addition to the previous supply, and it was only a very limited amount which Germany was capable of supplying. Its exact amount may be unkown, or known only to initiated bureaucrats, but according to a recent and very careful analysis of official data,* cannot have much exceeded four millions sterling, and whatever the total, Germany would have been careful, for her own sake, not to flood the market with it, nor to offer it for sale in portions much larger than those actually adopted, or, on the average, about seven millions yearly. But, seeing that India alone has been able to absorb nearly sixteen millions in a single twelvemonth without apparent discomposure, we cannot suppose that he annual distribution during some half-dozen years over the whole commercial world of less than half that quantity annually could have occasioned any sensible disturbance. It is now indeed well understood that the past action of Germany and of the Latin Union combined, has been much rather indirect than direct. It was far less what they did than uncertainty as to what they might either do or leave undone, that occasioned those violent fluctuations in the price of silver which are but faintly indicated by the average rates stated some pages back. This it was, together with the occasional panics occasioned by the wildly exaggerated rumors frequently arriving from the American mines, that by leaving bullion dealers without any firm data for calculation, often induced them to sell at heavy loss rather than risk heavier loss by waiting, and deterred them from purchasing except for immediate purposes.

* "Notice Historique sur la Réforme Monétaire en Allemagne," les Malou. Bruxelles, 1879.

Thus it was that the price of silver fell once to 46*d.* per oz., the lowest price ever known, and this, too, is by far the principal, if not the sole reason why the price is at this moment little higher than 52*d.*

It is all but certain, however, that neither the present depression nor anything like it can endure much longer, and would indeed be quite certain but for the doubt hanging over the American mines. It is of course conceivable that these may more that realize the wildest prophecies uttered regarding them. True, instead of an imaginary annual average of twenty to thirty millions, they have never yet yielded more than nine millions in any one year, and they may possibly be approaching exhaustion. Yet who can say what the unexplored bowels of the earth may have in store? But on the other hand when was there a time at which any one could say any better than he can now? The possibilities on either side are quite as evenly balanced as they ever were before, and there is no more reason now than there has always been why they should cause uneasiness or be taken at all into account: while, apart from these, there is solid ground for assurance that all assignable causes for the depreciation of silver must soon cease to operate. "Germany," according to a report made a few months back by Lord Odo Russell to Lord Salisbury, "has at last found out that she is herself a loser by her sales of silver, and has in consequence decided to suspend them, and is, moreover, generally believed by financial men to be preparing to introduce and adopt the double standard as in France," while France and the other Latin confederates must likewise discover very shortly the error of their ways, or at all events must act as if they had become aware of it. In 1886 at latest, according to a recent agreement between them, they must inevitably remove all restriction from the coinage of silver, but they will scarcely wait until then: they can scarcely fail very much earlier to perceive that they will ultimately have no choice between returning to unqualified bi-metallism and completely demonetizing silver and monomonitizing gold – an enterprise which, in view of the enormous rise in the price of gold that would result from their attempting it, would, without some such extraordinary aid as Germany in like circumstances derived from her war indemnity, be utterly beyond their resources. But every assignable cause for depreciation having thus been withdrawn, silver must presumably recover its old value, and the Indian Government which, as we have seen, has hitherto remained unharmed by the depreciation, may assure itself that it has no more to dread in future from that quarter than it has actually suffered during the past.

Repeating then, by implication, the assertion with which I started, I can see but one reason for even slightly modifying it. Just as the monetary policy of Germany and of the Latin Union has, so to speak, acted rather morally than materially, so the vague apprehensions created by the depreciation of silver may have aided to produce effects of which the depreciation itself was utterly guiltless. Although the depreciation has not as yet diminished the purchasing power of the rupee in respect to any thing except bills of exchange, people engaged in Indian commerce have from time to time very naturally assumed that it must almost immediately raise Indian prices generally; and seeing the price of silver bullion drop from 60*d.*, to 59*d.*, 58*d.*, 56*d.*, 54*d.*, and 52*d.*, successively, and at one time sinking as low as 46¾ *d.*, they never, when tendering for Council Bills, could do more than guess what those bills would be worth when they reached India, and they may probably enough have reduced their tender accordingly a good dial below the rates which they would otherwise have been content to pay. The close coincidence in point of time between the lowest price to which silver and the lowest rate to which the exchange ever fell, must be admitted to be all in favour of this supposition, for it was purely when the former dropped suddenly to 46¾ *d.* that the latter dropped with equal suddenness to 1*s.* 6*d.* Nevertheless, a comprehensive comparison of all the statistics will show how exceedingly fitful and transient in its operation must have been of the constant and potent agency which, I maintain, to have been the true cause of the depression of the exchange.

The Indian Government, if persuaded to accept the views set forth above, may perhaps be disposed somewhat over-hastily to congratulate itself that it has hitherto been occasionally panic-stricken by what, so far as India alone was concerned, was little more than a bugbear, and seeing that it has no evils to apprehend from the depreciation of silver, it may without any extraordinary magnanimity persist in the resolution, announced on its behalf in the last session of parliament, to face those evils manfully. Some relief it may derive, too, from perceiving that, in the actual circumstances of the case, alterations of its Currency Laws will not serve the turn, and that it may therefore cease to perplex itself with any of the currency schemes devised by Colonel Smith and others – schemes of which, let me say in passing, that, being myself the author of one of them, I am by no means disposed to speak disparagingly. But let it not therefore too hurriedly take heart of grace. Proceed they whence they may, the fall of the exchange, and the Government's loss in consequence, are none the less dire realities; and if ascribable, not to depreciation of silver but to excessive issue of Council Bills, they are due to a cause with which it may be even more difficult to deal. One true ground of consolation the Government may at first sight appear to have. One important difference between the present depression of the exchange, if due to depreciation of silver, and if due to superabundance of bills of exchange, deserves particular attention. In the one case, the depression would, for reasons already stated, last as long as the depreciation, and so too would any loss to Government resulting from it; but the Government would be the only permanent sufferer. Creditors would incur more or less loss, and debtors obtain more or less gain, but both loss and gain would be only temporary, and might too, in a national sense, be regarded as counterbalancing each other; and all fresh mercantile transactions would adapt themselves to the new monetary values; but a Government dependent as that of India is, for the greater part of its revenue, on contributions of predetermined sums of rupees, would necessarily remain at a disadvantage as long as the rupee remained depreciated, unless it could venture, as the Government of India cannot, to supplement its diminished revenue by additional taxation. In the other, and, as I contend, the actual case, the exchange may really be trusted to right itself, in a certain sense, by a process nearly identical with the one indicated by Mr. Bagehot. For whereas, in the former case, all Indian prices would rise in much about the same proportion as that in which the price of Indian bills on India fell, in the latter, all prices would remain for awhile unaffected, with the exception of those of bills of exchange, the prices of these being raised in India and lowered elsewhere by variations in the proportion between supply and demand, applying to them only and not extending to any other commodity. In these circumstances, an English merchant, procuring for £100 a bill on India for, say, 1110 rupees, instead of only 1000 as formerly, will not with that £100 have acquired purchasing power over Indian produce greater by one-tenth than before, and his profit, by bringing to England the goods therewith purchased, will be proportionately increased, while an Indian merchant, obtaining for 1000 rupees a bill on England for only £92 instead of £100, will exercise over English goods little more than nine-tenths of his previous purchasing power, and his profit by transferring his English purchases to India will be proportionately diminished. India's import trade will thus really be stimulated and her export trade checked until, by reason of the gradually increasing dearness of English goods in India, and the gradually increasing cheapness of Indian goods in England, the profit to be made by trade between England and India in either mode becomes the same. While this is going on, the amount of foreign bills on India will gradually diminish, and that of Indian bills on England increase, the exchange value of the rupee creeping up simultaneously until the two amounts become equal, and the Indian exchange stands again at par. According to Mr. Bagehot the evil will then have cured itself, since Government, receiving in full tale its accustomed due of rupees, will be able to obtain in exchange for those rupees gold for its English payments on as advantageous terms as ever, and the prime cause of its financial distress will thus be removed. Perhaps so, but if Mr. Bagehot had inquired at what cost to the people of India this cure will have been effected, he would have discovered that the remedy will be many times worse than the disease. He might almost as well have talked of a patient being cured of his complaint by the atrophy that killed him. For an obvious effect of the augmentation of India's export and diminution of her import trade will be to make all Indian produce probably cheaper abroad than before, and all foreign produce dearer in India than before – in other words, to compel India to accept a proportionately smaller quantity of foreign produce in return for any given quantity of Indian goods. If the excess of Bills on India, over and above those drawn on commercial account, be taken at its present amount of fourteen millions sterling, it will, in order that the Indian exchange should be restored to par by the process described, be necessary for India to barter for less than her present total of foreign imports a quantity of her own produce which, at the prices of the present day, would be worth more than those imports by fourteen millions. Thereupon, the profits of all Indian producers will of course be reduced in corresponding ratio. Capital, if not withdrawn from productive industry, will at least be discourage from resorting to it, and production, if not thrown back, will be prevented from advancing. To such fatally disastrous results, the risk of the Indian taxpayer being disabled from meeting his fiscal engagements in full, is by comparison a very insignificant addition. Now this is really what, if things are allowed to go on as at present, India has to look forward to, and the prospect is not one to be contemplate with equanimity. It plainly will not do, then, for India to be kept waiting until the "laws that govern foreign exchange" shall have obviated the exchange difficulty. Her Government, if sincerely resolved to face that trouble manfully, must also resolve that the issue of Council Bills shall, by some means or other, be materially lessened. Yet by what means? The problem is of the hardest, but where there is a will there is generally a way.

Experience, as usual, deferring until too late her captious counsels, at last teaches us clearly enough how serious an oversight there has been in an important branch of the domestic policy instituted by the Government of India some five-and-twenty years ago, and steadily pursued ever since. Every one could see that railways which has so marvellously developed the resources of Europe, were equally desirable for India; but neither did it occur to any practical administrator to inquire, nor did any theoretical economist volunteer to point out, how greatly the investment of British capital on Indian Public Works must, by necessitating the remittance to England of annual interest or profit on the investment, derange the Indian exchange, nor how grievous would be the effects of the derangement. Railways are good; irrigation is good, but neither on nor the other good enough to compensate for the opening and continual widening of a drain which has tapped India's very heart's blood, and is drying up the mainsprings of her industrial energy. So grievous an error of the past having been at length, however tardily, detected, will scarcely be persevered in, and we may reasonably assume, therefore, that there will be no more guaranteeing of private British enterprise, nor any more raising in Europe of Public Works Loans on any pretext whatever: while as for foreign loans for less plausible purposes, to denounce *them* would be superfluous. There is for India just now no other public work half so urgent as the restoration of equilibrium between income and expenditure, and all the rest should be imperatively required to wait until there shall be surplus revenue applicable to them, unless, perchance, the requisite funds can be intermediately borrowed from local capitalists content to receive their interest on the spot. Precautions like these, however, can but help to prevent the exchange difficulty from becoming aggravated, and a question that will not brook delay is by what means it can be abated. For this purpose, mere economy, economy in the abstract, will not suffice; not only must the aggregate and general expenditure of government be brought within more moderate limits, but expenditure in England – home expenditure, as it is officially termed – that expenditure which insists upon exhausting remittances from India and necessitates the drawing of Council Bills, must in especial be reduced to a minimum. How then is this indispensable reduction to be effected? The problem, as I said, is of the hardest, "but where there's a will there's a way," and I should myself be tempted to suggest several paths all tending in the right direction, if certain personal considerations, in addition to want of space, did not forbid my entering into detail upon this part of the subject. Here, then, I bring my story to a close by drawing from it the pregnant moral that it is India's tribute which is so balefully weighing down the Indian exchange, and that the same burden threatens, unless speedily and materially lightened, to break the Indian camel's back - miracle of endurance though the animal be. To the Indian Government, if persuaded fo the truth of these propositions, and of its consequent obligation to modify its past policy in some essential respects, it belongs to determine, with its own abundant light and knowledge and with the aid of the numerous accomplished experts at its disposal, what precise line of action it shall henceforth pursue. Certainly it cannot be too expeditious in acting upon Mr. Fawcett's advice, and commencing an entirely "new departure in Indian finance."

Our readers will be sorry to learn that the distinguished author of the foregoing Article died on the 17th ult., from the effects of a severe cold. – Ed. Of Westminister Review

TO JOHN STUART MILL, ESQ.

Thornton, William, "To John Stuart Mill, Esq., in imitation of an Epistle from Horace to Mæcenas", *Zohráb; Or, a Midsummer's Day's Dream: and other Poems*, (London: Longman, Brown, Green and Longmans, 1854).

This was originally the last in the collection of Thornton's poems. In it he expresses disappointment with political economy in the form of an epistle to Mill and predicts the long pause in his own ouput in political economy.

To
John Stuart Mill, Esq.,
In Imitation of an Epistle of Horace to Maecenas.

Dear Mill, whose friendship's kindly emphasis
Approved my first work, and encouraged this,
Scarce will you ask, why, from old studies turned,
My name unknown, a pension yet unearned,
Problems abstruse and tough, no more I try,
Of dark Political Economy,
Digging no more in serious dissertation
To trace the source of "Over-population,"
Nor publishing what hidden treasure lies
Deep in the soil of "Peasant Properties."
Age tells on mind, and though my well used quill,
Not quite worn out, may do some service still,
Not less my inward warning I regard,
And fear to ride my hobby-horse too hard,
Lest the tired jade, urged on beyond his strength,
In some absurd extreme break down at length.
Therefore I change my steed, and soaring higher,
Of loftier truth and nobler good enquire,
And in this quest, for my whole heart is in't,
Cull and compose what presently I print.
Now, would you know whose doctrine I profess,
Truly, I'm bound by no man's sentences.
Chance leads me on, and wheresoe'er I roam,
An easy guest, I make myself at home;
Mix with the busy world, and take a share
Of the opinions I find current there,
Yet steering heedfully by virtue's course,
And borrowing something of the Stoic's force,
Wherewith to face life's storms, their fury stem,
And make them yield to me, not I to them.
Long is the night to one whose mistress cheats,
Slowly the bondslave's day its term completes,
Immortal seems the tiresome dowager,
Whose lengthening years the stepson's hope defer.

As heavily for me the time drags on,
Whose frequent obstacles my hope postpone
Of perfecting some moral digest, which
May profit equally both poor and rich,
And whose neglect must hurt both young and old,
And by whose rules myself may be controlled.
  Scarce can weak eyes to lynx's strength attain,
Yet few the aid of spectacled disdain.
Though dietetics make no second Parr,
Freedom from chalk-stones, sure, is worth some care.
Do but aim high, and though the mark you miss,
'Tis something to have got as near as this.
Does grovelling avarice burrow in your breast?
A charm there is to rid you of the pest.
Does love of praise your panting bosom swell?
Ease shall be given by a thrice-told spell.
Envy or anger, sloth or wine, or love,
All mental ills wise counsel can remove.
No case so desperate, but its cure is near,
When good advice obtains a patient ear.
  Virtue's chief essence is from vice to flee,
And wisdom's sum from folly to be free.
See how men shun the evils they dread most,
A narrow income, an election lost.
Before no labour mind or body quails:
To farthest Ind the eager merchant sails,
Flying from poverty through fire and flood,
And rocky strait, with hidden peril strewed,
Nor heeds the monitor who bids him spurn
The yellow dirt he goes so far to earn.
  What jockey at Newmarket stays his horse,
When for the cup he need but walk the course?
As gold than silver, even so than gold
Is virtue better, though, 'tis true, we're told
First to get money – before virtue, coin.
Round the Queen's statue jobbers thus enjoin;
And docile lads repeat their seniors' rule,
With slate and satchel trudging on to school.
  If by some thousands of a plum you fail,
Will wit, faith, breeding, eloquence avail?
Spite of these gifts, you're no-one after all,
For none but Eton's young collegians call
Their cleverst, captain; yet with wall of brass

Is he surrounded, who a conscience has
Void of offence. And tell me, which is best
The schoolboy's, or the legislator's test?
This chooses worth that other worth excels;
That on the qualifying rent-roll dwells.
And whose the better maxim? his, who says
"Make money, if you can by honest ways;
But, any how, make money, which unlocks
Wealth's prime recognizance, the opera box;"
Or his, whose hopeful watchword is "Advance,
Firm and erect, meet fortune's arrogance?"
  But, if folks ask, why this eccentric,who
Lives with his fellows, can't live like them, too,
Seeking and shunning what they love and hate?
The cunning fox's answer I translate,
Who kept outside of the sick lion's den,
"All footmarks here lead in; none, out again."
Besides, oh! public, many-headed beast,
If you must lead me, condescend at least
To say how I can follow, what or whom?
For, of your heterogeneous items, some
Are ambushed in Stags' Alley; some, perhaps,
With fruit and dainties bait their widow traps;
Some fatten up old men, in hopes, of course,
That they'll cut up well; with as small remorse,
Others, with gloating eyes on spendthrifts bent,
Fatten themselves on loans at cent. per cent.
Thus different persons different courses choose,
But how long, think you, the same whims amuse?
The wealthy idler in the Isle of Wight
Fancies a villa – here's the very site!
He buys the ground, but ere the work's complete
A new thought strikes, he'll have a hunting seat.
"Off, Workmen, to the Highlands – haste, despatch."
Next, mark the victim of a new-made match.
See how he mourns his single blessedness.
When last he sighed, 'twas for the chaste caress
Of a fond wife. But how can be confined
In matrimonial noose, that Protean mind?
Such are the rich man's freaks; now, note the range
Of his poor neighbour, through as frequent change
Of garret, truckle-bed and shaving-shop.
Not twice at the same parish bath he'll stop,

And the same Sunday steamer bores him not
Less than if sailing in his private yacht.
If awkward barber cut my hair awry,
You laugh, of course, or if by chance you spy
Beneath my satin vest a tumbled shirt,
Or if my cloak hang trailing in the dirt.
Yet, if my humour, with itself at strife,
Change the whole tenor of my former life,
Seek what it spurned, and spurn the sought when found,
Pull down, build up, transforming square to round,

ZOHRÀB; OR, A MIDSUMMER DAY'S DREAM

Thornton, William, "Zohráb; Or, a Midsummer's Day's Dream", *Zohráb; Or, a Midsummer's Day's Dream: and other Poems*, (London: Longman, Brown, Green and Longmans, 1854).

This was the first and eponymous piece in the collection of Thornton's poems and it includes both the Preface and Dedication to the collection. Edward Zohráb, to whom this collection was dedicated, was Thornton's cousin.

Preface

I SHALL not in these few lines of introduction be guilty of the transparent affectation, so frequently committed by writers on their first appearance in poetical costume, of depreciation my own performances; for if I thought ill of them myself, I should of course not needlessly expose them to the scrutiny of a tribunal whose judgment I could scarcely expect to be more lenient than my own. But though I may as well honestly confess, what it would be useless to deny, that I believe my "Attempts in verse" to be not inferior to those of many other authors, whose productions have been received with considerable favour by the public, and though unable to plead "hunger or request of friends" in excuse for publishing them, I may at the same time declare that few of them would have been written, and none of them, assuredly, would have been printed, at least in this form, unless I had had in view a much higher object that that of either contributing to popular amusement or competing for popular applause. What that object is, unless I have missed my aim, will be sufficiently obvious to any one who may think it worth while to read the earlier pieces of this collection in the order in which they are placed.

Marlborough Hill, St. John's Wood.

To
Edward Zohrab, Esq.,
Turkish Consul-General in London.

This Memorial
Of His Celebrated Namesake
Is Inscribed
In Token of Esteem and Affection,
By His Cousin,
The Author.

Zohràb;
or,
A Midsummer Day's Dream.

In the cool shadow, which, midway
Up Ashley's hill, twin beeches throw,
Upon the new-mown sward I lay
And gazed upon the vale below,
Where, frolicking through flowery meads,
Smooth stones and tufted reeds among,
Young Exe his jocund waters leads
And prattles as he trips along.

A lovely vale, nor lovelier ever
Than while, as then, the noonday sun
Expends his strength in vain endeavour
To mar it; for, though elsewhere, none
But, drooping, pined beneath his power,
Here, his fierce radiance only drew
Still livelier tints from rill and bower,
Made earth more green, the stream more blue.

A lovely vale, and oft have I,
Reclined in this, my favourite nook,
Laid Lalla Rookh or Wordsworth by,
Delighted, up its course to look,
From where, on Collipriest's domain,
Thick woods the sheltering uplands crown,
To where St. Peter's hoary fane
Towers o'er sequestered Tiverton.

But now, though gazing steadfastly
On blooming field and shining river,
The landscape vainly bids the eye
Its message to the mind deliver.
I gaze, but see not; for a spell,
Wrought by the volume in my hand,
Has done its mystic office well,
And borne me to the Magian's land.

Behold! A mountain-chain displaces
The long, low line of leafy hills;
A parched and stony plain effaces
Green meadows moist with tinkling rills;
Gone are church-tower and gabled hall,
And where deep clefts the ridge divide,
A fort with white, embattled wall,
Spans the defile from side to side.

Above the indented parapet
Wave time-worn pennons, soiled and dim;
Thickly is each embrasure set
With turbaned heads and faces grim;
And mustering in the crowded court,
In haste their steeds caparison
Troopers, whose numbers more import
An army than a garrison:

Though but the van of following bands;
For see, – beyond the battlements,
Where at its mouth the gorge expands,
The wider space is black with tents;
And, closely ranked, or loosely grouped,
Legions of savage warriors
Mingle with sheep and camels cooped
Within the rocky barriers.

What means this menacing array?
Persia's north gate those ramparts close.
Are these then wardens of the way?
Say rather, Persia's bitterest foes.
The horsehair tent, the sheepskin vest;
The scattered camp's uneven plan
The desert's denizens attest,
The brigand hordes of Turkestan.

Weak bulwark against border raid,
The fort has bowed at their assault.
Then wherefore is their onset staid?
What bids the bold marauders halt?
Of late, like stream that seeks the sea,
They bounded down the mountain side;
Now, heave and chafe, impatiently,
Like torrent met by ocean's tide.

Yet ask not, why no further sped.
Turn southward; there may'st thou descry,
In gallant order garlanded,
The flower of Persian chivalry.
The Tartar slogan, far around,
Like tocsin's tongue, has rung the ban,
And when was Iran recreant found
At challenge of the Turcoman?

Outstretched in broad, beleaguering crescent,
Below the fort their camp is traced;
A various host, for there are present
Levies from six score nations raised;
Six score and seven* : no fewer bend
beneath imperial Khosrou's sway;
Khosrou, whose empire's bounds extend
From Ethiopia to Cathay.

Himself the tried militia heads
Assembled for the realm's defence.
Through the front ranks his presence spreads
A halo of magnificence.
There, within curtains of brocade,
(Yellow embroidered on Vermillion,)
Girdling a spacious esplanade,
Stands the "great king's" superb pavilion.

Without, are silken tissues, dight
With orient pearl and costly stone;
Within, soft gleams of azure light
Flicker about a sapphire throne.
The oriflamme of Feridoon†
In front a banner-staff upholds,
Radiant with jewelled sun and moon
Emblazoned on its purple folds.

* *Levies from six score nations raised; Six score and seven.*
"This is Ahashuerus which reigned from India even unto Ethiopia, over an hundred and seven and twenty provinces." – *Esther,* i. 1.

† *The oriflamme of Feridoon.*
"This famous standard was a blacksmith's apron set in jewels, and was long the imperial standard of Persia. Gâveh was a blacksmith; he overthrew the cruel tyrant Zohak, and placed Feridoon on the throne of Persia. When collecting followers, he carried his apron as the standard of revolt against Zohak. This apron remained the standard of the empire till taken by Saadben-wakas, who commanded the Mahometan army that conquered Persia."—*Sketches of Persia,* vol. i. p. 208. The sun and moon were anciently the armorial bearings of Persia. According to Sir William Ouseley (*Travels,* vol. iii. p. 564.), the present emblems of the kingdom, the Lion and Sun, were not assumed till the thirteenth century of our era.

A hundred elephants are ranged
In line before the outer screen;
Courtiers, their courtly garb exchanged
For plate and mail, parade within;
And lions guard the open gate.
And crouch submissive by the throne;
Insignia these of highest state
Assumed by royalty alone.

Flanking the monarch's central post,
On either hand, at intervals
Disposed throughout the embattled host,
Other pavilions rise, by walls
Enclosed of varied tapestry,
Above whose gaily coloured screens
Distinctive standards bear on high
Scutcheons of peers and paladins.

Princes Friborz and Tooz are there,
Whose boast of royal lineage
Heraldic elephants declare;
Goodurz, whose steel-clad equipage
A lion on their banner bear;
Gouraz, whom bristly boar denotes;
And mightiest Rustam, camping where
Aloft a fiery dragon floats.

His own distinctive colour too
Each chieftain's quarter notifies,
Known by its yellow, green, or blue,
Orange or crimson draperies.
Their followers' tents are spread between,
In strong contrasted whiteness shining,
As when in festal wreath are seen
Lilies and tulips intertwining.

But not beneath their canvass shades
Are Iran's warriors loitering now:
Drawn up in front, their mixed brigades
War in his richest vesture show.
How dazzlingly their gorgeous line
To the sun's eye its pomp presents!
Bright as if gnomes of Ophir's mine
Had fashioned their accoutrements.

For gold the glossy tunics sprinkles,
And burnished helm and hauberk gilds,
Gold on the spangled buskins twinkles,
And smoulders on the inlaid shields;
And mark, too, how the glittering crowd
Casts o'er the plain a saffron hue.
Might'st thou not deem a sunlit cloud
Had sunk distilled in golden dew?

Now hark! how from the Turkish hold
Sound signals of the coming fray.
Through the wide portals backward rolled,
A young commander leads the way.
Long files of horsemen, streaming after,
Quickly in wedge-shape order form,
With clamour, like the surly laughter
Of Ocean preluding a storm.*

Brief pause, in sooth, ere suddenly
Forth breaks the impatient hurricane.
Shrill shrieks the border battle cry
Of clansmen dashing o'er the plain.
A prairie fire their charge appears,
(Forked flame with smothering smoke contending,)
As, through the dust that veils them, spears
Start up, the hazy mantle rending.

Foremost in that tempestuous race
The ardent chief his train outrides;
T'wards the king's tent, at whirlwind pace,
His eager cavalry he guides.
Before his onslaught breaks away
The royal guard's unstable line:
So springs the lion on his prey;
So scattered fly the timid kine:

* *Like the surly laughter*
Of Ocean preluding a storm.
A similar expression appears to have been similarly employed by the Welsh Bard Taliessin. See *Life of Mrs. Hemans,* by her Sister.

And, as a lion that espies
The vengeful herdsman hovering near
Stops short, and with enkindled eyes
Waits his attack, – in full career
So halts Zohrab; so sternly glares
With scorn and wonder on the knight
Who midway meets him unawares
And challenges to single fight.

"And whither," this assailant cries,
"And wherefore thus at headlong speed?
Deem'st thou, perchance, the victor's prize
Shall be the fleetest courier's meed?
'Twixt thee and me must first be played
A match performed with bloodier rite;
So shalt thou have my falchion's aid
To goad thee to yet hastier flight."

Proud words, but which not ill beseem
Him in whose wrath such taunts are flung.
That sinewy frame may well redeem
The pledges of a wanton tongue.
Such stalwart strength not often Earth
Has seen among her sons enrolled,
Since her primeval powers gave birth
To giants in the days of old.

Nor need'st thou lightly question who
So threatening stands, his name and race.
Mark his crisp beard of tawny hue,
His quaintly bossed, bull-headed mace,
The skin of brindled leopard thrown
Athwart his ample chest; by these
May every where be surely known
Rustam, the Persian Hercules.*

* *Rustam, the Persian Hercules.* "Roosum," says Sir W. Ouseley (*Travels*, vol. ii. p. 505.), "is perhaps the only character, real of fictitious, of whom the Persian painters seem to have entertained but one idea; for, in the illuminated manuscripts, they generally represent him of the same complexion (his hair and beard being tawny or reddish brown), in the same singular dress, and with the same weapons, the mace, noose, and other attributes. His mace was crowned with a ponderous knob resembling the head of a bull, and appears in some pictures resting on the pommel of his saddle. Although shields are often used by his friends and enemies; I do not recollect any picture that assigns one to Roostum, who possessed a fighting dress, which miraculously protected its wearer from most personal dangers. It was made of a skin "brown coloured, with whitish stripes." From this it would seem that the skin had belonged to a tiger, but it is most frequently described as a leopard skin, which had the magical "property of resisting the impression of every weapon, was proof against fire, and would not sink in water." See Atkinson's *Soohrab*, p. 9.

Yet to Zohrab, it seems, unknown,
Who to his haughty foe replies
With like disdain of look and tone,
Unskilled in him to recognise
The hero, of whose conquering might
Hyrcania's demons, muttering, tell;
Whose seven-fold toils* have scaled the height
Of glory's loftiest pinnacle.

With short and sharp response, he bends
His head in token of assent.
Brief ceremonial now suspends
The concourse of the tournament.
Called from pursuit, or turned from flight,
Both armies closing, form the lists,
In semicircles which unite
Round the well paired antagonists.

Fair flaunts the living palisade,
Which yet in vain the eye invites,
For, in close orbit now arrayed,
The serried bands of satellites
Around the central champions are
As though outshone and lost to view.
When Dian mounts her crystal car,
Who heeds her starry retinue?

And who, as worthy of regard
Now deems the circling throng's display,
While its great leaders stand prepared
Their equal prowess to essay?
Equal, for if, in Rustam's guise,
Alcides stems the tide of war,
Scarce less Zohrab's high port implies
Some Eastern Mars's avatar.

* *Whose seven-fold toils*

As the Grecian Hercules is celebrated for his Twelve Labours, so is his eastern counterpart renowned for the Heft Kh'an, the Seven Labours, or, more properly, the Seven Stages, Which distinguished the expedition undertaken by him into Hyrcania, the modern Mazanderan, for the purpose of liberating his suzerain, the King of Persia, from the captivity in which he was held by the demon inhabitants of that province. A humorous summary of these exploits is given by Sir John Malcolm in his *Sketches of Persia,* vol. i. pp. 217–34.

Rustam himself admiringly
Compares his rival's form and face,
Stature which with his own may vie,
Herculean strength and Phidian grace;
And kindlier thoughts within him spring,
And unaccustomed phrased teach,
With rugged court'sy tempering
His wonted arrogance of speech.

"In paths with deadly foes beset,
Ever my pastime have I sought,
Nor man nor fiend encountered yet,
Whom, for assault or safeguard, aught
Availed, or force, or skill, or guile;
And will thy youth my power defy,
Lured by vain hope's perfidious smile
To court malignant destiny?

"Tempt not thy fate. Since form like thine
Sure ne'er was cast in Turkish mould,
O'er desert wolves thy sway resign
For worthier charge in Iran's fold.
Vengeance dismisses thee, nor needs
Inflict the penance thou hast dared.
The vultures whom my bounty feeds
Shall not lack meat though art spared."

Thus he; nor deigns Zohrab to speak
His outraged spirit's generous ire,
But flashing eye and flushing cheek
Glow with his bosom's inward fire,
Which into flame breaks forth amain,
As now, first sharply reining back
His horse, more vigorous spring to gain
And freer scope for his attack,

He gallops forward. Forward too
Rustam his foaming steed impels;
Crossed in his gentler mood, anew
His heart with hate and anger swells.
Grasping mid-shaft their levelled spears,
They charge at speed, and when within
Due distance, each at once uprears
And hurls his ponderous javelin.

Back from Zohrab's steel-sheltered breast
Flies the split lance with harsh rebound;
His own, from Rustam's furry vest
Drops heavily, with sullen sound.
Little he recks of hostile dart
Whom spoils of slaughtered pard defend;
That mantle, wrought with magic art,
No point can pierce, no edge can rend.

Unchecked in their impetuous charge,
The knights have swept each other by,
But, ere they reach the arena's marge,
Wheel round, and, spurring eagerly,
Straightway retrace their rapid course,
Not, as at first, content to greet
In passing, but, with hatred's force
And fervour, grappling as they meet.

Fairly confronted, hand to hand,
Close and assiduous strife they wage,
Where brand opposed by answering brand
Seems but to fan their mutual rage;
For fast and faster yet the clash
Of the commingling blades recurs,
And livelier yet the frequent flash
Glancing from off the cymeters.*

Both practised horseman, both essay
Whate'er long use of arms has taught:
Feint, double, foin and foil display
Science with sharp experience bought.
The horses, too, in battle tried,
The falchion's force, curvetting, aid,
Or backward starting, or aside,
Retaliatory pass evade.

* *Glancing from off the cymeters.*

The ancient Persian cymeter, as is evident from the representations of it in the bas-reliefs at Persepolis and elsewhere, was very different from the corresponding weapon at present in use among Asiatic nations, being straight or only slightly curved, and pointed as well as sharp-edged, and adapted, therefore, both for thrusting and cutting.

Every resource of art they try,
Nor vigour nor address prevails.
Shrewd scheme of covert strategy,
By eye as shrewd detected, fails,
And forward thrust, and downward stroke,
Which dexterous ward or parry meets,
Counter attack in turn provoke,
Which skill of fence in turn defeats:

Till Rustam, whom such dallying shames,
His sabre with both hands upheaves,
And at the Turkman's morion aims,
Nor yet that mark attains, but cleaves
The buckler's interposed defence,
Tough hide and triple brass beaks through,
Though at the misused sword's expense,
Which the same shock has shivered too.

Cursing the brittle steel, he flings
Its remnant at the jeering foe,
The massy wedge of bronze unslings
Dependent from his saddle bow,
And with the club none else may wield
The dauntless youth anew attacks,
Who, promptly quitting sword and shield,
Meets him with lifted battle-axe;

But now at disadvantage meets.
Baffled by necromantic spells,
His fury fruitlessly repeats
Blows which the magic garb repels;
While 'neath his fell opponent's mace
Gorget and corslet piecemeal fall,
Like splinters from the crumbling face
Of leaguered city's battered wall.

By odds so desperate sorely prest,
New tactic he employs, with wary
Alacrity intent how best
To thwart his slower adversary,
Whose aim, (as brandished threateningly
The club, he sees, new raised to strike,)
Guiding his horse with tightened knee,
He shuns with demivolte oblique:

And rallying fast from plann'd retreat,
While Rustam, by false stroke borne over,
Leans from his horse, his balanced seat
Zohrab forbids him to recover,
Smiting his bended neck; for though
The leopard skin from open wound
Protects him still, that well timed blow
Plunges him headlong to the ground.

How now from out on the dense stockade
Of troops that hem the arena round,
By fear and hope discordant swayed,
Dismay and triumph's cries resound!
The Persians see their leader sink;
Their chief's success the Tartars see.
Shrink, Iran, back in terror shrink!
Shout, shout, Touran, for victory!*

Yet hold, – think not that thus in earth†
Zalzur's aspiring blood‡ can sink;
Behold! it mounts afresh, – with birth
Renewed, rebounds from ruin's brink.
§Behold! as steed inured to war,
Which from light sleep the trumpet wakes,
Scenting the battle from afar,
Starts up, in strength rejoicing, shakes

The thunders of his neck, and neighs,
Mocking at fear, and paws the ground;
E'en so, while hostile legions raise
Their noisy paean, – at the sound
To madness stung, the fallen knight
From momentary stupor springs,
With ardour quickened by the might
Which shame to passion's succour brings;

* *Shout, shout Touran.*
Touran is one of the names given by the Persians to the regions inhabited by the Tartar races, in contradistinction to Iran, the usual appellation of their won country.

† *Think not that thus in earth*
What, will the aspiring blood of Lancaster Sink in the ground? I thought it would have mounted." – *King Henry VI., Act 5.*

‡ *Zalzur's aspiring blood*
Zalzur was the father of Rustam.

§ *Behold! as steed inured to war*
"Hast thou given the horse strength? hast thou clothed his neck with thunder? . . . He paweth in the valley and rejoiceth in his strength . . . He mocketh at fear . . . He smelleth the battle afar off." – *Job, xxxix. 19–25.*

And rushing on the foe, he throws
His arms around, and interlaced
Once more in deadly strife they close,
Fiercely embracing and embraced:
But hardly now Zohrab maintains
His station, while, with phrenzied force,
For vengeance painting, Rustam strains
Struggling to drag him from his horse.

Yet still with knees that firmly clench
The saddle, he preserves his grasp,
Struggling in turn, with furious wrench
That sinewy girdle to unclasp;
And thus, in mutual fetters locked,
They tug, they heave, and to and fro
Are swayed, like mountain cedars rocked
When battling winds alternate blow.

Nor ends the conflict till, at length,
Rustam uprising, and again
Slow stooping, concentrates his strength
In one long effort, which in vain
Zohrab resists; his horse's girth
Snaps, severed by the twofold stress;
His saddle turns, and prone to earth
Bears him in heavy helplessness;

And at the instant, o'er him bent,
The conqueror kneels, and gripes his throat.
His shattered armour, seamed and rent,
In that last peril guards him not.
The fatal dagger, lifted high,
With aim, which naught may now arrest,
One moment hovers doubtfully,
The next, lies quivering in his breast.

As languishes dying flower
By ruthless ploughshare rooted up,
Or, as weighed down by recent shower,
The poppy hangs its dripping cup,
Such now Zohrab's last agony,
Stretched weltering in Death's cold embrace,
So on his shoulder wearily
Lean his weak neck and livid face.

Beside him, motionless awhile
Stands, and his bloody work surveys,
Its sobered author, nor with smile
Of scornful triumph, stops to gaze.
To the fierce lust of blinded hate
Regret and self-reproach succeed;
Compassion for untimely fate,
Compunction for unknightly deed.

He stoops to take his victim's hand.
But why that sudden start and why
Earnestly on the spiral band
Of gold and graven jewelry,
Whose coil the nerveless arm enclasps,
Fasten his strained and stony eyes?
And why? but hold – in faltering gasps,
The dying youth's last breath replies.

"Stranger, not thine the guilt, to thee
Albeit Death's fell shaft is lent.
I yield to Destiny's decree,
Thou but Fate's servile instrument.
Yet not the less, where'er retired,
Shall swift revenge thy path pursue;
Not less of thee shall be required
Thy forfeit blood for bloodshed due.

"Ay, note that gem's inscription well.
What ominous cypher, there, hast read?
Thy doom those characters foretell.
Ay! wert thou to earth's centre fled,
Or Ocean's depth, or, veiled in night,
Could'st thou ascend the starry sphere,
E'en there my sire should track thy flight,
And Rustam's vengeance seize thee there."

"Rustam! thou Rustam's son! ah me!
Of further witness needs there aught?
Alas! the bracelet-seal I see,
The parting gift Amina sought,
The token for our child, – for thee.
Ah! let this anguished heart aver
Thy father, yet thy murderer!"

One frantic burst of woe, – one cry
Of wild despair, – and now, with hands
Fast clenched, and eyes fixed vacantly
Upon the stiffening clay, he stands
Speechless, till horror's gloom enthrals
His darkened spirit, at its source
Curdling his life blood, and he falls
Senseless beside the senseless corse.

Nay, raise him not, – the mutual quest
Is ended here, – the lost are won.
After long search, together rest
Victor and victim, sire and son:
Pierced by one barb's envenomed force,
Crushed beneath misery's equal weight.
Sundered throughout life's devious course,
On life's last verge associate.

Such was the chequered vision's guise,
Summoned from Phantasy's domain,
To float before my wakeful eyes,
By echos of the far-famed strain,
With which, in Ghizni's palace hall,
While royal Mahmoud listening sate,
Erst, would Ferdousi's muse recall*
Of Zalzur's line the piteous fate.

Princes and lords beside their king
Were grouped, and oft, amid the throng
Stood rival poets, hearkening
With transport to the minstrel's song;
Unenvying rivals from the day
When to the court, till then unknown,
He came, and with his peerless lay
Contended for the laurel crown.

* *Erst would Ferdousi's muse recall*
Abool Casim Mansoor, surnamed Ferdousi, born at Toos in Khorasan, about A.D. 931, undertook the composition of his Shah Nameh, or Book of Kings, the most celebrated of oriental epics, by desire of Sultan Mahmoud the Ghaznevide. That monarch, wishing to have the achievements fo the ancient kings and heroes of Persia embodied in an historical poem, endeavoured to ascertain who was best fitted for the task, by requiring seven of the most distinguished poets of his court to execute, eacch, a metrical version of some legendary romance. In this trial of strength the most successful was Unsuri; for Ferdousi had not yet emerged from the obscurity of his native village; but he was now attracted to the capital by the fame of the patronage there afforded to literature, and submitted to the Sultan a poem on the subject of Rustam and Sohrab, with which Mahmoud was so much charmed, that he at once made choice of its author for the performance of the proposed work.

Then, as with voice companioning
The mellow lute's mellifluous measure,
He shook from every trembling string
Its secret hoard of dulcet treasure,
And drew from ancient chronicles
His theme of baleful destiny,
A theme, whence many a fountain wells,
Fed with the waters of the eye;*

At the first pause the chant allowed,
His seven compeers around him pressed,†
And kissed his garment's hem, while loud
Applauses his the palm confessed;
And "Not as to their Teacher, now,"
They cry, "disciples bend to thee.
Prince among bards, supreme, art thou;
The meanest of thy servants, we."

"Nay, though as partner of my throne,"
The monarch thus vouchsafes his praise,
"Such colleague proudly might I own,
More highly yet your plaudit raise.
Such rapture of celestial fire
Never from mortal bosom broke;
At mortal's touch, no earthly lyre
E'er to such ecstasy awoke.

* *Fed with the waters of the eye;*

The story of Sohrab, as told by Ferdousi, is now incorporated with the Shah Nameh. In commencing this episode, the poet says that he is about to relate "Ekee dastan pur abi chushum." "A tale full of the waters of the eye." Though I quote these words in the original for the edification of oriental scholars, I take this opportunity to confess that I have not the slightest knowledge of the Persian language, and that for my acquaintance with Ferdousi's narrative, I am entirely indebted to the English versions of Mr. James Atkinson (Calcutta, 1814) and Mr. W. Tulloh Robertson (Calcutta, 1829). I must also acknowledge, what will be at once perceived on reference to either of those translations, that I have taken from them little more than the bare outline of my theme, dilating, or compressing, or otherwise altering, incidents, character, and costume, without scruple, as best suited my purpose.

† *His seven compeers around him pressed,*

On one occasion after Ferdousi had been reciting before Mahmoud, seven poets, who were present, flocked round him and insisted on kissing his hand as an acknowledgment of superiority. Unsuri, in particular, was so far from taking umbrage at the preference shown to his rival, that in some verses written after the latter's death, he says, very nearly in the words introduced into the text, "Praise to the soul of Ferdousi, the essence of all that is illustrious. He was not a teacher, and we his pupils. He was our lord and master, and we his slaves."

"A wanderer from Eden's bowers,
No earthly chorister, is he
Who through our honoured mansion showers
This soft ethereal melody,
Which, as diffused through Memory's cells,
The notes in liquid cadence melt,
Of happier scenes and seasons tells,
While yet ourselves in Eden dwelt.

"Deep, deep within the boundless sea
Of Heaven's blue ether islanded,
A bright and blooming galaxy,
The Gardens of the Soul are spread.
There, endless day displaces night,
All seasons summer vesture wear,
Nor sun nor moon dispenses light,
For God's own glory lightens there.

"There, Beauty's self decks fairy bowers,
Festoons arcades and avenues,
And weaves the embroidery of flowers
That paints the ground with rainbow hues,
And, over sands of pearly glow,
Through banks o'erhung with emerald shades.
Bids crystal streams now smoothly flow,
Now leap in feathery cascades.

"There once, ere yet by hellish wiles
Ensnared, by fleshly fetters bound,
And banished from those radiant isles
To pace on earth life's weary round,
There once, in native purity,
The unfallen spirit had her home,
Through fields of changeful splendour, free,
In blest unprescience, to roam.

"Yea! there ourselves once habited,
Witless of prowling fiend's pursuit,
Refreshed with nectarous balm, and fed
With fragrance of ambrosial fruit,
With angel guests, through myrtle groves,
Wandering in colloquy divine,
Or lulled, in jasmine-wrought alcoves,
By seraph symphonies like thine.

"And now, while thy witching strain
The heart's long dormant joys are stirred,
The blissful scenes return again
Where kindred music once we heard.
Glimmerings of memory, half extinct,
Again with sudden brilliance shine;
Again, in vivid order linked,
Loose threads of tangled thought combine.

"Once more the flowery paths we tread,
Once more we breathe the scented air,
Once more, through sylvan mazes led,
In intercourse of angels share.
'Tis at thy call the forms appear,
Thy voice that bids the phantoms rise,
Ferdousi, thou, thy presence here
Makes of our court a paradise!"*

Low, now, lies Ghizni's buried pride,†
Dome, spire, and mural coronet,
And grassy mounds the ruins hide,
Save where the spider throws her net‡

* *Makes of our court* a *Paradise!*

The poet's surname "Ferdousi" signifies Paradise, and is said to have been given to him by Mahmoud in a burst of enthusiastic admiration at the close of one of his recitations, when the Sultan exclaimed, "By your presence here, you have made my court a paradise, O Ferdousi." The sentiments placed in the mouth of Mahmoud with regard to the pre-existence of the soul, and the secret of the charm of music, were suggested by those beautiful lines of Leyden:– *"Ah! sure as Hindoo legends tell, When music's tones the bosom swell, The scences of former life return; Ere sunk beneath the morning star, We left our parent climes afar, immured in mortal forms to mourn."* The conqueror of a considerable portion of Hindoostan may not unreasonably be supposed to have become acquainted with some Braminical notions.

† *Ghizni's buried pride,*

The Ghizni of Mahmoud was about three miles distant from the modern city, whose name has been rendered so familiar to English ears by the exploits and disasters of the late Afghan war. The ruins of the old city consist of a vast extent of shapeless mounds. "Copre i fasti e le pompe arena ed erba." The only remains of its former splendour are the tomb of Mahmoud, and two finely proportioned minarets, each a hundred feet high, and twelve in diameter. See E. Thornton's *Gazetter of the countries adjacent to India.* art. Ghuznee.

‡ *The spider throws her net*

In this passage, an attempt has been made to imitate "an elegant Persian distich on the instability of human grandeur, repeated by the Ottoman Sultan, Mahomet the Second, after the capture of Constantinople, when he entered the deserted palace of the last of the Caesars. "Perdè dary mikiuned ber kysr Kaisar ankebut: Bumy neubey mizened ber kuinbeti Efrasiab." "The spider holds the veil in the palace of Caesar. The Owl stands sentinel on the watch-tower of Afrasiab." *Perdè* is the curtain which is spread before the throne, or at the entrance of the hall of state, which the pages draw aside when strangers are admitted to an audience: but here the office of chamberlain is assigned to the spider. *Neubet,* the martial music, which from the turrets of the imperial residence announces the evening retreat, is replaced by the screechings of the owl." – Thornton, *Present state of Turkey,* vol. i. p. 22.

Athwart the broken arch, from whence
The audience hall's silk curtain fell,
And on the watchtower's eminence
The screeching owl stands sentinel;

Save where the sultan's tomb is left,
Sole relic of the dread mahmoud,
But of its sculptured portals reft,
The trophy gates of sandal wood:*
Those spoils of Somnauth's ravaged fane,
In retributive triumph borne
Back to their idol's realm, again
His vindicated shrine adorn.

But though Ferdousi's minstrelsy
Mid Ghizni's wreck is heard no more,
And owls and doleful creatures cry
Where warbled once his tuneful lore,
Yet honour still awaits his lay
In Monarch's court, in baron's tower;
Still kings and courtiers own the sway
Of the departed wizard's power.

Nor more the epic descant charms
In pillared hall, than peasant's shed;
Mid peaceful toil, mid clanging arms,
The rich romaunt is balladed.†
It cheers the jaded artisian,
Inflames the charging host's attack,
Revives the drooping caravan,
And soothes the nightly bivouac.

* *Trophy gates of sandal wood.*

These famous gates, which Mahmoud is believed to have brought away in triumph from the temple of Somnath in Guzerat, and which, after occupying the entrance to the conquerors tomb for more than eight hundred years, were, by order of Lord Ellenborough, carried back to India, in 1842, by the British army under Sir William Nott, "are of sandal wood eighteen feet high, each five feet broad and three inches thick, very beautifully carved in tasteful arabesques." A detailed description of them will be found in Thornton's *Gazetter of the countries adjacent to India.* art. Ghuznee.

† *The rich romaunt is balladed.*

The continued popularity of Ferdousi among Persians of all ranks is noticed by several travellers. Waring says an "amusement among those who can afford it, is listening to a Shah Namu Khoon, a person who repeats and acts various passages of Ferdousi's epic poem called the Shah Namu. This is an amusement of a very superior kind, and one which a stranger is sure to delight in. They act the different descriptions of the poet with great spirit, particularly the account of the battle between Roostum, the hero of the poem, and Sohrab." (*Tour to Shiraz,* p. 55) According to Sir John Malcolm, "it has long been the custom for persons to recite animating verses from the Shah Nameh at the commencement of and during battle. The late king, Aga Mahomed, was particularly fond of this usage and bestowed marks of his favour

Thus, still where'er through eastern clime
Flow the sweet tones of Persia's tongue,
How, by the unconscious father's crime
Zohrab was slain, the tale is sung.
Yet, though a native poet's lays
To Persia's sons the theme endear.
Well may my feeble paraphrase
Unheeded fall on English ear.

Nor, therefore, shall its sequel swell
The story's too protracted course,
Nor, save by brief allusion, tell
How the rack'd saticide's remorse
Sought vent in funeral pageantry,
Nor how, with shrieks and gestures wild,
And fitful peals of frantic glee,
The maniac mother mourned her child.

Else might my verse assert its claim
Elegiac cenotaph to rear
To one, whose old historic name
Still my own mother's kindred bear;
And to restore his mouldering tomb,
From me, perchance, were justly due,
Who, in his fame would fain assume
Hereditary interest too.

At least, from his illustrious race,
Boyhood's romantic vanity
Feared not our own descent to trace;
And oft, with strange delight, have I

---

on such minstrels." A nobleman who lived on terms of intimacy with Sir John "recited to him from the Shah Nameh the greater part of the episode of the combats between Roostum and his unknown son Soohr'ab," and if this friend were not at hand, there was no difficulty in finding some one of meaner station well qualified to take his place. On one occasion "during a long night march it was suggested that a minstrel was wanted to shorten the distance by tales of wonder. This want was no sooner hinted than an old groom called Joozee Bey came forward and offered his services. He belonged, he said, to the Zend tribe, and when its chiefs were kings of Persia he was not neglected. 'Moorad Ali Khan and Lootf Ali Khan, that miracle of valour,' said the old man, 'have listened to my voice when it was exerted to animate their followers to battle; but these days are gone; a Turkish family wears the crown of Iran. I am, like others of my race, in indigence and obscurity, and now recite verses, which princes loved to hear, to men, like myself, of low degree; but if the Elchee desires, I will repeat some lines fit for a soldier to hear, from the Shah Nemeh of Firdousee.' " – *Sketches of Persia*, vol.1. pp. 204, 205, and vol. ii. p. 94.

(For sportive fancy, too, was young
And rich in wild imaginings,)
Dreamed our neglected branch had sprung
From antique stock of Asian kings.

Baseless or real, such idle boast
Now would my tutored mind deride,
Of boyish follies, scorning most
The folly of ancestral pride.
Yet would I fain with Zalzur's line
Still deem our own associate,
If so the more the hope were mine
Ancestral deeds to emulate.

Wondrous, in sooth, what legends tell
Of deeds by that high lineage wrought,
Whose chiefs, by faith invincible,
Ofttimes with foes unearthly fought;
And banded fiends in arms withstood,
And realms, from bondage freed, o'er ran,
And to their mountain caves pursued
The demons of Mazanderan.

Still throughout Earth the power survives
Of the renewed demoniac brood;
Still Ahriman with Ormuzd strives,*
Not yet is Ill o'ercome of Good.
Fiends, in their proper shapes, unveiled,
Hold willing nations in their thrall,
Mammon, still Prince of this World hailed,
Moloch and subtle Belial.

And fearful too shall be the feud
Which Ormuzd's faithful followers wage,
Ere Ahriman, at length subdued,
Yield up his earthly appanage;
And dire the perils they must dare
Who seek God's kingdom to extend.
Lord! be it mine their toils to share!
Mine in Thy cause my life to spend!

* *Still Ahriman with Ormuzd strives,*
It is perhaps scarcely necessary to mention that Ormuzd and Ahriman are the good and evil principles of Zoroaster's theological system.

Oh! be it mine my part to bear,
Joint labourer with Thine own elect.
Lord! from thy suppliant's lowly prayer
Turn not, nor this my suit reject.
What though in bodily presence weak,
And in my speech contemptible,
Aid from thy grace I yet may seek
In that great strife to quit me well.

So shall I boldly venture on,
Following where'er thy banners guide,
In humble confidence, as one.
Who, fearing thee, fears none beside:
Nor fears e'en thee: Faith casts out fear.
In thy disposal of my lot
Calmly I trust; with awe revere,
Love and adore, but fear Thee not!

And whatsoe'er, not wholly vain,
My grateful service may present,
Haply, may more acceptance gain,
Through meanness of the instrument,
Which shall but more exalt Thy praise,
More honour to Thy name shall bring,
Who, from the dust recruits canst raise,
Strength in our weakness perfecting.